GOD
=OUR=
FATHER

John Koessler

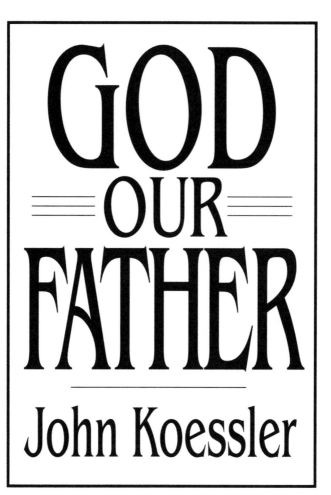

GOD
OUR
FATHER

John Koessler

MOODY PRESS
CHICAGO

This book is dedicated to the memory of my father,
George William Koessler, Sr.
His love for You was late, Lord,
but by Your mercy it was not too late.

"So he got up and went to his father. But while he was still a long way off, his father saw him and was filled with compassion for him; he ran to his son, threw his arms around him and kissed him." Luke 15:20

CONTENTS

ACKNOWLEDGMENTS

I am grateful to Jim Bell for suggesting that I take on this project and for his enthusiasm over the initial proposal. I am also thankful for the patient work of Cheryl Dunlop, whose editing skill has helped me to be a better writer. I owe a debt to my wife, Jane. She is my friend, mentor, and first proofreader. In addition, I want to express my appreciation to Harry Shields, chairman of the pastoral studies department at Moody Bible Institute, both for his insight and for his effort in arranging my schedule so that I would have the freedom to write. Most of all, I want to acknowledge the mercy and grace of the Lord Jesus Christ, who has shown me the way to the Father.

INTRODUCTION

A little boy was busily working with pencil and crayon when an adult asked him to describe what he was drawing. The boy was so intent upon his work that he barely looked up as he answered, "I'm drawing a picture of God." The adult chuckled and said, "But nobody knows what God looks like." Unmoved, the boy continued to draw and replied with confidence, "Well, when I'm done they will."

It is easy for us to laugh at his childlike certainty. The same endeavor, however, may seem arrogant when taken on by an adult. It is said that the theologian Thomas Aquinas, after he had begun to compile the *Summa Theologica*, a massive treatise intended to bring together the entire body of revealed truth in one work, abandoned the effort after celebrating mass in the chapel of St. Thomas on December 6, 1273. Impressed with the vastness of eternity and the immensity of the Father, he determined never to write about God again. His secretary, Reginald, attempted to persuade him to continue but was unsuccessful. Aquinas flatly refused, saying, "Reginald, I can do no more. Such things have been revealed to me that all I have written seems as so much straw."

I think I understand what Aquinas meant. The portrait of God the Father that you will find in these pages is by no means exhaustive. Its subject is too vast to be comprehended in a single volume. If John could say that the world itself does not have the room for the books that could be written about all that Jesus Christ did while on Earth, it must certainly be true that the universe cannot contain all the books that could be written to describe all that the Father is.

This book may only be a child's stick figure drawing of God, yet I believe that it can serve as a good starting point for those who would like to understand the heavenly Father better. In it I attempt to sketch the broad outlines of the Father's nature, character, and work. The primary focus of this book is the first person of the Trinity. However, any understanding of the Father inevitably leads to a better understanding of the other two members of the Trinity, and it will also give you a greater appreciation for the ministry of the Son and the Holy Spirit. Along the way I attempt to draw out some of the practical implications that these truths have for us as children of the Father. Consequently, I believe you will have a better understanding of the Christian life after reading this book. Its subject matter is theological, but its aim is devotional. This is a reflection of my conviction that the ultimate goal for all theological reflection ought to be application. When theological facts are not applied to life, they tend to poison the soul. It is my hope that you will know more about God the Father as a result of what you read here. But my real prayer is that you will love *Him more* and have a greater desire to serve Him as a result of your study.

If my depiction resembles a child's crude sketch of the Father, it is one that is based upon a more substantial image. It is a picture that is grounded in the Father's own self-portrait contained in the Scriptures. I hope that you will read this book with Bible in hand. Looking up the biblical references can be tedious, but the effort will be well rewarded.

Many of the footnotes address academic or controversial issues, and some contain helpful comments from other writers. The questions at the end of each chapter may be used to generate group discussion or for personal reflection.

When Philip asked the Lord Jesus to show him the Father, the Savior replied: "Don't you know me, Philip, even after I have been among you such a long time? Anyone who has seen me has seen the Father. How can you say, 'Show us the Father'?" (John 14:9). If you want to know the Father, you must do as Philip did. You must come to know Him through the person of His Son. Jesus said: "All things have been committed to me by my Father. No one knows who the Son is except the Father, and no one knows who the Father is except the Son and those to whom the Son chooses to reveal him" (Luke 10:22). Knowledge of the Father is not the exclusive possession of scholars and theologians. It is a gracious gift offered to all who come to Jesus Christ in faith. Lord Jesus, show us the Father.

.

1

"I BELIEVE IN
GOD THE FATHER . . ."

Whether he is called "Poppa," "Daddy," or even "Abba," the word for father is one of the first to be spoken by people of every language and culture. The same is true of the family of God. For two millennia Christians have been taught to pray by addressing God as "Our Father . . ." (Matthew 6:9). For slightly less than that they have confessed their faith by reciting the Apostles' Creed, beginning with the affirmation: "I believe in God the Father almighty . . ." Yet despite this apparent familiarity, God the Father may be the most neglected member of the Trinity. A quick search through your favorite hymnal will reveal an abundance of songs focusing on Jesus Christ and even more dealing with the Christian's experience of salvation, but relatively few that have the Father as their primary focus. Many books and articles concentrate on the work of the Son, the Holy Spirit, and even the Trinity, but few are devoted solely to God the Father.

A columnist in a national magazine recently observed that God the Father seems to have fallen on hard times. Evangelical Christians focus on Jesus, Pentecostals dwell on the power of the Holy Spirit, and Roman Catholics are deeply interested in Mary. Meanwhile a growing number of mainline denominations are removing male-centered language from their hymnals, their prayer books, and even their Bibles. Tongue in cheek, the author asks: "How can God the Father compete with a divine Son, a perfect Virgin Mother and the anti-patriarchal spirit of the times?"[1]

THE USE OF FATHER LANGUAGE
IN THE OLD TESTAMENT

The church was not the first to address God as Father. Although it appeared considerably less frequently than in the New Testament, the word *father* was used by some Old Testament writers to refer to the God of Israel. For example, at the end of his life Moses criticized God's people for their rebellious attitude and asked: "Is this the way you repay the Lord, O foolish and unwise people? Is he not your Father, your Creator?" (Deuteronomy 32:6). The prophet Isaiah used the term when appealing to God for a demonstration of parental compassion: "But you are our Father, though Abraham does not know us or Israel acknowledge us; you, O Lord, are our Father, our Redeemer from of old is your name" (Isaiah 63:16; cf. 64:8). Israel was criticized for calling God "my Father" and "my friend from my youth" in times of trouble, while refusing to turn from her disobedience (Jeremiah 3:4).

The parallel construction used in these passages points to the significance of this title. God was "father" of Israel in the sense that He was Israel's creator (Deuteronomy 32:6). In this respect He is universally the father of all humankind. Centuries later, while preaching the gospel in Athens, the apostle Paul emphasized that the same God who "made the world and everything in it" also made every nation on earth "from one man" (Acts 17:24, 26).

According to Isaiah 63:16 God was the father of Israel because He was its "Redeemer from of old." The "Redeemer" or "Redeemer Kinsman" was a near relative who was obligated to help a kinsman who had been sold into slavery or whose poverty threatened the loss of family property. According to Leon Morris: "The verb may be used of redeeming a relation from a state of slavery into which he has fallen (Leviticus 25:48f.), or redeeming his field (Leviticus 25:25)."[2] God the Father had acted as Israel's redeemer when He rescued the nation from slavery in Egypt. This action was described by Moses as a purchase or "ransom" of God's people (see Exodus 15:16).

In Jeremiah 3:4 the title *Father* is in parallel construction with a Hebrew term that means "friend." This broad term could refer to a family member, a spouse, the head of a tribe, or even an animal. It reflected the wide range of help God had provided for His people.[3]

In addition to these titles, God's personal names were combined with the Hebrew term for father in many of the names of people in the Old Testament. The name Joab, for example, meant "Yahweh is my Father." Similarly, the name Abijah meant "my Father is Yahweh." The name Abihu, which meant "He is my Father," probably combined a circumlocution for God's name with the term for father. The name Abimael combined the divine name El with the term for father to mean "my Father is God."

God's role as Israel's Father was further emphasized in the Old Testament by the use of parental metaphors—word pictures that compared God's care for His people to the treatment of a loving father. The father metaphor helped the Israelites to understand God in personal terms. God Himself employed this metaphor when He commanded Pharaoh to release the Israelites from their slavery. He described Israel as "my son" and "my firstborn son" (Exodus 4:22–23). The emphasis behind this metaphor was threefold. First, it was used to underscore the divine origin of the people of Israel. They were the children of the living God and were to live as such (Deuteronomy 14:1). Second, it served as a reminder of divine authority. Speaking for God, the prophet Malachi complained: "'A son honors his father, and a servant his master. If I am a father, where is the honor due me? If I am a master, where is the respect due me?' says the Lord Almighty" (Malachi 1:6). Third, the father metaphor was used in the Old Testament to illustrate God's nurturing character. It helped the Israelites to understand God in personal terms. It described God as One who delighted in His children, disciplined them when they

erred, and longed for restoration when separated from them
(Proverbs 3:11–12; cf. Hebrews 12:5–6; Jeremiah 31:20).

THE USE OF FATHER LANGUAGE
IN THE NEW TESTAMENT

In the New Testament the use of the term "Father" to refer to
God continued with an important new emphasis. It is there that the
person of the Father is most fully revealed. In His teaching and by
His example Jesus raised the biblical concept of God as Father to an
entirely new level by exhibiting an unparalleled degree of intimacy
in His personal prayer life. When Jesus addressed God as Father, He
did so using a term that was so intimate that it was normally used
by members of one's immediate family (Mark 14:36). In particular,
it was a familiar term used by children. Joachim Jeremias observes
that the Palestinian Jews of Jesus' day did not usually address God in
this way:

> We first meet the title "Father" as a direct address in prayer in
> ancient Judaism; but there are only isolated instances in Palestine. In
> the Diaspora there are rather more. By and large other titles for God
> are far more frequent in Jewish prayers. From the first two centuries
> A.D. we can mention with certainty *only two prayers* from Palestine
> which address God as Father.[4]

The church followed Jesus' example and employed the term
Abba in its own prayer life (Romans 8:15; Galatians 4:6). This term
has been compared to the diminutive "Daddy." However, James Barr
has pointed out that it is probably better to understand it as an
emphatic form that meant either "my father" or "*the* father."[5] Jesus'
use of such language revealed that the fatherhood of God was more
than a mere metaphor. It identified the Father as a distinct person of
the Godhead. This person was the Father first and foremost because
He was Father in relation to the Son. Jesus was "the only begotten
Son" sent by the Father to provide salvation for the world (John
3:16–17 KJV). Jesus was the object of the Father's love and pleasure

(Matthew 3:17; 17:5; John 5:20). More important, Jesus was the embodied revelation of the Father. So much so, in fact, that He could say: "Anyone who has seen me has seen the Father" (John 14:9). Jesus also taught that this same person was Father to all who would trust in the Son. The disciples' relationship to Jesus not only enabled them to learn about the person of the Father, but ushered them into an intimate relationship with Him. This intimate relationship became the basis for their confidence in prayer (John 16:23–24). On the night of His betrayal and arrest Jesus comforted the disciples, saying: "Though I have been speaking figuratively, a time is coming when I will no longer use this kind of language but will tell you plainly about my Father. In that day you will ask in my name. I am not saying that I will ask the Father on your behalf. No, the Father himself loves you because you have loved me and have believed that I came from God" (John 16:25–27).

In other words, Jesus taught His disciples not only to pray to the *Father* but also to pray to Him as *their* Father. This link between the work of Christ and the believer's experience of the Father became the central theme of New Testament theology. It also raised a practical question. If Jesus was the primary mediator of the disciple's knowledge and experience of the Father, how would the believer gain access to this knowledge and experience in the physical absence of Jesus? The solution was to be found in the person of the Holy Spirit, whom Jesus said would come upon the disciples after His departure. He promised to ask the Father to send "another Counselor to be with you forever" (John 14:16). Upon His arrival the disciples would realize "that I am in my Father, and you are in me, and I am in you" (v. 20).

Jesus referred to the Holy Spirit as "the Spirit of your Father" (Matthew 10:20). He said that the Father would be pleased to give the Holy Spirit to those who asked (Luke 11:13; cf. John 15:26). Later, the apostle Paul linked the believer's access to the Father to the ministry of both Christ and the Spirit by saying: "Through him [i.e., Christ] we both have access to the Father by one Spirit" (Ephesians 2:18). According to Paul, Christ's work makes access possible to Jews and Gentiles alike, while the Holy Spirit makes such access a reality in their experience. Jesus Christ gives us the right to have access to the Father, and the Holy Spirit actualizes it for us.

Consequently, the image of the Father cast in the New Testament is one that has been refracted through the prism of Trinitarian theology. This is what Cornelius Plantinga Jr. described as the "uniquely Christian claim about the divine."[6] The New Testament reaffirmed Old Testament monotheism but also asserted that this same God existed in a unity of three persons: Father, Son, and Holy Spirit. It made the shocking claim that the Father could only be truly known in conjunction with the Son and the Spirit. One of the church's earliest struggles was the challenge of defining this relationship and defending it against those who objected to such a doctrine.

WHAT DOES THE FATHER METAPHOR SAY ABOUT GOD?

What, then, does the Father metaphor tell us about God? To answer this question we must first understand how metaphorical language functions. A metaphor uses one thing to explain another. Metaphors employ the concrete to explain the abstract and are an integral part of human communication. Indeed, most concepts are "partially understood in terms of other concepts."[7] This is doubly necessary where God is concerned, because "No one has ever seen God" (John 1:18; 1 John 4:12).

Jesus used the Father metaphor to illustrate the Father's willingness to give "good gifts" to His children (Matthew 7:11). His pointed analogy recognized the vast difference between the Creator and His creatures by acknowledging that we are by nature "evil." Yet Jesus' application clearly indicated that there is also some point of contact between an earthly father and the heavenly Father. According to Jesus, the commonality they share is the quality of compassion: "Which of you, if his son asks for bread, will give him a stone? Or if he asks for a fish, will give him a snake?" (Matthew 7:9–10). Bread and fish were the two primary staples in the diet of His audience. Jesus' words do not imply that every parent will automatically show compassion to his children. The Scriptures acknowledge the possibility of neglect (Isaiah 49:15). Yet even in an age where cases of neglect have increased sharply, it must be granted that most parents still consider it an obligation to meet their child's most basic needs. To use the language of Jesus, the child who asks for a loaf gets a loaf.

Children have an innate awareness of this parental sense of obligation that renders them fearless when making requests. They consider no request too small or too large, and no circumstance is too inconvenient to keep from asking. In time, of course, a child learns that there are limits to a father's patience and resources. The underlying assumption behind Jesus' words, however, is that God's children tend to underestimate their heavenly Father's willingness to answer prayer. At the same time, Jesus' words make it equally clear that God's answers to our prayers often depend upon the nature of the request. He is not the genie in the bottle who will grant any request that is made. God's answers are filtered through His wise and loving awareness of our true need. Part of the confidence that believers have when they pray is the assurance that God will sort through their requests and grant only those things that qualify as "good." If this were not the case, who would dare to pray? The same Father who will not give His son a snake when he asks for something to eat will also refuse to give His son a snake when he asks for a snake.

There is an equally important assumption about human nature behind Jesus' words. If God is like an earthly father, then it can also be said that earthly fathers are, in some measure, like God. All people are bearers of the divine image (Genesis 1:26; 9:6). This is both a blessing and a responsibility. It is a blessing because it provides a universal starting point for the knowledge of God, even for those who do not have access to special revelation. Although it does not provide enough knowledge to lead to salvation, it does offer a starting point. Theologian Charles Hodge observed: "If we are like God,

God is like us. This is the fundamental principle of religion."[8] It is also the ground for all moral behavior.

This is not to say that all humans acknowledge the same moral standard. Clearly, they do not. We cannot even say that all humans acknowledge that their sense of right and wrong comes from an innate awareness of what God is like. In reality the opposite is true. The impediment of sin guarantees that our natural response will be to suppress what can be known about God (Romans 1:18–20). What is certain is that all humans have *some* moral sense. They have an innate sense that there is a standard by which actions must be measured. C. S. Lewis refers to this as "the rule of fair play" and notes that this Law of Human Nature comes to the surface every time we feel we have been mistreated. Lewis explains that people who are wronged universally appeal to a standard of behavior, one which they expect others to know about. When this happens the other party rarely rejects the standard itself: "Nearly always he tries to make out that what he has been doing does not really go against the standard, or that if it does there is some special excuse."[9]

This, then, is the responsibility that comes with being created in God's image: All human beings are to reflect His character in their actions. This is especially true of those who name God as their heavenly Father as a result of the work of Christ: "As obedient children, do not conform to the evil desires you had when you lived in ignorance. But just as he who called you is holy, so be holy in all you do; for it is written: 'Be holy, because I am holy'" (1 Peter 1:14–16). If God is our Father, then we have an obligation to reflect His image in our actions. To do this we must know something about God's attributes. Some of these are shown through His names.

NAMES OF THE FATHER

My father had several names. His colleagues at work called him George. My mother, on the other hand, called him Bill, because his middle name was William. His best friend referred to him as "Father," based (I think) on the nickname of the jazz pianist Earl

"Fatha" Hines. I called him Dad. God the Father also has several names. Each one reveals an important dimension of His character and work. Geerhardus Vos explains: "In the Bible the name is always more than a conventional sign. It expresses character or history. Hence a change in either respect frequently gives rise to a change of name. This applies to the names of God likewise. It explains why certain divine names belong to certain stages of revelation. They serve to sum up the significance of a period. Therefore they are not names which man gives to God, but names given by God to Himself."[10] These divine names were revealed, not only so that we would know how to address our heavenly Father, but primarily so that we would know what He is like.

God of Power

According to Vos, the oldest and most common divine names are *El* and *Elohim*.[11] Both terms are usually translated "God" and come from a Hebrew root that means "strength." *Elohim* is the most general name for God and is also used to refer to false gods and idols. It occurs first in Genesis 1:1: "In the beginning God created the heavens and the earth." It is the name of God the Creator who brought all things into existence by His own power. As such, He is not merely the God of Israel but was first and foremost the God of all the nations.[12] In Deuteronomy 32:37–39 the Lord used the term Elohim to refer to Himself and to the false gods worshiped by the nations and declares that He alone is God. The first commandment also uses it when it warns: "I am the Lord your God, who brought you out of Egypt, out of the land of slavery. You shall have no other gods before me" (Exodus 20:2–3). These names are often used in a way that emphasizes the personal relationship that exists between the Father and His children. He is called "my God" and "your God."

The name *El* is sometimes compounded with other terms and phrases that reflect the Father's attributes. Hagar used the term El when she referred to the Lord as "the God who sees me" (Genesis 16:13). Interestingly, the same title appears in Isaiah 45:15, which says: "Truly you are a God who hides himself, O God and Savior of Israel." He is a God who sees but is not Himself seen. Other uses indicate that He is the "faithful God" and the "holy God" (Deuteronomy 7:9; Isaiah 5:16). He is the God of "knowledge," "glory," and "truth" (Psalm 29:3; 31:5; 94:10). El Shaddai means God Almighty (Genesis 17:1; 28:3; 35:11; 43:14; 48:3; Exodus 6:3).[13] In Genesis 14:18–22 the name El is coupled with Elyon and is translated "God Most High." He is the God who "saves the upright in heart" and "fulfills His purpose" for His people (Psalm 7:10; 57:2). He is their Redeemer (Psalm 78:35). In general, combinations employing the term El stress the Father's superiority, ability to save, and awesome power. He has no equal among the nations and alone is to be worshiped with holy fear. Yet He is also deeply concerned about the needs of His people.

God of Authority

The name Adonai could be translated "Lord," "Master," or even "Ruler," and it emphasizes the Father's authority. A form of this word is sometimes used to refer to human authorities. For example, it is used in Genesis 24:9 to refer to Abraham's relationship to his servant (cf. Genesis 24:12, 14, 27). Sarah used the term to refer to her husband Abraham (Genesis 18:12). Interestingly, Rebekah also used it as a title of respect when she addressed Abraham's servant (Genesis 24:18). It is the term used to refer to the king (1 Samuel 16:16; 2 Samuel 14:9). Israel's God, however, is the supreme authority and the source from which all other authority is derived. He is "God of gods and Lord of lords, the great God, mighty and awesome, who shows no partiality and accepts no bribes" (Deuteronomy 10:17).

The recognition of God's authority is an important aspect of faith. The Gospels tell how a centurion from Capernaum asked Jesus to heal his servant. The servant was so ill that he could not be brought to Jesus. Yet despite the urgency of his case, the centurion did not ask Jesus to come personally. Instead, when Jesus offered to come, the centurion replied, "Lord, I do not deserve to have you come under my roof. But just say the word, and my servant will be healed. For I myself am a man under authority, with soldiers under me. I tell this one, 'Go,' and he goes; and that one, 'Come,' and he comes. I say to my servant, 'Do this,' and he does it." When Jesus heard this He praised the centurion for his "great faith" (Matthew 8:8–10; cf. Luke 7:9–10). This man's request did not stem only from his recognition of Christ's authority. It was ultimately grounded in his trust in Christ. He was confident that Jesus would be sympathetic to his need and respond to his request. In the same way, our recognition of the Father's authority over our lives should not be an exercise in cringing obedience but should be grounded in the confidence that His will for us flows from His unfailing love. Psalm 32:10 promises: "Many are the woes of the wicked, but the Lord's unfailing love surrounds the man who trusts in him."

God of Promise

Another name became prominent during the Mosaic period. Usually translated Jehovah or Yahweh, this name was based upon the Hebrew verb "to be." J. Barton Payne describes it as "the most important single definition of God's name."[14] This was God's personal name and the name associated with His covenant promises to Israel. Its meaning, according to Exodus 3:14, is "I AM WHO I AM." It was revealed in response to Moses' question: "Suppose I go to the Israelites and say to them, 'The God of your fathers has sent me to you,' and they ask me, 'What is his name?' Then what shall I tell them?" (Exodus 3:13). When Moses first received God's call to bring the Israelites out of Egypt, he objected that he was unqualified for the task. The Lord, in return, replied that His own presence was qualification enough (Exodus 3:11–12). Moses' question arose from his expectation that the elders of Israel would ask for evidence for the claim that God was with him. How would the divine name be proof? Perhaps Moses recognized that the Israelites would expect their God to follow the same pattern He had with the patriarchs by linking this new revelation of Himself with a distinctive name (cf.

Exodus 6:3).[15] Brevard S. Childs notes, however, that the Lord's
answer is somewhat ambiguous:

> The formula is paradoxically both an answer and a refusal of an
> answer. The tenses of the formula indicate that more than a senseless
> tautology is intended, as if to say, I am who I am, a self-contained,
> incomprehensible being. Moses is not simply refuted as was Manoah
> (Judg. 13:18). Rather God announces that his intentions will be
> revealed in his future acts, which he now refuses to explain.[16]

In other words, the essence of the Lord's response was that
Moses' experience of God's presence would itself be the proof of
God's presence. The truth of this is reflected in the "sign" promised
to Moses in Exodus 3:12: "And God said, 'I will be with you. And
this will be the sign to you that it is I who have sent you: When you
have brought the people out of Egypt, you will worship God on this
mountain.'" Unlike the miraculous signs granted to the elders of
Israel that served to confirm Moses as God's representative, this was
a sign granted after the fact. The only way that Moses would ever
see it was to obey God's call. Not surprisingly, many combinations
with the divine name Jehovah emphasize the experiential dimension
of our relationship with the Father. He is the Lord who provides for
us (Genesis 22:14). He is the Lord who heals us (Exodus 15:26). He
is the Lord who is our banner and who protects us (Exodus 17:15).
He is the Lord who makes us holy (Exodus 31:13). He is the Lord
who is the source of our peace (Judges 6:24). He is the Lord of hosts
who defends those who cannot defend themselves and preserves His
people (1 Samuel 17:45; Isaiah 1:9; Romans 9:29; James 5:4).

DYSFUNCTIONAL VIEWS OF THE FATHER

Like many children, four-year-old Paul has begun to ask questions about God. After serious reflection, he announced that he
thought he had figured out just who God was. "Is he Dad?" he
asked.[17] Paul's experience is not at all unusual. Indeed, it seems to be
part of God's original design that our first impressions of what He is

like should come from our experience with our earthly parents. What happens, however, when the model provided by our parents is dysfunctional? Nancy J. Duff, Associate Professor of Christian Ethics at Princeton Theological Seminary, has warned that the "emotional fallout" in such cases may have permanently distorted the truth that is meant to be conveyed by the biblical use of the term "Father" to refer to God. Duff explains: "While defenders of the Reformed tradition maintain that we should not understand the fatherhood of God by looking first at earthly fathers, they refuse to acknowledge that some people's experience with abusive fathers means that the word 'father' itself cannot be recovered."[18] In fact, some who have grown up with abusive fathers have commented that even those with deficient fathers know what a father *should* be, and those children see in God what a father is supposed to look like.

Some have attempted to solve the apparent problem by removing such language from our translations. If, however, God's use of the term Father is intentional, as the Scriptures seem to indicate, such a solution is unwise. What is more, any relief it provides will only be cosmetic. The lesson that fatherhood teaches about God is ultimately to be found in the experience of parenting itself. It is the image of God itself that has been distorted in man, and not merely one of His titles. What is really needed is a renewed perception of what God the Father is truly like. The only way to do this is to examine and expose the false images that sinful parenting has created.

Your heavenly Father is not an angry father. The Bible does speak of God's "wrath." His anger, however, is not like the rage that some of us experienced as children. In our case parental anger was unpredictable. The punishment it provoked was either unwarranted or wholly out of proportion to our actions. God's anger, on the other hand, is directed "against all ungodliness and unrighteousness of men, who hold the truth in unrighteousness" (Romans 1:18 KJV). Although those who have not trusted in Christ are "children of wrath" and in danger of judgment, God the Father deals patiently with them (Exodus 34:6; Ephesians 2:3 KJV; 5:6; Colossians 3:6). He loves them despite their sin and does not enjoy the prospect of punishing them. Instead, He gives them time to repent and pleads with them to turn from sin (Ezekiel 18:31; 33:11; 2 Peter 3:9). He is the Father who loved us before we loved Him, while we were still dead in our sins (Ephesians 2:4–5; 1 John 4:10). What is more, He did not even spare His own Son, but gave Him up for us so that we would not have to experience His wrath (Romans 8:32).

Your heavenly Father is not an absent father. Many children are the victims of parental abandonment and neglect. Recently I noticed a billboard emblazoned with the question "Who's the father?" and a toll-free number. Presumably, a mother who calls this number will receive information about DNA testing that will enable her to discover who is the father of her child. In other cases the father is known but absent, either as a result of divorce or abandonment. David Blankenhorn, president of the Institute for American Values, reports that about 40 percent of children in the United States live apart from their fathers. Blankenhorn argues that one of the factors that has contributed to this trend may actually be a lack of knowledge about God: "Several years ago I wrote a book about fatherlessness, arguing that it is the most harmful social trend of our generation. In it I only asked: Do children need fathers? But what if the deeper question is: Do fathers need God? Does knowledge and love of God help a man to be a good father and a good husband?"[19] God the Father is "an ever-present help in trouble" (Psalm 46:1). He has promised to never leave or forsake His children (Deuteronomy 31:6, 8; Joshua 1:5; 1 Kings 8:57; cf. Matthew 28:20). If our earthly parents abandon us, God the Father will accept us (Psalm 27:10).

Your heavenly Father is not a silent father. Some parents find it so difficult to communicate to their children that they have never said the words "I love you." Perhaps it is because they assume that such things are so obvious they do not need to be stated. They may be too embarrassed to say what they are feeling. God the Father, on the other hand, has no such qualms about expressing Himself to His children. He has spoken to us by word and by deed. He has provided an unwritten testimony of His glory in creation and spoken to us in human language through His Word. He has given us a permanent proof of His unfailing love for us by sending His Son to speak on His behalf, so that Jesus could say: "Anyone who has seen me has seen the Father" (John 14:9). The Father has communicated to us in so many ways that the hymnwriter asked: "What more can He say than to you He hath said, To you who for refuge to Jesus have fled?"

Your heavenly Father is not a dependent father. Dysfunctional parents often seek from their children the things that they failed to receive from their own parents. The result is a tragic reversal of roles. Those who should receive the care of their parents become the caretakers. Unlike these earthly parents the heavenly Father has no needs. Acts 17:24–25 declares: "The God who made the world and everything in it is the Lord of heaven and earth and does not live in temples built by hands. And he is not served by human hands, as if he needed anything, because he himself gives all men life and breath and everything else." The Father's actions toward His children are never driven by selfish motives. The fact that He uses us is for our sake, not for His.

The reality of sin means that all parents are dysfunctional parents to some degree. None of us can perfectly model what God is like. It is this very fact that makes it so important that we know God as Father. David Blankenhorn points out that in order for a society to produce good fathers, it must first have a clear sense of what a good father looks like. He suggests: "For people of faith, the ultimate reality of 'Father,' in whose likeness humans are created and toward which they are ordinated, is the reality of God, the pattern of all parenthood."[20]

RETURNING TO THE FATHER

Jesus once told a story about a father who had two sons. The older son was responsible and cautious. He never took a risk and always had his nose to the grindstone. The younger son was a daredevil. Between the two, he was always the one out in front. Given the choice between work and play, play won out every time. One day the younger son came to his father, demanded his share of the estate, and left home. It was a rash and foolish decision. Before long

the young man's funds had run out and he found himself living a
life of virtual slavery. In desperation he decided that, no matter how
embarrassing it might be, he would go home to his father and fall
on his mercy.

As he walked along the dusty road he imagined what it would
be like to see his father again. He even memorized the first words he
would say once their eyes met. No doubt he wondered about the
kind of reception he would have once the two finally met. He did
not have to wait long to find out. Jesus told us that while the prodigal was still a long way off, his father saw him and was filled with
compassion for him. He ran to his son, threw his arms around him,
and kissed him. It is clear that the father had been watching for his
return. The boy began to make a confession and to plead with his
father to let him return as a servant, but he was interrupted.
"Quick!" the father commanded his servants. "Bring the best robe
and put it on him. Put a ring on his finger and sandals on his feet.
Bring the fattened calf and kill it. Let's have a feast and celebrate.
For this son of mine was dead and is alive again; he was lost and is
found" (Luke 15:22–24).

While the father and the servants celebrated the younger son's
return, the older son approached the house. He too was covered
with dust, but of a different kind. As usual he had spent the heat of
the day laboring in his father's field. When he heard the commotion
in the house he called for one of the servants and inquired about it.
Perhaps he was surprised by the unplanned party and felt uncomfortable about entering the house while still covered with the grime
of the workday. Or did he ask because he already knew the answer?
Had he somehow anticipated or even seen his brother's return? The
servant joyfully replied: "Your brother has come, . . . and your father
has killed the fattened calf because he has him back safe and sound"
(Luke 15:27). The older son was furious and refused to join the
party. When his father came to plead with him, he spat back:
"'Look! All these years I've been slaving for you and never disobeyed
your orders. Yet you never gave me even a young goat so I could celebrate with my friends. But when this son of yours who has squan-

dered your property with prostitutes comes home, you kill the fattened calf for him!" (vv. 29–30).

Here is the wonder of the story. The prodigal had asked to be a slave and was restored as a son. Yet after all these years it was the "good" son who felt like a slave. He complained that he had "slaved" for his father and "never disobeyed" his orders. He did not think of himself as a son but as an employee. It is true that the younger son had squandered his inheritance, but the older son had done something far worse: He had forfeited his relationship with his father by serving him with the mentality of a wage earner. The older son's words reveal his fundamental error. He had not earned what was his any more than his younger brother had. It belonged to him by virtue of his relationship with his father. This is precisely what the father said as he patiently pleaded with his older son to join the party. "'My son,' the father said, 'you are always with me, and everything I have is yours. But we had to celebrate and be glad, because this brother of yours was dead and is alive again; he was lost and is found'" (Luke 15:31–32).

In the Father's eyes we are all wanderers and rebels. We cannot earn His forgiveness, and we do not deserve it. The only ground for acceptance is the ground of mercy. That is why Jesus Christ died and rose again. We can know the Father and experience His love only as a gift that comes through faith in Jesus Christ. God the Father does not want any of His children to linger on the threshold of a relationship with Him like outsiders.

QUESTIONS FOR DISCUSSION

1. Why do you think some people object to the use of the term "Father" when referring to God?

2. In what sense did Jesus "raise the biblical concept of God as Father to an entirely new level"?

3. In what way did Jesus use the Father metaphor to help us understand God better?

4. What does God's use of the title Father to refer to Himself teach us about ourselves?

5. What do the divine names El and Elohim reveal about the Father's relationship to the nations?

6. What does the name Adonai emphasize about the Father?

7. Why would the removal of the term "Father" from our translations be an inadequate solution for those who have a dysfunctional view of God the Father?

2

THE ROLE OF THE FATHER

The teenage son of the famous Scottish novelist Sir Walter Scott once listened to a group of older adults discussing the literary work of his father. When one of them described the elder Scott, the author of *Ivanhoe*, as a genius, the son readily agreed, but for different reasons. "Aye," he observed, "it's commonly him is first to see the hare."

It is natural for a child to hold his or her father in high esteem. What, however, are we to make of Jesus' statements about His Father? At times Jesus spoke of God the Father as an equal. On other occasions He used language that seemed to speak of the supremacy of the Father. What is the Father's relationship to the other members of the Trinity?

Throughout history the doctrine of the Father has brought objections from heresies that have sprung up within the church. The focus of those challenges has varied but has tended to fall into one of two divisions.

ANCIENT OBJECTIONS TO THE THEOLOGY OF THE FATHER

The earliest objections the church faced regarding its teaching about the Father were concerned primarily with His relationship to the Son. By the end of the second century and into the third century, the church was forced to respond to a form of teaching known as Monarchianism. This heresy had grown out of two older heresies, Ebionism and Docetism, that had appeared during the second century. All of them reflected the church's struggle to understand the relationship between Jesus Christ and the Father. The Ebionites had rejected the divinity of Christ. Many of them regarded Him as nothing more than a Rabbi. Other Ebionites claimed that the Christ had descended upon Jesus in the form of a dove at His baptism and later departed from Him. Docetism denied the Incarnation and taught that Christ only appeared to have a body. Its name is derived from the Greek word δοκέω, which meant "to have the appearance of."

Monarchianism emphasized the oneness of God but rejected the idea of distinct persons. Dynamic Monarchianism taught that Jesus was a mere man who had been indwelt with divine power. Modalistic Monarchianism affirmed Christ's divinity but at the expense of His humanity. One form of Modalistic Monarchianism, known as Patripassianism, taught that it was really the Father who suffered on the cross. Sabellius, who taught in Rome in the early third century, regarded Christ and the Holy Spirit as modes of the Father. The New Testament does say "God was reconciling the world to himself in Christ" (2 Corinthians 5:19). The context suggests, however, that Paul used the preposition "in" to signify that Christ was the means used by God to reconcile the world to Himself rather than to imply that the Father had somehow inhabited the human Jesus or that God had merely appeared to take a human form.

One of the most serious doctrinal challenges of this era came from a church leader from Alexandria by the name of Arius (d. 336). Arius was one of several presbyters who had been summoned by the bishop of Alexandria to a conference for the purpose of discussing the meaning of Proverbs 8:22–23: "The Lord brought me forth as the first of his works, before his deeds of old; I was appointed from eternity, from the beginning, before the world began." Arius argued that God was originally alone (μόνος). When Christ was begotten, God became a dyad and then a triad when the Spirit was produced. He was convinced that to say that Jesus Christ was of the same substance as the Father detracted from God's transcendence. According to Arian teaching God "had not always been a Father."[1] Jesus Christ was the only begotten Son who was less than God but more than man.

The emperor Constantine became concerned about this dispute when the conflict created within the church by this doctrine threatened the political stability of his empire. Consequently, he called a general church council to resolve the matter. Between two hundred fifty and three hundred eighteen church leaders gathered at Nicea in June of A.D. 325 to debate the issues. Athanasius, who attended the conference with Alexander the bishop of Alexandria and acted as his secretary, later went on to write a treatise defending both the true deity and genuine humanity of Christ and emphasizing the deity of the Holy Spirit. Athanasius warned that Arian theology ultimately called into question the validity of Christ's sacrifice. He argued that the value of Christ's sacrifice was dependent upon Christ's nature.

Other councils followed, each one dealing with the theological implications of the church's teaching about the Father, Son, and Holy Spirit. Among the most important were the councils at Constantinople, Ephesus, and Chalcedon. The council of Constantinople in A.D. 381 addressed the teaching of Apollinarius, which claimed that Christ had a real body but one that functioned, more or less, as a container for the Logos. The Logos took the place of what would have normally been the soul in an ordinary human being. This meant that He was divine but not truly human. The creed issued by the council emphasized the reality of the Incarnation and reaffirmed that Christ was truly God ("very God of very God, begotten not made, being of one substance with the Father") and also truly man ("incarnate by the Holy Ghost and the Virgin Mary, and was made man"). It also affirmed that the Holy Spirit was to be worshiped along with the Father and the Son.

The council of Ephesus in A.D. 431 dealt with a reaction to the

teaching of Apollinarius known as Nestorianism. Nestorius, a pres-
byter at Antioch who became the patriarch of Constantinople in
A.D. 428, taught that Christ had both a human and a divine nature
and that these natures were distinct. Those who opposed him
accused Nestorius of teaching that Christ was really two distinct
persons, one human and the other divine. The practical result was to
minimize Christ's divine nature, which Nestorius taught could not
take part in His human experiences.

The council of Ephesus condemned Nestorius and removed
him from office. The council of Chalcedon in A.D. 451 continued to
grapple with the theology of Christ's two natures, responding to the
teaching of a monk from Asia Minor by the name of Eutychus.
Eutychianism is also known as Monophysitism because it taught
that Christ did not really have two natures but one, a kind of
divine/human hybrid. The council of Chalcedon, under the leadership of Pope Leo I, rejected this view and affirmed that Christ had
two permanently distinct natures that cannot be separated or confused, joined in one hypostatic union. The Greek noun from which
the term *hypostatic* is derived meant "being."

These discussions may seem obscure and strangely irrelevant to
many of us today. However, this is primarily because we now take
for granted the theological foundation that these early church leaders labored to establish. They recognized the importance of a proper
understanding of the relationship between the three members of the
Trinity. We cannot correctly view the Father apart from an understanding of His Son Jesus Christ and the Holy Spirit. Indeed, we
cannot really worship the Father apart from Christ and the Holy
Spirit. A God who is Father alone is not the God of the Bible and is
really a false god.

MODERN OBJECTIONS
TO THE THEOLOGY OF THE FATHER

While Jesus Christ was the focus of theological controversy for
the early church, it is the Father who is the object of discussion for

many today. In recent days the church's use of the term "Father" to refer to God has itself come under fire, with many objecting that such language is both misleading and a form of gender-based oppression. Feminists like Mary Daly have objected to such language, saying that it promotes sexism: "Since God is male, the Male is God."² Others have complained that this type of language alienates worshipers who are not male.

In addition to this social question, the Bible's use of gender-specific language to refer to God raises an important theological question. The Bible clearly teaches that both men and women are made in the image of God (Genesis 1:27). Why, then, are so many of the Bible's references to God couched in male terms? Is God male? Interestingly, the God of the Bible used both male and female images to describe Himself. Whereas He used the title Father to reveal Himself in Scriptures, He also compared His compassion to that of a nursing mother: "Can a mother forget the baby at her breast and have no compassion on the child she has borne? Though she may forget, I will not forget you!" (Isaiah 49:15). Elsewhere, God promised to comfort Israel as a mother comforts her child (Isaiah 66:13). Jesus compared His yearning for Jerusalem to a mother hen who "gathers her chicks under her wings" (Matthew 23:37; Luke 13:34). Deuteronomy 32:18 may even mix these images when it says, "You deserted the Rock, who fathered you; you forgot the God who gave you birth." The Hebrew text is somewhat ambiguous, however, since the term that is here translated "fathered" is used of both women and men. What is clear from these descriptions is that both genders reflect God's image.

However, theologian Donald Bloesch has suggested that such language also implies that the idea of gender is not entirely alien to God. While it is wrong to say that God is male rather than female, it is not entirely correct to say that God is genderless:

> In striking contrast to the deities upheld by the fertility cults of the ancient Mideast, the God of the Bible infinitely transcends human sexuality and gender. And yet since God fashioned man and woman in

his own image, we must surmise that gender is not foreign to his nature. His actions create the impression of gender and are so described in the Bible. He is the ground of both the masculine and the feminine, yet he chooses to relate to us in the form of the masculine— as Lord, Father, Son and so on. God is described in feminine imagery as well, but the masculine is always dominant, and God is never addressed as "Mother."[3]

Bloesch makes an important point. The term Father is used in the Bible to refer to God, not because of social convenience, but because it is the language God has chosen to use to reveal Himself and His character. It is revelatory language. If His goal had merely been to accommodate the cultural expectations of those who were to receive His Word, it seems likely that He would have been more inclined to speak in feminine terms since female deities were commonly worshiped by Israel's contemporaries. Some might argue that, if God were to reveal Himself today, He would not use the title Father. However, such a suggestion fails to do justice to the fact that God Himself selected both the Father metaphor and the historical context in which to reveal Himself. Wolfhart Pannenberg describes this as "the scandal of historical particularity that is the burden of the Christian faith in God's incarnation and history."[4] We are bound by the language that God Himself has chosen to use.

What is more, if God's goal in communicating in this way to humanity was self-revelation, then His use of gender-specific language is significant. It tells us something about God that other language cannot. This is consistent with what the Bible tells us about itself. According to 2 Timothy 3:16 all Scriptures are "God breathed"; they are the words breathed out by God Himself. Although He used human instruments without blotting out their personality, history, and vocabulary, the Holy Spirit superintended the process so that the result would include only those words He wanted to be recorded. Those who wrote the Scriptures were moved or "carried along" by the Holy Spirit (2 Peter 1:21). The control of the Holy Spirit in this process extended even to the very letters used to form the words

(Matthew 5:18). Consequently, when the Bible calls God "Father," it means just what it says.

IS THE FATHER GREATER THAN CHRIST?

Jesus clearly saw Himself as an equal with the Father. He claimed: "I and the Father are one" (John 10:30). His enemies correctly understood this to be a claim to deity (John 10:33). Jesus' language in this statement was reminiscent of the Jewish confession known as the "Shema," which was often recited as part of the synagogue service. Specifically, Jesus' words focused on the foundational statement of the Shema, which was drawn from Deuteronomy 6:4 and asserted that Israel's God was "one." Some commentators have suggested that the Hebrew term "one"(אֶחָד) actually functioned as a title for God in this verse.[5] Its sense was not merely to emphasize the monotheistic nature of Israel's religion, but to underscore the uniqueness of Israel's God as the one and only Jehovah. Old Testament commentators C. F. Keil and Franz Delitzsch explain that "what is predicated here of Jehovah *(Jehovah One)* does not relate to the unity of God, but simply states that it is to Him alone that the name *Jehovah* rightfully belongs, that He is the one absolute God, to whom no other *Elohim* can be compared."[6] If the term "one" in Deuteronomy 6:4 was a title for God equivalent to the name Jehovah, Jesus' statement could be understood to mean: "I and the Father are Jehovah."

However, Jesus did not mean by this that He and the Father were identical. The use of the neuter rather than the masculine form for the term "one" in John 10:30 implied unity of essence rather than identity of person.[7] This is a subtle but important distinction. To say that Jesus was identical with the Father would mean that He was merely a manifestation of the Father in another form, rather than a person distinct from the Father. At the same time, to affirm that Jesus (or the Spirit for that matter) is a divine person without also recognizing that He is of the same essence (οὐσία) as the Father would be equal to saying that He is another god along with the

Father. This would mean that the Christian doctrine of the Trinity was actually a form of polytheism! Theologian Herman Bavinck has pointed out the importance of understanding the implications of both affirmations. He has identified the three fundamental questions that must be answered if we are to understand the doctrine of the Trinity:

> For a proper understanding of the doctrine of the trinity three questions must be answered: What is the meaning of the term "essence," "being"? What is indicated by the word "person"? What is the relation between essence and person, and between the persons severally?[8]

The Father, Son, and Spirit are one in essence. They all possess the same divine nature. Yet They are distinct in their persons. In other words, the Father is not the Son nor is He the Spirit. Each is distinct from the other. Origen, an important church leader and theologian who taught in Alexandria in the third century, used the Greek term ὑπόστασις (hypostasis) to refer to this personal dimension of the Trinity. This term was originally synonymous with οὐσία (ousia) and had been employed by the Greek philosophers to refer to "real existence or essence, that which a thing is . . ."[9] Origen, however, distinguished it from οὐσία and used it in a way that emphasized the reality of the individual subsistence of each of the members of the Trinity.[10] Later theologians followed this example and maintained a distinction between the two terms, asserting that the three hypostases of the Trinity were one in *ousia*. This has become the classic definition of the Trinity: of one substance, in three persons.

The term *hypostasis* has also figured importantly in the church's effort to describe the relationship between the two natures of Christ. The council of Chalcedon held in A.D. 451 focused on the relationship between the human and divine natures of Christ. Jesus differs from the Father and the Holy Spirit because He alone possesses both a human nature and a divine nature. These two natures are united in one person (hypostasis). Theologians refer to this as the hypostatic union. Just as it is important to recognize the subtle distinction between the unity of nature and individual subsistence of the three members of the Trinity, it is equally important to understand that the two natures of Jesus are united in one person. Neither of these natures is mingled with the other. For example, we cannot say that Jesus is a kind of divine/human hybrid that is neither really human nor truly divine. Jesus is both truly human and truly divine. Yet neither can we say that each of these natures reflects a distinct person within Christ. We should not view Him as two persons, one human and the other divine, somehow cohabiting the same space.

Additionally, it is important to recognize that neither of Christ's two natures detracts or changes the other. His human nature does not "humanize" His divine nature, and His divine nature does not make His human nature less human. His divine nature remains divine and His human nature remains human. Theologian Charles Hodge has pointed out that Christ's *person* is theanthropic (a mixture of divine and human) but not His *nature:*

> Christ's person is theanthropic, but not His nature; for that would make the finite infinite, and the infinite finite. Christ would be neither God nor man; but the Scriptures constantly declare Him to be both God and man. In all Christian creeds therefore, it is declared that the two natures in Christ retain each its own properties and attributes.[11]

This clarification enables us to understand some of Jesus' most difficult statements about Himself and His relationship to the Father and helps us to see how Jesus could make assertions about Himself with respect to His human nature that would not apply to His divine nature. For example, Jesus could say, "The Father is greater than I" (John 14:28) without contradicting His earlier claim to equality with the Father. As far as Jesus' human nature was concerned, the Father was greater. Speaking from His human nature Jesus could legitimately say, "There is only One who is good," without denying the reality of His own goodness or His divine nature (Matthew 19:17). As a person with a truly human nature, Jesus could experience the kind of limitation of knowledge that caused Him to admit that the Father alone knew the day of His return (Matthew 24:36).

During His incarnation Jesus seems to have had access to the attributes of both natures, at times exercising the omnipotence and omniscience of His divine nature, while at others acting in the weakness and limitations of His human nature. The same person who possessed the power to raise the dead, feed the multitudes, and heal the sick was Himself subject to hunger, thirst, and weariness (John 4:6–7). He saw Philip beneath the fig tree before meeting him and knew the intimate details of the Samaritan woman's personal life without being told (John 4:17–18). Yet He needed to ask who had touched Him when a woman grasped the hem of His garment as He passed by in a crowd (Luke 8:45). Primarily He chose not to exercise the powers of His divine nature during His earthly ministry.[12]

The Father and the Son

It is significant that Jesus' equality with the Father did not exempt Him from the practice of submission. He did not see it as inconsistent with His position as the divine Son to do only what He saw the Father doing (John 5:19). Jesus said: "By myself I can do nothing; I judge only as I hear, and my judgment is just, for I seek not to please myself but him who sent me" (John 5:30). The submission of Christ reached its peak in the Garden of Gethsemane, where He pleaded with the Father to let the cup of suffering pass from Him with the stipulation "yet not my will, but yours be done" (Luke 22:42).

J. I. Packer has pointed out that this submission was not limited to Christ's incarnation. Instead, it was "a continuation in time of the eternal relationship between the Son and the Father in heaven."[13] In its attempts to explain the nature of this relationship, the church has not always been successful in maintaining the difference in role between the Father and Son without implying that the Son is somehow less than the Father. The technical term for such teaching is "subordinationism." Subordinationism teaches that the difference between the members of the Trinity is not merely one in Their order of being and their ministry but is more fundamental. It says that the Father, Son, and Spirit are not equal, but that the Son and the Spirit are inferior to the Father. For some, like Origen, this took the form of implying that Jesus was still God but in a lesser sense than the Father. Origen felt, for example, that it was inappropriate for believers to address their prayers to Christ. He taught that prayers should be addressed to the Father alone:

> If we understand what prayer is, perhaps we ought not to pray to anyone born [of woman], nor even to Christ himself, but only to the God and Father of all, to whom also our Saviour prayed, as we have mentioned before, and teaches us to pray. For when he heard "Teach us to pray," he did not "teach" them "to pray" to himself, but to the Father, saying, "Our Father which art in heaven," and so forth. For if, as is shown elsewhere, the Son is different from the Father in person and in subject, we must pray either to the Son and not to the Father, or to both, or to the Father alone.[14]

Others, like Arius who lived nearly a century after Origen, took a more extreme position and asserted that Jesus was actually a creature who had been brought into existence before time by the Father and was not God.

One of the important theological terms in this debate was the Greek word μονογενής, a term that is usually translated "only begotten" or, in the NIV, "one and only" (John 1:14, 18; 3:16, 18; 1 John 4:9). The fact that this word was linked etymologically to the verb γεννάω, which meant literally "to become the father of" and figuratively "to bring forth" or "produce," led to speculation about the "generation" of the Son by the Father. Origen had taught that the Son was begotten by an act of the Father's will. For Arius this could only mean that the Son had a beginning. Athanasius, who had attended the council of Nicea and would go on to become one of the most articulate spokesmen for its theology, countered that the Son was begotten by an internal, necessary, and eternal act of the

Father.[15] Simply put, the Father did not choose to beget the Son but did so because of His nature as Father. It was an act fundamental to His very nature that took place from all eternity. The conclusion of the church at the council of Nicea was that the Father had always been the Father, generating the Son from all eternity, and the Son had always been the Son, existing in a filial relationship to the Father. There was never a time when the Father was not the Father, nor was there ever a time when the Son was not the Son. The council of Nicea concluded that this filial relationship meant that the Son possessed the same divine nature and equality with the Father.

Although They are one in substance, distinct in person, and equal in glory, power, and divinity, the Father and the Son have distinct roles. The Father occupies a unique place in this intra-Trinitarian relationship. Jesus repeatedly pointed to the Father when referring to His own purpose, authority, and power. When His opponents tried to kill Him for failing to observe their Sabbath traditions and for making statements that implied that He was equal with God, Jesus responded that His ministry agenda had been determined by the Father. Jesus said: "I tell you the truth, the Son can do nothing by himself; he can do only what he sees his Father doing, because whatever the Father does the Son also does" (John 5:19; cf. John 5:30).

When the mother of Zebedee's sons came to Jesus and petitioned Him to grant James and John a place of prominence in the kingdom, Jesus replied, "To sit at my right or left is not for me to grant. These places belong to those for whom they have been prepared by my Father" (Matthew 20:23). Jesus also said that the Father had granted Him authority and that His unique relationship with the Father meant He alone had the power to reveal the Father (Luke 10:22). According to Jesus, it was the Father who had conferred the kingdom upon Him (Luke 22:29). Jesus even traced His authority to grant eternal life to the Father. The Son gives life to whomever He pleases, but this is because the Father has granted (literally "given") the Son to have life in Himself as the Father has life in Himself (John 5:26). Those who come to the Son in faith are those whom the Father has given to the Son (John 6:37).

Certainly, some of these statements can be understood as referring to conditions that were the result of Jesus' representative role as
the Second Adam. Jesus' deference to the Father and His obedience to
the Father's commands were part of His overall obedience on our
behalf. Yet the Scriptures use language that assign the Father the role of
initiator even prior to the Incarnation. It was the Father who sent the
Son: "For what the law was powerless to do in that it was weakened by
the sinful nature, God did by sending his own Son in the likeness of
sinful man to be a sin offering. And so he condemned sin in sinful
man, in order that the righteous requirements of the law might be fully
met in us, who do not live according to the sinful nature but according
to the Spirit" (Romans 8:3–4). Moreover, it is significant that following His resurrection and restoration to glory at the right hand of the
Father, Jesus continued to use language that implied some kind of dif-
ferentiation between their roles (Revelation 2:27).

These passages suggest that some aspects of this "division of
labor" between the Father and the Son are eternal in nature and not
limited to the period of Christ's humiliation. Can we conclude from
this that Jesus is dependent upon the Father? This was certainly true
of His human nature during His earthly ministry. To say any more,
however, might seem to detract from His divine nature. In fact, this
is one question that may actually be better answered in negative
rather than in positive terms—it is easier to say what is not true
than what is. If it seems too strong to say that the Son is fundamentally dependent upon the Father, it is at least clear that He is not
independent of the Father. In this respect the three members of the
Trinity are interdependent.

Jesus' statement in John 5:30 that by Himself He could do
nothing was not an admission of weakness but a declaration of
power and a testimony to His unity with the Father. It was part of
His overall defense to those who had condemned Him for making
Himself equal with God (v. 18). Far from being a denial of their
accusation, it was a bold admission that Jesus could do what the
Father could do. Like the Father, He raised the dead and gave them
life (v. 21). He was given the authority to act as the Father's repre-

sentative and judge sin (v. 22). As a result, He deserved the same honor that rightfully belonged to the Father (v. 23). In effect, Jesus put His enemies on notice that those who opposed Him also opposed His Father.

Submission Not Subordination

In reality, the Bible does not speak of Christ's "subordination" to the Father but of His submission. In Philippians 2:5–11 believers are told:

> Your attitude should be the same as that of Christ Jesus: Who, being in very nature God, did not consider equality with God something to be grasped, but made himself nothing, taking the very nature of a servant, being made in human likeness. And being found in appearance as a man, he humbled himself and became obedient to death— even death on a cross! Therefore God exalted him to the highest place and gave him the name that is above every name, that at the name of Jesus every knee should bow, in heaven and on earth and under the earth, and every tongue confess that Jesus Christ is Lord, to the glory of God the Father.

These verses reveal four important facts about Christ's submission to the Father:

1. *It was voluntary.* Although equal with the Father, Jesus did not cling to that equality. He "made himself nothing" (Philippians 2:7). The word order in this phrase places a slight emphasis on the pronoun "himself."[16] During the Incarnation Jesus "emptied" or stripped Himself of the prerogatives that were His by virtue of His divine nature. He was not compelled to do this by the Father. He freely took it upon Himself. That He did not cease to be equal with the Father in nature is clear from the fact that He continued to make claims of equality during His incarnation. He did, however, choose not to exercise His equality and instead took upon Himself the role of a servant. According to the writer of Hebrews He "learned obedience" during this period (Hebrews 5:8).

2. *It was linked to the Incarnation.* Jesus set aside the rights and privileges that were His in order to take to Himself a human nature. The "nature of a servant" referred to in this passage is further described as "being made in human likeness" and "being found in appearance as a man."

3. *It was functional.* Jesus humbled Himself in order to complete a specific task. He submitted to death on the cross. The Father did not die on the cross; Jesus did. Nor did the Father humble Himself. It was the Son who took the form of a servant. Yet the Son was not any less the Son, nor was He any less equal with the Father in nature and power when He chose to submit to the Father's will. This may be one of the reasons Jesus occasionally chose to exercise His divine attributes during the Incarnation: These actions demonstrate that He did not cease to be God when He became man.

4. *It was temporary.* Although Jesus is still incarnate, He is no longer in a state of voluntary humiliation. He has been exalted to the highest place. His prayer on the night of His betrayal indicated that He expected to be restored to the position of glory that was His prior to the incarnation (John 17:5). His present place at the right hand of the Father is one of equality. He is not second in command in the heavenly order but is co-ruler, seated with the Father on His throne (Revelation 3:21; 7:17; 22:3).[17] Yet even when Christ is in this exalted state, the Father occupies a unique place in relationship to the Son. Those who will bow the knee and confess that Jesus is Lord will do so "to the glory of God the Father" (Philippians 2:11). The post-resurrection relationship between God the Father and Jesus Christ is characterized by the apostle Paul as one in which the Father is "the head of Christ" (1 Corinthians 11:3).

The Father and the Spirit

The early church also struggled to understand the relationship between the Father and the Holy Spirit. Although the Scriptures clearly affirm the deity of the Holy Spirit, some church leaders taught that He was less divine than the Father. Gregory of Nazianzus, one of three important theologians from Cappadocia who lived in the late fourth century and played a significant role in shaping the church's statements about the doctrine of the Trinity during that era, wrote that some in his day understood the Holy Spirit to be an impersonal force. Others viewed Him as a created being. Gregory argued that what was true of Jesus Christ with respect to deity must also be true of the Holy Spirit. Like the Son, the Holy Spirit is of the same essence as the Father and is equally divine. Also like Christ, although equal with the Father, the Holy Spirit plays a distinct role in God's plan of redemption.

Jesus had said that the Holy Spirit "goes out" or "proceeds" from the Father (John 15:26). For Gregory this was proof enough that the Holy Spirit was God. Gregory maintained the deity of the Holy Spirit and the distinctiveness of the three persons of the Trinity, while affirming their unity. He wrote: "For neither is the Son Father, for the Father is one, but he is what the Father is; nor is the Spirit Son because he is of God, for the only-begotten is one, but he is what the Son is. The three are one in Godhead, and the one three in properties."[18]

However, a disagreement over the Holy Spirit's relationship to the Father and the Son became one of the factors that eventually alienated the Eastern branch of the church from its Western division. The Eastern church objected to the West's addition of the term *filioque* to the Nicene creed at the council of Toledo in A.D. 447. This addition clarified that the Holy Spirit proceeded from the Son as well as the Father. The volumes of speculative theology that resulted from this controversy did not really clarify the issue but only served to divide the church further. Gregory admitted that the question of the Holy Spirit's "generation" or "procession" from the Father was subtle and hard to understand. In his most important work, entitled *The Theological Orations,* he wrote: "What, then, is procession? Do you tell me what is the unbegottenness of the Father, and I will explain to you the physiology of the generation of the Son and the procession of the Spirit and we shall both of us be frenzy-stricken for prying into the mystery of God."[19]

Similarly, twentieth-century theologian Clark Pinnock has characterized the Holy Spirit as the most "mysterious" of the members of the Trinity:

> Spirit is not as clearly defined for us as Father and Son, because the Son became visible and renders the Father visible, while the Spirit remains invisible and not as easily known. It is easier to assign a face to the Son than to the Spirit, because of the historical concreteness of incarnation. By comparison, the Spirit is less well defined. Images like dove, water and fire (for example) are evocative but do not reveal the face of a Person; the Spirit remains somewhat anonymous.[20]

This "anonymity" appears to be intentional. If Jesus' words reflect a deference to the Father, this is doubly true of the work of the Holy Spirit. The nature of His ministry is one in which our attention is naturally directed away from the Spirit Himself. Instead, the Holy Spirit's words and works cause us to focus upon the other two members of the Trinity. For example, the Holy Spirit was God's agent in creation (Genesis 1:1; Psalm 33:6). This was a role He shared with Jesus Christ (John 1:3). He is the source of both physical and spiritual life (Genesis 2:7; John 6:63; 2 Corinthians 3:6). The Holy Spirit speaks, but not for Himself. In the Old Testament He was the agency of inspiration that enabled the prophets to speak on behalf of the Father (Ezekiel 37:1; Micah 3:8). After the coming of Christ His ministry was to bring glory to Christ and draw attention to His words: "But when he, the Spirit of truth, comes, he will guide you into all truth. He will not speak on his own; he will speak only what he hears, and he will tell you what is yet to come. He will bring glory to me by taking from what is mine and making it known to you" (John 16:13–14). He is the One who convicts of sin and unites the believer to Christ (John 16:8; Romans 8:9). He is the source of our assurance (Romans 8:15–16). He prays for us— another ministry that He shares with the Son (Romans 8:26–27; cf. Hebrews 7:25).

Although it is something of an oversimplification, the division of labor between the three members of the Trinity can be generally described this way: The Father sends, the Son redeems, the Spirit applies. The Holy Spirit unites us to Christ, who reveals to us what the Father is like. Their work might even be described as "patrocentric" (i.e., centered on the Father). The Son and the Spirit both work together to reveal the Father. The Spirit points to the Son, who in turn points to the Father. The Father in turn glorifies the Son, while the Holy Spirit does not begrudge the attention given to the other two members of the Trinity. How could He? Since They are one in essence, power, and glory, the glory given to one is also received by the others. There is no competition between Them.

The cooperation between the members of the Trinity serves as a model for the church's ministry relationships. This is especially true of Jesus' relationship to the Father, because it provides clear evidence that submission is not a sign of inferiority. Jesus was equal with the Father, yet He submitted to the Father. His relationship to the Father also indicates that differences in role do not diminish one's value. The Father's role as initiator in the plan of redemption did not detract from the Son's glory or equality in any way.

Those who follow in Christ's steps as His disciples are called to imitate our Lord's example (Luke 22:25–27). There is an important parallel between the relationship that exists between the three members of the Trinity and that which exists between believers. There is a "division of labor" between believers much like the one between the Father, Son, and Holy Spirit. All believers are equal, yet not all believers serve the same function. Some have "greater gifts," and some have lesser gifts (1 Corinthians 12:31). In Christ, "there is neither Jew nor Greek, slave nor free, male nor female, for you are all one in Christ Jesus" (Galatians 3:28). Yet believers in general are told, "Submit to one another out of reverence for Christ" (Ephesians 5:21).

This mutual submission was reflected in the social life of the New Testament church. Christian slaves were told to submit to their masters (Ephesians 6:5–6). Husbands were to love and respect their wives and to provide sensitive leadership in the home (Ephesians

5:25; Colossians 3:19; 1 Peter 3:7). Wives were to submit to their husbands (Ephesians 5:22–23; Colossians 3:18). Men were assigned the responsibility of primary leadership in the home and in the congregation (1 Timothy 2:11–15).

Many of these distinctions are now commonly criticized. This is especially true of those passages that seem to imply that some aspects of the church's leadership structure should be gender specific. To those who interpret the Bible through a lens colored by egalitarian culture such statements are embarrassing at best. They are often explained away as well meaning but misguided accommodations to a less enlightened age or as temporary restrictions that are no longer binding on the church. The most explicit passages, those in the Pastoral Epistles, are sometimes dismissed as being the inauthentic creations of the later church that were falsely ascribed to the apostle Paul to provide divine sanction for a patriarchal structure that God did not originally intend. This assumption is based upon a circular argument that focuses primarily on the content and vocabulary of these epistles. Those critics who argue that the Pastoral Epistles cannot have been written by Paul claim that the themes and vocabulary of these letters reflect issues that faced the church much later in its life. For example, they do not think that the leadership structure described in the Pastoral Epistles was a feature of the church in the New Testament era. Yet we know from the book of Acts that Paul and his companions appointed leaders in the churches and that these leaders were given the same titles that appear in the Pastoral Epistles (Acts 14:23). There is no historical or manuscript evidence to contradict the testimony of the letters themselves that they are the authentic work of the apostle Paul.

Those who must submit to others in the church do not do so because they are any less than those to whom they must submit. All are equal in Christ. Yet equality of position does not guarantee identity of function. Not everyone serves in the same capacity. This is certainly true in the case of spiritual gifts. Spiritual gifts are not distributed on the basis of personal merit but upon the basis of divine sovereignty (1 Corinthians 12:18). Those who possess one of the

"lesser" gifts cannot conclude from this that they are any less a part
of the body of Christ or any less valuable to it: "And if the ear
should say, 'Because I am not an eye, I do not belong to the body,' it
would not for that reason cease to be part of the body. If the whole
body were an eye, where would the sense of hearing be? If the whole
body were an ear, where would the sense of smell be?" (1 Corinthians 12:16–17).

Conversely, the example of the Father provides those who have
been charged with the responsibility of exercising leadership with a
much-needed model that shows them how they should fulfill their
calling. If Jesus' experience demonstrates that there is nothing inher-
ently demeaning in the practice of submission, it is equally true that
the church's history has often shown that leadership can be exercised
in a way that makes it so. God's leaders must exercise their authority
in a way that reflects the loving sensitivity of their heavenly Father.

While we may not be able to understand the "theological
physics" of the relationship between the Father, the Son, and the
Holy Spirit, the Scriptures can help us to understand something
about the role each of these members has in the work of redemption
and how They relate to one another. Even more important, God's
Word tells us how we are to respond to Their work in our lives. We
do not need to understand all the mechanics of Their relationship to
one another in order to benefit from Their ministry.

QUESTIONS FOR DISCUSSION

1. Why is it important to recognize that the unity between Jesus
   Christ and God the Father is a unity of essence rather than identity of person?
2. How would you characterize the difference between the Ebionite,
   Docetic, and Monarchian views of Jesus Christ?
3. What is meant by the "hypostatic union"?
4. What essential roles do the Son and Holy Spirit play in our
   understanding of God the Father?
5. What is meant by "subordinationism"?

6. Why might "submission" be a better term to use when describing the Son's relationship to the Father than "subordination"?

7. Describe four characteristics of Christ's submission to the Father.

8. Why might the work of the Son and the Holy Spirit be described as "patrocentric"?

9. What practical implications can be drawn from the relationship between the Father, the Son, and the Holy Spirit for relationships within the church?

3

THE NATURE OF THE FATHER

Helen Keller lost her sight, hearing, and the capacity to make most sounds as a result of a disease that she suffered during infancy. Deprived of these abilities, her initial awareness of the world around her was drawn from the three senses that remained. She used her sense of smell to locate her favorite food and to identify her own clothes from those of the rest of her family when they came back from the laundry each week. Her sense of taste enabled her to distinguish between the foods she liked and those she didn't. She used her sense of smell and the ability to feel her way around the house to find her way into her mother's garden.

She later explained that her dependence upon these three senses made her aware of many subtleties that others miss. For example, the difference in vibrations enabled her to tell whether the person walking across the floor was a child, a middle-aged adult, or a youth. She could even tell something about the person's emotional state from these vibrations: whether he was weary, distressed, or impatient. Although she could not see the sun, she could tell the difference between the cold light of a winter sun and the warm light of the summer rays. Although she did not have direct access to much of the world around her, she learned about it from its effects.

This is also true of much of our knowledge of God the Father. We know Him primarily by His effects.

THE INVISIBILITY OF THE FATHER

According to the Scriptures, God the Father is invisible. He is "the King eternal, immortal, invisible, the only God" (1 Timothy 1:17). When the Bible says this of Him, does it mean that it is impossible to see the Father, or simply that He is hidden from our view? At least one passage suggests the former. According to 1 Timothy 6:16, God the Father is the One "who alone is immortal and who lives in unapproachable light, whom no one has seen or can see" (1 Timothy 6:16). This description is reminiscent of the Lord's response to Moses when he asked to be shown God's "glory." The Lord replied that He would cause His "goodness" to pass before Moses but warned, "You cannot see my face, for no one may see me and live" (Exodus 33:20). More importantly, Jesus taught, "No one has seen the Father except the one who is from God; only he has seen the Father" (John 6:46; cf. John 1:18). He told His opponents that, unlike Him, they had never heard the Father's voice or seen His "form" (John 5:37). The Greek word that is translated "form" in this verse is the term εἶδος, which referred in other contexts to the "form" or "outward appearance" of something.

Is it possible, however, that the Father who is presently invisible to us actually possesses a substance that is at least potentially visible? The fact that Jesus could say that He *had* seen the Father may suggest that the Father is capable of being seen. Moreover, several passages seem to imply that it is possible for believers to see the Father. These fall into two major categories. First, there are statements that indicate that some believers have actually seen God. Such appearances are called "theophanies." A theophany is a manifestation of God in human form. For example, the patriarch Jacob dreamt of a stairway that reached from earth to heaven. It had angels ascending and descending upon it, and the Lord stood above it. When Jacob woke up he described the place as "the house of

God" and "the gate of heaven" (Genesis 28:17) and said: "Surely the Lord is in this place, and I was not aware of it" (v. 16). During the era of the judges the Angel of the Lord appeared to Samson's parents and predicted that they would have a son who would deliver Israel from the Philistines. After the experience, Samson's father Manoah was afraid that they would die because they had "seen God" (Judges 13:21–22). In his classic treatise on the existence and attributes of God, Puritan theologian Stephen Charnock explains that when God manifested Himself to Old Testament believers in this way, He did not reveal Himself to them in His essence:

> Though God hath manifested himself in a bodily shape (Gen. xviii. 1), and elsewhere Jehovah appeared to Abraham, yet the substance of God was not seen, no more than the substance of angels was seen in their apparitions to men. . . . Sometimes a representation is made to the inward sense and imagination, as to Micaiah, and to Isaiah (vi. 1); but they saw not the essence of God, but some images and figures of him proportioned to their sense or imagination. The essence of God no man ever saw, nor can see.[1]

Many think that Old Testament theophanies could also be described as "christophanies," appearances of Jesus Christ in human form prior to the Incarnation. If this is true, those who saw God on these occasions did not actually see the Father but saw Christ. The New Testament confirms that this was true in at least one instance. The apostle John explained that when the prophet Isaiah saw the Lord seated on a throne, high and exalted, in reality he "saw Jesus' glory and spoke about him" (John 12:41; cf. Isaiah 6:1).

A few passages reveal that it was not God Himself that was seen but some accompanying manifestation. This was the case with the elders of Israel, who were invited to fellowship in God's presence while encamped at Sinai. Although Exodus 24:11 says that they "saw God," the previous verse indicates that all they really saw was the pavement under His feet.[2] The case of Moses is more difficult. Despite the Lord's warning in Exodus 33:20 that no one could see

His face and live, the Lord later described their relationship as one in which He communicated with him "face to face" (Numbers 12:8). Numbers 12:8 also says that Moses saw the "form" (תְּמֻנָה) of the Lord. This is the same Hebrew term used in Exodus 20:4 and Deuteronomy 5:8 to prohibit the making of an idol in the "form of anything in heaven above or on the earth beneath or in the waters below." Gordon Wehnam noted that it normally used of visual representations, such as pictures or images.[3] In view of the Lord's warning in Exodus 33:20 and Jesus' statement that He alone had seen the Father, the phrase "face to face" must refer to the clear and intimate communion Moses enjoyed with the Father. It cannot mean that He had literally seen the Father's face. If such a thing had been possible, Moses would not have survived the experience.

A second class of passages indicates that believers will see the Father at some point in the future. This was Job's confidence during his time of trial: "I know that my Redeemer lives, and that in the end he will stand upon the earth. And after my skin has been destroyed, yet in my flesh I will see God; I myself will see him with my own eyes—I, and not another. How my heart yearns within me!" (Job 19:25–27). The psalmist expected to see God's "likeness" (Psalm 17:15). Jesus promised that the pure in heart would "see God" (Matthew 5:8). The apostle Paul says that we will see God "face to face," and the apostle John promises that we will see Him "as he is" (1 Corinthians 13:12; 1 John 3:2). It would be a mistake, however, to press this anthropomorphic language too far. The biblical language of "seeing" in these verses is not concerned with visual experience so much as it is with understanding. To "see" God is to "know" God. An overly literal interpretation of such language makes the mistake of assigning material attributes to an immaterial being. Theologian Charles Hodge observes:

> It is impossible, therefore, to overestimate the importance of the truth contained in the simple proposition, God is a Spirit. It is involved in that proposition that God is immaterial. None of the properties of matter can be predicated of Him. He is not extended or

divisible, or compounded, or visible, or tangible. He has neither bulk nor form.[4]

The language of seeing and knowing are combined in 1 Corinthians 13:12, where our present limited apprehension of God is compared to the experience of seeing a "poor reflection as in a mirror" and our future hope is that of seeing "face to face." This seeing is further described as knowing fully "even as I am fully known." We cannot see the Father, but we do know Him and will one day know Him better.

THE POSSIBILITY OF KNOWING THE FATHER

This raises a number of important questions. How can we know a God we cannot see? Who can know Him? More important, what can we know about Him? In the first chapter of his most famous work, *Institutes of the Christian Religion,* Reformation theologian John Calvin observed that all the wisdom we possess consists of two parts: the knowledge of God and the knowledge of ourselves. Calvin went on to explain that these two are related. The knowledge of ourselves points us to God, and the knowledge of God enables us to understand ourselves. When we examine ourselves and note the "mighty gifts with which we are endowed," it becomes clear to us that these do not come from ourselves.[5] At the same time, honest self-examination will inevitably lead to a painful discovery. We will find that we are sadly and deeply flawed:

> For, as a veritable world of miseries is to be found in mankind, and we are thereby despoiled of divine raiment, our shameful nakedness exposes a teeming horde of infamies. Each of us must, then, be so stung by the consciousness of his own unhappiness as to attain at least some knowledge of God. Thus, from the feeling of our own ignorance, vanity, poverty, infirmity, and—what is more—depravity and corruption, we recognize that the true light of wisdom, sound virtue, full abundance of every good, and purity of righteousness rest

in the Lord alone. To this extent we are prompted by our own ills to contemplate the good things of God; and we cannot seriously aspire to him before we begin to become displeased with ourselves.[6]

There is within us a dim reflection of the Father's image. We know something about Him by looking at ourselves. Jesus acknowledged this when He used human experience to explain the character of God (Matthew 7:9–11). However, Jesus also acknowledged something else. God is in some measure like us, but we are not entirely like God. To use the language Jesus used in Matthew 7:11, we are "evil." The entrance of sin into human experience has marred our ability to function as bearers of the divine image. We reflect the Father, but only imperfectly. Consequently, we can understand what the Father is like by noting the flaws of human nature and reasoning backward. We can say, in effect, "If this is what we are like in our sin, we can be certain that this is *not* what the Father is like." This is the kind of reasoning used in Numbers 23:19: "God is not a man, that he should lie, nor a son of man, that he should change his mind. Does he speak and then not act? Does he promise and not fulfill?"

The possibility of knowing the Father is further complicated by God's own nature. He is incomprehensible. To say that God is incomprehensible does not mean that He is confusing or unknowable, only that it is impossible to know Him exhaustively. Theologians have used the words immanence and transcendence to refer to these aspects of God's nature. When we say that God is immanent, we imply that He is knowable and involved in our lives. The Bible teaches that every person possesses an inherent knowledge of God. Because all humans possess this knowledge, it is often referred to as *general* revelation. It is general *revelation* because its existence depends upon God's own initiative in making Himself known. This is because God is transcendent as well as immanent. We are made in the image of God but we are not God. He is so far removed from us that, if He did not make Himself known to us, we would not know Him: "'For my thoughts are not your thoughts, neither are your ways my ways,' declares the Lord. 'As the heavens are higher than the earth, so are my ways higher than your ways and my thoughts than your thoughts'" (Isaiah 55:8–9).

External and Internal General Revelation

Fortunately, the Father has taken steps to ensure that we would know Him as He truly is. He did this first by leaving His imprint upon creation itself. According to Psalm 19:1 the heavens "declare" the glory of God and the skies "proclaim" the work of His hands. The first term (סָפַר) is used in the Old Testament of both counting and writing. It means to "recount" or "tell" something to somebody. The second term (נָגַד) is often used in the Bible to speak of revelation. This means that creation itself is a form of revelation. It tells us something about God. Specifically, it speaks of His glory. According to the psalmist, no place or people group is out of reach of this non-verbal form of divine self-disclosure. It reaches every corner of the globe and communicates regardless of any language (Psalm 19:3–4). Because its message is conveyed through the medium of creation, the conclusions drawn from this form of revelation have been called "natural" theology. Gerald Bray has pointed out that God's invisibility poses a significant problem for natural theology:

> This unavailability of God is in fact the greatest argument against natural theology, at least in the forms which it has traditionally taken. God's activity may always be "read into" the universe, the origins of which may even be attributed to him. But as far as hoping to find him in his creation by scientific means is concerned, natural theology is a complete non-starter. There is simply no way in which God can be measured or his existence made necessary to explain the course of events. In strictly scientific terms, therefore, God's existence is superfluous, because it does not come within the scope of scientific investigation.[7]

General revelation, however, is not confined to that which is seen in creation. In addition to being external and empirical, it is internal and subjective. Indeed, this internal dimension is necessary if we are to make any sense of external general revelation:

> God reveals Himself to the inner sense of man through the religious consciousness and the moral conscience. He also reveals himself in the works of nature without. It is obvious that the latter must rest on the former. If there were no antecedent innate knowledge of God, no amount of nature-observation would lead to an adequate conception of God.[8]

This is why the apostle Paul could later assert that God was just in revealing His wrath against all those who suppress the truth about God: "since what may be known about God is plain to them, because God has made it plain to them. For since the creation of the world God's invisible qualities—his eternal power and divine nature —have been clearly seen, being understood from what has been made, so that men are without excuse" (Romans 1:19–20).

Unfortunately, while this external and internal revelation is universal, it is also limited. It is thorough enough to tell us about God's eternal power and divine nature, but it does not tell us everything that should be known about God and His plan for us. It does not even tell what is most important about God. It only reveals enough to leave us "without excuse" when judged by God. The problem does not lie with general revelation but with us. Sin has not only damaged our ability to reflect God's image; it has also distorted our perception of Him. We perceive something about God in the world around us but not clearly. Romans 1:18 says that our natural response to the message of general revelation is to "suppress" it. Even worse, sin has spoiled our "taste" for the divine. We still hunger for God, but we find ourselves compelled to satisfy this desire with that which is not God (Romans 1:21–23). The reality of our sinful condition now demands a more explicit revelation that will show us the remedy for our alienation from the Father. Such a message could only come to us by special revelation.

Special Revelation

The names given to general revelation and special revelation themselves signal the significant difference between them. General revelation is accessible to all because it comes through nature. Special revelation "comes to a limited circle for the reason that it springs from the sphere of the supernatural through a specific self-disclosure of God."[9] General revelation is addressed to all, while special revelation is addressed to a particular audience. Special revelation is also more specific in its content than general revelation. General revelation tells us about God's attributes, while special revelation tells us about God's plan for dealing with humanity's sin.

The greatest difference between these two forms of revelation, however, is that special revelation is more direct than general revelation. This is exemplified by the biblical prophets' frequent use of the phrase "this is what the Lord says" to introduce their messages. In general revelation the heavens and Earth are declaring something about God. In special revelation it is God Himself who speaks. Special revelation, then, is a direct and personal revelation of God in word and deed. In special revelation God intervened in human events and then explained the significance of His actions. This explanation came through human instruments like Moses, the prophets, and the authors of Scripture who wrote under the inspiration of God's Spirit. Special revelation reached its apex in the person of Jesus Christ and has been preserved in the Scriptures. The message of general revelation has been objectified. It is cast in the form of physical symbols and visible analogies. Special revelation has the distinction of being verbal in nature. It has come to us in the form of propositions. Hebrews 1:1 says that God "spoke" to our forefathers. This statement underscores the remarkable truth that the God whose attributes are described to us in such general terms in creation has also communicated to us in human language.

Although special revelation is more direct than general revelation, our knowledge of the Father continues to be mediated knowledge, even when He speaks for Himself. Hebrews 1:1 says God spoke to our forefathers, but it also states that He did this "through the prophets." Moreover, the author went on to say that in these last days the Father's ultimate self-revelation has come through the person of Jesus Christ. The Son is not the Father, but He is "the radiance of God's glory and the exact representation of his being" (Hebrews 1:3). When the disciple Philip asked Jesus to "show" him the Father, the Lord replied that the disciples had already seen the Father: "Jesus answered: 'Don't you know me, Philip, even after I have been among you such a long time? Anyone who has seen me has seen the Father. How can you say, "Show us the Father"? Don't you believe that I am in the Father, and that the Father is in me? The words I say to you are not just my own. Rather, it is the Father, living in me, who is doing his work'" (John 14:9–10).

God's Word and Christ's works are inseparably bound together. Jesus has shown us the Father, but our knowledge of Him comes only through the Scriptures. In a sense, this was true even of those who had the opportunity to observe Jesus firsthand. He told His opponents: "You diligently study the Scriptures because you think that by them you possess eternal life. These are the Scriptures that testify about me, yet you refuse to come to me to have life" (John 5:39–40).

The Father's word is active and powerful. In the Old Testament the Hebrew term *dabar* (דָּבָר) can mean both word and act. What the Father speaks comes to pass in the very act of speaking (Genesis 1). Words figure importantly in the work of the other members of the Trinity as well. One of the titles of the Lord Jesus Christ is "the Word" (John 1:1). He was addressed as Teacher, and He promised a blessing to those who would obey His words (John 13:13, 15; 15:7). He warned that His response to us on the Last Day would be determined by our response to His words (Luke 9:26). The Holy Spirit was the Father's agent of inspiration, who "carried along" those who penned the Scriptures (2 Peter 1:21). Moreover, the Holy Spirit plays a critical role in our understanding of these same words. We do not need the Holy Spirit in order to possess a cognitive knowledge of what the Scriptures have to say about the Father, but without His help we cannot hope to benefit from that knowledge. Without the intervention of the Spirit our compulsion to suppress the truth about God will become too strong. We need the Spirit to truly understand and accept what God is saying about Himself in the Bible (1 Corinthians 2:14; cf. 1 John 2:27).

THE FATHER'S ATTRIBUTES

What, then, does the Bible say that God the Father is like? It is important to remember that biblical revelation was progressive and usually related to specific redemptive acts. No single book provides us with an exhaustive list of the attributes of God. As a result, our theological portrait of God must be culled from the entire body of Scriptures. Even the best attempt to synthesize this information will inevitably fall short of the reality.

It is not surprising, then, that theologians have disagreed with one another about how God's attributes should be categorized. Most divide God's attributes into two main groups. Some divide them into incommunicable and communicable attributes. Incommunicable attributes are those attributes of God that have no analogy in His creatures. Communicable attributes are those that have some analogy in His creatures. Others have divided them into absolute and relative attributes. Absolute attributes are those that can be ascribed to God in His essence, while relative attributes are those that describe God in relation to His creation.[10] Another approach has been to divide the attributes into moral and non-moral attributes. Henry Thiessen, former chairman of the faculty of Wheaton Graduate School, describes the nonmoral attributes as "those necessary predicates of the divine essence that do not involve moral qualities," but he points out that even God's nonmoral attributes have moral implications because they "have a direct bearing on human conduct."[11] Still others, like the authors of the Westminster Catechism, simply list the attributes.[12]

Perspective poses an additional problem for those who attempt to formulate a theological portrait of God from His attributes. Our view of God changes radically if we emphasize one attribute over another. For example, if we consider God's righteousness and holiness apart from His love and mercy, the resulting perception will be of a God who is harsh and more inclined to damn than redeem. If, on the other hand, we emphasize the love of God at the expense of His holiness, we will be tempted to explain away those passages that speak of God's anger, judgment, and eventual punishment of the wicked.

There are many reasons for this kind of theological imbalance. One of them comes from the Bible itself. The same Scriptures that teach that God is "slow to anger" also say that He is "a righteous judge, a God who expresses his wrath every day" (Psalm 7:11; cf. Exodus 34:7). It is easy to focus on certain passages while neglecting others, especially if we feel uncomfortable with the attributes described in those Scriptures that we ignore. The most common cause of such a "one-sided" view of God, however, is our own experience. Many of us have experienced one of God's attributes to a greater degree than any of the other attributes, often as a result of our conversion experience. One person has lived an immoral life and is made aware of God's law and the inevitability of judgment and is frightened into the arms of Christ. Christ's patience and mercy toward sinners attracts another. Our personal experience often serves as a filter that colors our view of God.

The limitation of human language is a third factor that complicates the task of formulating a theological portrait of God based upon His attributes. We often depend on the known reality of human experience to explain the unseen reality of God. The validity of such statements is demonstrated by God's own choice of human language as a vehicle for self-revelation. We know that human language can be used to accurately speak of God because God Himself has chosen to use human words to tell us what He is like. Those words are characterized as "truth" (Psalm 119:142, 151; John 17:17). This does not mean, however, that such statements speak exhaustively of God. Nor does it mean that there is always a literal correspondence between the divine reality behind the metaphors, analogies, and concepts that God uses to describe Himself and their earthly counterparts. As Thomas F. Torrance explains:

Catholic theology is bound to recognize that there is a measure of impropriety in all human language of God, and therefore must ever be ready to call a halt in its speaking of him, in humble acknowledgement of the fact that our human thought cannot travel beyond a certain point, and be ready at the same time to let the human speech used by the Holy Spirit in the Scriptures point far beyond itself to the sheer reality and glory of God who alone can bear witness of himself and create in us, beyond any capacity of our own to achieve it, genuine knowledge of God.[13]

It is appropriate to use human language to explain what God is like, especially when we are using language that God Himself has chosen. But such terms should not be made to bear more weight than is fitting. God uses creation as an aid in our understanding of Him, but He is also unlike His creation.

God Is Independent

Nowhere is the distinction between God and His creation more evident than in the attribute of independence. The Scriptures teach that, although God is active in the universe and is deeply involved with His creatures, He is not dependent upon them. He exists in and of Himself and does not require anything from His creation: "The God who made the world and everything in it is the Lord of heaven and earth and does not live in temples built by hands. And he is not served by human hands, as if he needed anything, because he himself gives all men life and breath and everything else" (Acts 17:24–25). God alone is capable of existing apart from creation. Everything else, whether animate or inanimate, is ultimately dependent upon God for its existence. This independence also means that God is superior to His creation. Not only does it depend upon Him; it also belongs to Him and is answerable to Him.

The reality of God's independence from His creation means that it is impossible for us to manipulate God. Although He desires and enjoys our worship, He gains no benefit from it. We cannot use our worship of Him or our service to Him as a bargaining chip. Such a view is really a pagan notion of God, often reflected in idol worship, where the gods were thought to have been sustained by the offerings presented to them by their followers. Israel's God warned against such faulty thinking through the psalmist when He said: "I have no need of a bull from your stall or of goats from your pens, for every animal of the forest is mine, and the cattle on a thousand hills. I know every bird in the mountains, and the creatures of the field are mine. If I were hungry I would not tell you, for the world is mine, and all that is in it. Do I eat the flesh of bulls or drink the blood of goats?" (Psalm 50:9–13).

The Scriptures teach that God is both the source of all creation and the ground for its continuing existence. According to 1 Corinthians 8:6 He is "the Father, from whom all things came and for whom we live" (cf. Romans 11:36). Nevertheless, an important distinction must be made here. God is the source of all creation, but creation itself is not God. Pantheism teaches that God is the source of all that exists but also teaches that all that exists *is* God. According to pantheism the paper and ink you now hold in your hand are divine because they are a manifestation of God. Pantheistic assumptions are an important part of the teaching of many popular spiritual writers. Douglas Groothuis cites the example of one best-selling author who assured his readers that they are "divinity in disguise" and promised to teach them how to release the divinity that is resident within them. Groothuis observes: "This is classic New Age teaching: everything is one (monism); everything is divine (pantheism); we are divine (self-deification); and we have unlimited potential to shape our destiny apart from any Creator who stands over us as Lord."[14]

Such teaching is really a sign of humanity's rebellion against God, because it blurs the distinction between the Creator and His creation (Romans 1:23). Speaking through the prophet Isaiah, God the Father called upon Israel to remember His uniqueness: "Remember this, fix it in mind, take it to heart, you rebels. Remember the former things, those of long ago; I am God, and there is no other; I am God, and there is none like me. I make known the end from the beginning, from ancient times, what is still to come. I say: My purpose will stand, and I will do all that I please" (Isaiah 46:8–10). In this passage the attribute of independence is linked with another equally important attribute: divine sovereignty.

God Is Sovereign

All would agree that God exercises a measure of control over His creation. If we do not agree formally, we at least do so informally whenever we pray, because the fundamental assumption behind prayer is that God will intervene on our behalf.[15] Christians disagree, however, about the extent of God's control. When we pray for the salvation of a friend or a loved one, what exactly is it that we expect God to do? Some believe that the best God can do is to arrange circumstances so that the one we are praying for will have an opportunity to hear the gospel. How the person eventually responds to that message is beyond His control. Others have a much different view. They not only believe that God can arrange for others to hear the gospel; they are also convinced that He has the power to create a responsive heart within those who hear its message.

The Bible speaks of God's control in absolute terms. He is the God who "does whatever pleases him" (Psalm 115:3; 135:6). This means that He has control over natural events. For example, the Bible says that He sent a wind over the earth and caused the waters to recede after the great flood (Genesis 8:1). He sent venomous snakes to bite the Israelites when they rebelled in the wilderness (Numbers 21:6). The Lord sent the great storm that nearly destroyed the ship Jonah had embarked upon to flee from God's presence. He also sent the great fish that swallowed Jonah and the small worm that destroyed the vine that shaded him after delivering his message to the people of Nineveh (Jonah 1:4, 17; 4:7). Amazingly, God takes responsibility for calamities as well as blessings in the Scriptures: "I form the light and create darkness, I bring prosperity and create disaster; I, the Lord, do all these things" (Isaiah 45:7).

The Scriptures speak of God as "sending" thunder, hail, lightning, earthquakes, famines, and even wild beasts (Exodus 9:23; Numbers 16:30–35; Deuteronomy 32:24; 1 Samuel 12:18).

Should we, then, think of God the Father like the gods of the Greek and Roman antiquity, who were said to mischievously harass mortals by sending storms and hurling lightning bolts at them? It is important to recognize that when God uses the language of responsibility for such events in the Bible, it does not always mean that He is the immediate cause. He does not stand upon Mount Olympus with a fist full of lightning bolts, hurling them to the earth in a fit of rage. He often works through the laws of nature and through secondary agents. When it comes to disaster, divine control is often exercised in the form of permission. God does not cause the suffering of others but allows them to suffer.

This was clearly the case with the Old Testament patriarch Job. The troubles he experienced were only secondarily caused by God. Their immediate cause was Satan, who had challenged God: "Stretch out your hand" against Job and "strike everything he has." The Lord responded to this request with a remarkable permission: "Very well, then, everything he has is in your hands, but on the man himself do not lay a finger" (Job 1:11–12). Later, when Job suffered from painful sores from head to foot, it was because God had again placed him in Satan's hands (Job 2:6). Job's troubles included natural disasters, supernatural events, and even those that involved human causality—all instigated by Satan. Each time, however, the Lord set limitations upon Satan's actions (Job 1:12; 2:6; cf. 1:10).

God's ultimate control over the terrible circumstances experienced by Job becomes even more evident when we consider that it was God Himself who had pointed Job out to Satan (Job 1:8). Is it reasonable to think that the Father was unaware of what Satan's response would be or that He regretted His words once He saw the result? This certainly does not seem to be consistent with His response to Job's complaint. When Job asked "Why me, God?" the Lord could have replied, "It wasn't Me; it was Satan," or "If I had known what Satan would do, I wouldn't have pointed you out to him." Instead, the Father responded to Job's questions with a question of His own: "Where were you when I laid the earth's foundation? Tell me, if you understand" (Job 38:4).

In the chapters that follow the Lord fired a series of questions at Job. He repeatedly asked questions that begin with phrases like, "Have you . . . ?" "Can you . . . ?" "Will you . . . ?" God's questions all have to do with the operation of the universe. He took full responsibility for the circumstances in Job's life. When Job asked "why," the Lord replied, in effect, "Because I am in control and this is part of My plan for you." This answer will offer small comfort to those who want a "manageable" God—a God who will fit neatly into our theological and philosophical boxes. The God of the Bible is a God of love who wills only the best for His children, but sometimes that best includes pain. We will not always understand or even appreciate His ways, but we can always trust His plan.

Divine Sovereignty and Human Responsibility

God's control over natural events raises another important question. Just how much control does God exercise over the actions of those who have been created to be "free" moral agents? Here, again, the Bible appears to speak in absolute terms. When the prophet Habakkuk complained about God's apparent refusal to respond to the injustice of His people, the Lord replied: "Look at the nations and watch—and be utterly amazed. For I am going to do something in your days that you would not believe, even if you were told. I am raising up the Babylonians, that ruthless and impetuous people, who sweep across the whole earth to seize dwelling places not their own" (Habakkuk 1:5–6). The Lord hardened Pharaoh's heart so that he would not free the children of Israel (Exodus 4:21). He has the power to direct the king's heart (Proverbs 21:1).

In fact, God's control is so great that He can take all the events that come into the life of the Christian, whether good or bad, and in all of it, "God works for the good of those who love him" (Romans

8:28). He does not approve of the evil actions that people commit and is Himself incapable of committing such acts (Deuteronomy 32:4; James 1:13). Yet He has the power to take the evil acts of His creatures and turn them to suit His purposes. Joseph acknowledged this power after he had been sold into slavery by his brothers. Joseph explained to his brothers: "You intended to harm me, but God intended it for good to accomplish what is now being done, the saving of many lives" (Genesis 50:20).

In spite of this sovereign power, we should not think of human beings as mere automatons that respond like puppets to the control of their Creator and act without personal will. The Bible emphasizes both divine sovereignty and human responsibility. People are said to act according to their own initiative: They take counsel from others, plan, and make choices that shape the course of events. From the human perspective, some actions can even change the future. The prayer of faith results in answers to those prayers. Those who do not pray do not receive (James 4:2). Those who sin are held accountable for their actions (Deuteronomy 24:16). Those who turn from their sin can avoid judgment (Ezekiel 33:11). It is even possible to "speed" the day of the Lord's return (2 Peter 3:12). None of these actions is inconsistent with divine sovereignty.

The harmony between divine sovereignty and human responsibility is aptly illustrated in Luke 1:3 where the author says that it "seemed good" to him to write an orderly account of events of Christ's life. Yet 2 Peter 1:21 says that the writers of Scripture were "carried along" by the Holy Spirit. This is the same term used in Acts 27:15 and 17 to describe the effect upon a ship that was "driven" by the wind. This divine control enabled Paul to characterize Scripture as "God-breathed" (2 Timothy 3:16). Yet despite this divine power, Luke used his own initiative, experience, vocabulary, and personal research to write his Gospel account. The Holy Spirit did not blot out his personality, nor did He circumvent the normal human processes of evaluation, decision making, and action.

J. I. Packer uses the term "antinomy" to describe the relationship between divine sovereignty and human responsibility. According to Packer: "An antinomy exists when a pair of principles stands side by side, seemingly irreconcilable, yet both undeniable."[16] Both truths are indispensable, and the relationship between them cannot be fully comprehended by us:

> What should one do, then, with an antinomy? Accept it for what it is, and learn to live with it. Refuse to regard the apparent inconsistency as real; put down the semblance of contradiction to the deficiency in our own understanding; think of the two principles as, not rival alternatives, but, in some way that at present you do not grasp, complementary to each other. Be careful, therefore, not to set them at loggerheads, nor to make deductions from either that would cut across the other (such deductions, would, for that very reason be certainly unsound). Use each within the limits of its own sphere of reference (i.e., the area delimited by the evidence from which the principle has been drawn). Note what connections exist between the two truths and their two frames of reference, and teach yourself to think of reality in a way that provides for their peaceful coexistence, remembering that reality itself has proved actually to contain them both.[17]

God Is Immutable

Divine sovereignty is closely related to the Father's attribute of immutability. Although many analogies have been used in an attempt to explain this divine characteristic, there is no parallel in human experience. They fall short because all of creation is subject to change. This is especially true of human beings. We grow and learn. We may vacillate in our opinions or break our word. Of God alone can it be said that He "does not change like shifting shadows" (James 1:17; cf. Malachi 3:6). He remains the same (Hebrews 1:12). His word is firm; He does not lie or change His mind about what He has purposed to do (Numbers 23:19; 1 Samuel 15:29).

Recently, some have rejected traditional views of divine immutability by proposing a theological model that they refer to as divine "openness." The "open view of God" limits immutability to God's ethical nature:

For the open view, then, God is both changeless and changeable, in distinctly different ways. So while proponents of divine openness emphasize the biblical evidence that God is affected by what happens in the world (suffers) and that he changes his mind (repents), they fully accept the biblical affirmations of divine changelessness. They apply the "changeless" statements to God's existence and character, to his love and reliability. They apply the "changing" statements to God's actions and experience.[18]

These critics of the traditional view of immutability raise an important point. A number of passages in Scripture seem to give the impression that God *does* change. According to Genesis 6:6–7: "The Lord was grieved that he had made man on the earth, and his heart was filled with pain. So the Lord said, 'I will wipe mankind, whom I have created, from the face of the earth—men and animals, and creatures that move along the ground, and birds of the air—for I am grieved that I have made them.'" He sent the prophet Jonah to Nineveh with the message: "Forty more days and Nineveh will be overturned," but He did not destroy Nineveh until much later because they repented (Jonah 3:4, 10). Are these, however, instances in which it can truly be said that God "changed His mind"? The proponents for the "open view" argue that God is dynamic in His relationship to His creatures and limited in His knowledge of the future. He knows some aspects of what will take place but does not know the future "exhaustively."[19] Yet the Scriptures indicate that God's knowledge of what will take place is so detailed that He knows my words even before I speak them (Psalm 139:4).

God is dynamic in His relationship with His creatures to this extent: He enters into a relationship with them, feels for their suffering, and is not merely passive in His experience. Furthermore, God has had a succession of self-experiences that can be understood within a framework of past, present, and future. For example, God existed both before and after creation. It is possible to speak of a "pre-creation" experience of God and a "post-creation" experience. There was a point in the experience of the Trinity when the Son had not become incarnate. In both cases a change took place in terms of God's experience, but not in God's nature. In the Incarnation the Son changed in the sense that He took to Himself a human nature, which He did not previously possess, but this change did not affect His divine nature. There have also been instances in Scripture in which God's actions toward His creatures changed. On occasions His attitude changed from satisfaction to regret (Genesis 6:5–7; 1 Samuel 15:10–11). In other instances He did not follow through on a proposed threat (Exodus 32:7–14; Jonah 3:10). There is no indication, however, that any of these "changes" was unforeseen by God.

In summary, then, we can say that God is immutable in the following respects:

1. He does not change in His nature or His divine attributes.
2. His eternal plan regarding Creation, the Fall, and redemption does not change.
3. He is not limited in foreknowledge, and there is no evidence that He must modify His plans to provide for contingencies to deal with unforeseen emergencies.
4. God's Word does not change, nor do His promises. He does exactly what He says He will do, except in those cases where God's actions are said to be contingent upon human response. In such cases the human response was foreseen by God and was part of His plan.

Like Helen Keller, we can know a great deal about what is unseen by relying upon the limited perception we do possess. We know about the attributes discussed above because we can read about them in God's Word and experience His work in our lives. Our inability to fully grasp them does not keep us from knowing and experiencing the God to whom they belong.

Who has seen the wind?
Neither I nor you:

But when the leaves hang trembling,
The wind is passing thro'.

Who has seen the wind?
Neither you nor I:
But when the trees bow down their heads
The wind is passing by.

Christina Rossetti

QUESTIONS FOR DISCUSSION

1. What do you think the Bible means when it refers to God the Father as being "invisible"?
2. How should we understand those passages that seem to speak of believers as having "seen" God?
3. In what way does looking at ourselves help us to understand God the Father better? What potential problems are there with this approach to understanding God?
4. Explain the difference between external and internal general revelation.
5. What are the limits of external and internal general revelation?
6. How does special revelation differ from general revelation?
7. What is the difference between God's communicable and incommunicable attributes?
8. Why do our experiences with God sometimes pose a problem in our understanding of His attributes?
9. How would you describe the relationship between divine sovereignty and human responsibility?

4

THE FATHER ALMIGHTY

*S*uperman was my favorite television show when I was a small boy. I would often tie an old bath towel around my neck as a cape and run through the house with my arms outstretched pretending to fly like my hero. One day, however, I decided that pretending wasn't enough. I would learn to really fly. But how? I thought about it for a few minutes, and then the answer came: I would ask my father. Imagine my shock and dismay, however, when he told me that he didn't know how to fly! "Yes you do!" I protested. "Superman does it all the time on TV!"

Learning that our parents have limitations is a normal part of growing up. When we are very young, we are convinced that our parents know the answer to every question and can fix any problem. We come to them with our disappointments and give them the broken pieces, confident that they will be able to hand them back to us like new. Eventually we discover that this is not always the case. When it comes to our relationship with God the Father, however, we have the opposite problem. Our struggle with our heavenly Father is to learn that He is entirely without limitations.

THE FATHER IS INFINITE

When we say that the Father is infinite, we are not speaking primarily in spatial terms. Theologian Louis Berkhof warns that God's infinity "should not be confused with boundless extension, as if God were spread out through the entire universe, one part here and another there, for God has no body and therefore no extension."[1] When we speak of infinity with reference to God, we refer to His freedom from limitations. He is unlimited in His presence, power, and perfection.

Unlimited in Presence: Eternal and Omnipresent

God is not bound by the constraints of the universe. He is not confined to it, nor is He limited by its natural laws. In the previous chapter we noted that there is a temporal dimension to God's experience. This does not mean, however, that He is temporally limited. He is called "the Eternal God" in Genesis 21:33 and Deuteronomy 33:27. Two different Hebrew words are used to refer to God's eternal nature in these verses. The term used in Genesis 21:33 (עוֹלָם) is used most often to refer to an indefinite period in the future. The term used in Deuteronomy 33:27 קֶדֶם, a word that means "ancient" or "aforetime," refers to the past. Together these terms indicate that God's eternity stretches in two directions. It reaches into the past and points toward the future.

God has no beginning or end. Unlike us, He did not come into being as a weak and dependent creature that needed to increase in knowledge and in strength. He will not reach a "peak" in His ability and then decline in power. He does not have "good days" and "bad days." Because of His eternal nature, God the Father is as able to deliver today as He ever was. He will always be able to deliver His people. In Deuteronomy 33:27 the Father is pictured as one who holds His people securely in His "everlasting" (עוֹלָם) arms. He is also described as the "Rock eternal" who provides His people with protection from their enemies (Isaiah 26:4). Because of this, He provides peace for the one who trusts in Him.

Since God is eternal, His word is also eternal. It "stands firm in the heavens" (Psalm 119:89). The eternal nature of God's Word is a basis for hope for God's people. It is God's living and enduring Word that provides us with an understanding of the gospel and enables us to be born again (1 Peter 1:23–25). Its promises are always true, and their fulfillment is certain: "Your kingdom is an everlasting kingdom, and your dominion endures through all generations. The Lord is faithful to all his promises and loving toward all he has made" (Psalm 145:13; cf. Joshua 23:14). God's eternal nature is reflected in the blessings He bestows upon His people. They demonstrate His eternal love for those who are His (1 Kings 10:9). Although God's people are sometimes inconsistent in their obedience, His love for them is unfailing (Exodus 15:13; Psalm 6:4; 32:10; Lamentations 3:32).

There is, however, a sobering counterpart to this truth. If God's promises are eternal, so are His threats! In his book entitled *A Body of Divinity,* Puritan Thomas Watson observed:

> Here is thunder and lightning to the wicked. God is eternal, therefore the torments of the wicked are eternal. God lives for ever; and as long as God lives he will be punishing the damned. This should be as the handwriting upon the wall, it should "make their joints to be loosed," &c. Dan v 6. The sinner takes liberty to sin; he breaks God's laws, like a wild beast that breaks over the hedge, and leaps into forbidden pasture; he sins with greediness, as if he thought he could not sin fast enough. Eph iv 19. But remember, one of God's names is Eternal, and as long as God is eternal he has time enough to reckon with all his enemies. To make sinners tremble, let them think of these three things: the torments of the damned are without intermission, without mixture, and eternal.[2]

Jesus characterized God's final judgment upon the wicked as an eternal fire (Matthew 18:8). This punishment was originally prepared for the devil and his angels (Matthew 25:41). Its only alternative is eternal life, which comes through faith in the person and work of the Lord Jesus Christ (John 3:14–16, 36; Romans 6:23).

God the Father is not bound by the limitations of space any more than He is bound by the limitations of time. He is omnipresent. The psalmist drew comfort from this attribute when he asked: "Where can I go from your Spirit? Where can I flee from your presence?" (Psalm 139:7). The biblical concept of God's omnipresence differed greatly from the view of many of Israel's contemporaries. Pagan deities were often linked to specific locations or natural events. This was not true of Israel's God. He had no territorial boundaries, nor was His power limited to a single sphere of activity. He was not merely the God of the hills but the God who created the heavens and Earth and all that is in them (Genesis 1:1; 1 Chronicles 16:26; Nehemiah 9:6; Jeremiah 32:17; Revelation 14:7).

In view of this attribute, how should we understand those passages where God identifies Himself with a particular location? In the Mosaic Law, the tabernacle was designated as the Lord's "dwelling place" (Leviticus 15:31). This label was later transferred to the temple in Jerusalem. When Solomon dedicated the temple in Jerusalem he prayed: "May your eyes be open toward this temple night and day, this place of which you said, 'My Name shall be there,' so that you will hear the prayer your servant prays toward this place" (1 Kings 8:29; cf. Nehemiah 1:9). It is clear that Solomon did not think that God's presence was limited to the temple, because in the same prayer he also referred to heaven as God's dwelling place (1 Kings 8:30, 39, 43, 49). Moses used similar language when he spoke of heaven as the Lord's "holy dwelling place" (Deuteronomy 26:15).

When God's presence was linked to a particular location, it did not mean that He was confined to that place. Instead, such statements identified Him with the promises or events that were associated with the name. Consequently, He referred to Himself as "the God of Bethel" (Genesis 31:13).[3] He consecrated the temple in Jerusalem with His presence and said of it: "I have heard the prayer and plea you have made before me; I have consecrated this temple, which you have built, by putting my Name there forever. My eyes and my heart will always be there" (1 Kings 9:3). Some Israelites misunderstood this promise and made the mistake of viewing the temple in Jerusalem as a talisman that would protect them from divine judgment despite their sinful behavior. They concluded that since Jerusalem was God's own dwelling place, He would not allow the Babylonians to capture the city. In response, the Lord warned that He would allow the inhabitants of Jerusalem to remain only if they changed their ways (Jeremiah 7:4–7). They did not, and they were eventually driven into exile.

One of the most valuable lessons God's people learned during this period of exile was that they could experience God's personal presence wherever they lived. God Himself promised to be their sanctuary: "Therefore say: 'This is what the Sovereign Lord says: Although I sent them far away among the nations and scattered them among the countries, yet for a little while I have been a sanctuary for them in the countries where they have gone'" (Ezekiel 11:16). Jesus later echoed this same truth when speaking to the woman of Samaria. He pointed out that God was no longer to be worshiped in a specific geographic locale but in spirit and truth (John 4:23).

Heaven and earth reflect the glory of God and are filled with His presence (cf. Isaiah 6:3). One practical implication of this is the comforting thought that there is no place or circumstance that is out of the reach of God's presence. Even the worst of circumstances has the potential to become a "holy place." God the Father does not limit His presence to places that are comfortable or attractive. Although it is easy for us to see His beauty in the sunset, we can also experience Him in the hospital room. Even the grave is not beyond His reach. The chief comfort to be derived from the doctrine of God's omnipresence comes from the assurance it provides that God will continue to be our guide regardless of our circumstances. This was the confidence of the psalmist when he declared:

> If I go up to the heavens, you are there; if I make my bed in the depths, you are there. If I rise on the wings of the dawn, if I settle on the far side of the sea, even there your hand will guide me, your right hand will hold me fast. If I say, "Surely the darkness will hide me and

the light become night around me," even the darkness will not be dark to you; the night will shine like the day, for darkness is as light to you. (Psalm 139:8–12)

In his book about the life of David, entitled *Leap over a Wall*, Eugene Peterson writes about the importance of the concept of sanctuary: "The spirituality of sanctuary is fundamental to the Christian life. We need sanctuaries to run to in order to sustain ourselves with what is necessary to life—God and God's provision for living in a world that's hostile to faith."[4] Peterson warns, however, about the danger of limiting our concept of places where we can experience God's presence only to those that are neat or beautiful:

> What I want to prevent is the kind of spirituality that turns us into aesthetes of the numinous, appreciating the fine points of liturgy and doctrine, meditating on the intricacy of roses and the rhythm of ocean waves, while escaping to quiet, secluded places from the grossness of the world and messiness of family.[5]

If it is true that we can experience the presence of God in the midst of the "grossness of the world and the messiness of the family," our personal "sanctuaries" may be found in some very unlikely places. They may take the form of a rebellious teenager, a boring job, an alcoholic loved one, a shattered relationship, or even a terminal illness. A friend of mine who is a Christian counselor recently told me that when he prays with people who are going through hard times, he likes to get behind them and place his hand on their back. "It's my way of helping them 'lean into' their troubles," he explained. I think his metaphor is very appropriate. The truth of the Father's omnipresence means that the difficult circumstance that we now dread could actually be the place where God has chosen to meet with us. By running from it, we could also be running from the one thing we want most in life—an unparalleled experience of intimacy with God.

The reality of God's infinite presence also means that there are no truly "dark" places in the world. Although there are locations where the knowledge of God has been dimmed and others where Christ is not yet known, God is equally present in such places. We should not think, however, that this absolves us of the responsibility to proclaim the gospel. It is true that God is "not far" from every human being. God has determined the times and location of those that dwell on the earth, so that "men would seek him and perhaps reach out for him and find him" (Acts 17:27). Despite this there is an infinite "distance" between God and His creatures. This distance is spiritual in nature rather than geographic. Sin has blinded us to God's presence to such an extent that we cannot find Him without the gospel message—a message that has been entrusted to the church. The same omnipresent God who is "not far from each one of us" has sent the church into the world in which He is ever present to preach the gospel.

This responsibility underscores an important truth. The fact that God is omnipresent does not automatically guarantee that everyone has individual access into God's personal presence. This was once possible but has now been lost to us as a result of Adam's sin. After Adam and Even had eaten from the forbidden tree, they "hid from the Lord God among the trees of the garden" as soon as they became aware of His presence (Genesis 3:8). The Hebrew text literally says that Adam and Eve hid from "the face of" the Lord. It is significant that the Hebrew term that is translated "hid" in this verse appears most often in the Old Testament in contexts that refer to those whose hiding was prompted by a fear of death.[6] In Genesis 2:17 the Lord had warned that death would be the penalty for disobeying the command not to eat of the tree. This curse involved more than cessation of physical life. Ultimately it meant alienation from God and expulsion from His presence. Geerhardus Vos explains:

> The Hebrew words cannot be translated "thou shalt become mortal" or "thou shalt begin to die". Nevertheless a deeper conception of death seems to be hinted at. It was intimated that death carried with

it separation from God, since sin issued both in death and in the exclusion from the garden. If life consisted in communion with God, then on the principle of opposites, death may have been interpretable as separation from God.[7]

This loss of access into God's presence was later symbolized in the Law of Moses, when all but the high priest were forbidden to enter into the Holy of Holies. The Holy of Holies was the inner room of the tabernacle where the ark of the covenant was kept. It was the premier symbol of God's presence with His people (Exodus 25:8; 29:42–46). The Lord was said to be "enthroned between the cherubim" who decorated the ark (1 Samuel 4:4; 2 Samuel 6:2; 2 Kings 19:15; 1 Chronicles 13:6; Psalm 80:1; 99:1; Isaiah 37:16). The prohibition that kept the ordinary Israelite, and even the priests, from entering the Holy of Holies symbolized the fact that the way into God's presence was closed until the coming of Jesus Christ (Hebrews 9:6–14). God had indeed promised to dwell with His people, but He dwelt with them at a distance.

This has changed now that Jesus Christ has come. Those who have trusted in Christ have direct access to the Father (Ephesians 2:18). What was once forbidden to all but the high priest is now the daily privilege of all who are in Christ: "Therefore, brothers, since we have confidence to enter the Most Holy Place by the blood of Jesus, by a new and living way opened for us through the curtain, that is, his body, and since we have a great priest over the house of God, let us draw near to God with a sincere heart in full assurance of faith, having our hearts sprinkled to cleanse us from a guilty conscience and having our bodies washed with pure water" (Hebrews 10:19–22).

Unlimited in Power: Omniscient and Omnipotent

The theological term that is commonly used to refer to God's unlimited power with respect to knowledge is *omniscience*. When we refer to His unlimited power to act, we say that He is omnipotent. God is omniscient in the sense that He knows all. He knows all that has taken place and all that will take place. This knowledge is not limited to the broad sweep of human events but also encompasses the intimate details of the individual's thought and life. He knows the hour of our death (Matthew 6:27). He knows our thoughts (Psalm 139:2). He even knows the words that we will speak before they have been uttered (Psalm 139:4). He anticipates our prayers and puts the events into motion that will provide the answer, even before we have made our request (Isaiah 65:24).

Some, however, feel that the doctrine of divine foreknowledge threatens the viability of free choice. They have argued that God's foreknowledge is limited.[8] The crucifixion of Jesus Christ offers clear evidence that divine foreknowledge includes even the smallest decisions we make. After the four soldiers who crucified Jesus determined to divide His clothing into shares, a common practice among those who were assigned to such duty, they noticed that His undergarment was woven together without a seam. Since they could not divide it among themselves, they decided to cast lots for it. This insignificant decision was predicted centuries earlier by the psalmist (Psalm 22:18).

Divine foreknowledge is not merely descriptive; it is also determinative. God does more than look into the future to see what people will do. His foreknowledge determines in advance what will take place. One proof of this is found in the Old Testament prophecy of the decree of Cyrus that granted permission to the Jews to return to Jerusalem after their exile in Babylon. The fact that Isaiah predicted this event a century before it actually took place and mentioned Cyrus by name is evidence that God's foreknowledge includes the free choices made by individuals. The language of Isaiah's prophecy indicates that God's sovereign purpose was the determinative factor in Israel's deliverance. Cyrus is said to have been "stirred up" by God Himself (Isaiah 41:25). He is referred to as the Lord's "anointed" (Isaiah 45:1), a term that indicated that he had been set apart by God for this mission. Although Cyrus does not seem to have been a believer, the Lord could say of him, "He is my shepherd and will accomplish all that I please; he will say of Jerusalem, 'Let it be rebuilt,' and of the temple, 'Let its foundations be laid'" (Isaiah 44:28). The emphasis in this section is upon God's controlling power (Isaiah 44:24–27).[9]

How can such statements be reconciled with the notion that human beings act as free agents? Theologian Charles Hodge has pointed out that foreordination does not compel people to act in ways that they would not otherwise, but renders events certain by divine permission. God often accomplishes His will through secondary causes and by taking into account the future choices that will be made by those He has created to be free agents:

> The decrees of God, therefore, which only secure the certainty of events, are not inconsistent with liberty as to the mode of their occurrence. Although his purpose comprehends all things, and is immutable, yet thereby "no violence is offered to the will of the creatures, nor is the liberty or contingency of second causes taken away, but rather established."[10]

The teaching of Scripture is unequivocal. God's knowledge is all encompassing and ultimately determinative. He is the One who has said of Himself: "I make known the end from the beginning, from ancient times, what is still to come. I say: My purpose will stand, and I will do all that I please. From the east I summon a bird of prey; from a far-off land, a man to fulfill my purpose. What I have said, that will I bring about; what I have planned, that will I do" (Isaiah 46:10–11).

We need to be careful, however, not to be so distracted by the difficult philosophical questions that are raised by this attribute that we fail to see that divine knowledge has an important relational dimension. The biblical phrase "to know" (יָדַע) often refers to more than a mere awareness of facts. It can also signify a deep and intimate relationship. For example, this Hebrew term is used in Genesis 4:1 to refer to sexual relations. When it is used of God and His people, it signifies a covenant relationship. This is reflected in the Lord's statement to Moses in Exodus 33:12: "I know you by name and you have found favor with me." The phrase "know you by name" is synonymous with "choose."[11]

The Lord used similar language later in Israel's history when speaking through the prophets (Isaiah 43:1; Amos 3:2). In the same way, the apostle Paul used the term "to know" (γινώσκω) in the New Testament to speak of God's relationship with the believer: "But now that you know God—or rather are known by God—how is it that you are turning back to those weak and miserable principles? Do you wish to be enslaved by them all over again?" (Galatians 4:9). To be known by God is to be bound to Him in a relationship of love (1 Corinthians 8:3). In such contexts the language of knowledge, like the biblical language of choice, gives priority to divine initiative in the relationship between the Father and His children. We know God because we are known by God. We love Him because He first loved us (cf. 1 John 4:19). Elsewhere Paul identifies divine foreknowledge and sovereign choice as two of the vital links in the chain of grace (Romans 8:28–30).

God's omniscience is related to His omnipotence. R. C. Sproul explains:

> God's omniscience also grows out of his omnipotence. God is not all-knowing simply because He has applied His superior intellect to a sober study of the universe and all its contents. Rather, God knows all because He created all and has willed all. As sovereign Ruler over the universe, God controls the universe. Though some theologians have tried to separate the two, it is impossible for God to know all without controlling all, and it is impossible for Him to control all without knowing all. Like all the attributes of God, they are codependent, two necessary parts of the whole.[12]

Divine omnipotence has two important aspects. It is expressed both in the power to rule and the power to do. God the Father exercises the power to rule by means of His authority. He is the "ruler of all things" (1 Chronicles 29:12). He is the ultimate Ruler over all the kingdoms of the earth, who establishes one ruler and deposes another (2 Chronicles 20:6; Psalm 46:6; 75:7; Jeremiah 1:10).

Most of the time, however, when the Bible uses the word *power* with reference to God, it is used in a context that speaks of His actions. Exodus 14:31 says that the Israelites saw the great "power" of the Lord displayed against the Egyptians. The Hebrew word that is translated "power" in this verse is actually the term for "hand" (יָד). The plagues suffered by Egypt in connection with Israel's deliverance were all displays of "his majesty, his mighty hand, his outstretched arm" (Deuteronomy 11:2). Many of the prayers in the book of Psalms that plead with God to display His power ask Him to save by His hand (Psalm 17:7, 14; 20:6; 21:8; 37:24; 44:2, etc.). God's power is also referred to in the Old Testament by the Hebrew term כֹּחַ, a word that often appears in contexts that speak of His strength. This is the power that was demonstrated at creation (Jeremiah 10:12; 51:15). In Psalm 66:7 it is linked with His authority to rule: "He rules forever by his power, his eyes watch the nations—let not the rebellious rise up against him."

In the New Testament these two aspects of God's power are both reflected in the risen Christ's reply to the disciples when they asked whether the time had come to restore the kingdom to Israel. Jesus answered: "It is not for you to know the times or dates the Father has set by his own authority. But you will receive power when the Holy Spirit comes on you; and you will be my witnesses in Jerusalem, and in all Judea and Samaria, and to the ends of the earth" (Acts 1:7–8). Although the disciples could not know the times or dates determined by God for the restoration of Israel, which was the province of the Father's personal authority, they would receive power from the Holy Spirit. From this promise we see that the Father exercises His power by empowering others. It is God's own power that enables us to obey His commands (2 Thessalonians 1:11). As we grow in Christ we are strengthened by God's power in the inner being (Ephesians 3:16).

God often mediates His power through others. He does this first and foremost through the preaching of the gospel. The power Christ promised His disciples in Acts 1:8 was the power to be His witnesses. This experience has two dimensions. First, those who preach the gospel are empowered by God. Second, as they preach they find that there is power in the gospel message itself. It is "the power of God for the salvation of everyone who believes" (Romans

1:16). God also conveys His power through the gifts of the Spirit. Every time we use our spiritual gifts to serve others we are "administering God's grace in its various forms" (1 Peter 4:10). In this way we become channels of God's power.

Unlimited in Perfection: Holy, Just, Good, and True

None of God's attributes can really be separated from any other. If we focus exclusively on one attribute and isolate it from the others, the inevitable result is a distorted picture of God. The attributes that we have already examined primarily describe divine experience and actions. However, these characteristics of the Father are grounded in God's moral attributes. All that God experiences and does reflects the fact that He is fundamentally holy, just, good, and true. These four attributes do more than help us to understand the nature of God. They provide the key to understanding the human spiritual dilemma. Our ultimate spiritual problem is not that we are unable to do what God can do. Rather, it is that we have lost the capacity to be like God.

When we say that God is holy, we must also affirm that we are not. This is the root idea in the biblical language for holiness. The most common Hebrew verb that is translated "to be holy" (קָדַשׁ) is rooted in the idea of separation. It is not merely used of God but also refers to places, events, and even items. The places and objects designated as holy in Scripture were those that were dedicated to special use. When Moses encountered God in the burning bush on Mount Sinai, he was told that he was standing on "holy ground" (Exodus 3:5; cf. 19:23). The "holy" or "sacred" furnishings of the tabernacle and the temple were set apart from common utensils because they were used in worship of God (Numbers 4:16; 1 Kings 8:4; 1 Chronicles 22:19; 2 Chronicles 5:5). Under the Law of Moses a field that was dedicated to the Lord was considered "holy" and became the property of the priests (Leviticus 27:21). Holy days were days in which the normal activity of life ceased and God's people were called to rest, pray, celebrate, and worship (Exodus 16:23;

20:8). In a similar way, God is characterized as holy because He is set apart from His creatures. In his song of victory after Israel's deliverance on the banks of the Red Sea, Moses declared: "Who among the gods is like you, O Lord? Who is like you—majestic in holiness, awesome in glory, working wonders?" (Exodus 15:11).

Theologians list holiness as one of God's "moral" attributes. This implies that it has an ethical quality. Holiness is reflected in righteousness (Isaiah 5:16; Mark 6:20; Luke 1:75). Viewed from another perspective, it might be said that holiness is the accumulation of righteousness. The apostle Paul described holiness as the ultimate goal of the practice of righteousness in the Christian life: "I put this in human terms because you are weak in your natural selves. Just as you used to offer the parts of your body in slavery to impurity and to ever-increasing wickedness, so now offer them in slavery to righteousness leading to holiness" (Romans 6:19).

GOD'S HOLINESS AND OURS

One of the unfortunate consequences of sin is that it causes us to be uncomfortable in the presence of holiness. When the prophet Isaiah saw the Lord in His glory and heard the cherubim declare the holiness of God, he became painfully aware of his own sinfulness. Overcome with a combined sense of awe and desperation, Isaiah cried out, "Woe to me! . . . I am ruined! For I am a man of unclean lips, and I live among a people of unclean lips, and my eyes have seen the King, the Lord Almighty" (Isaiah 6:5). The apostle Peter had the same reaction when he obtained his first glimpse of the true nature of Jesus Christ. This new knowledge of the person of Christ made Peter more fully aware of his own true nature. As a result, he pleaded with Jesus to leave, saying, "Go away from me, Lord; I am a sinful man!" (Luke 5:8). However, those who have placed their trust in Jesus Christ have been set free from sin and reap holiness as one of the benefits of Christ's work (Romans 6:22).

Holiness in the life of the Christian is both positional and practical in nature. It is a matter of position because the believer's holiness is God's gracious gift that comes as a result of the work of Jesus Christ. The writer of the book of Hebrews explained that "we have been made holy through the sacrifice of the body of Jesus Christ once for all" (Hebrews 10:10). Christian holiness is also a matter of practice because those who belong to Jesus Christ are commanded to offer their bodies as living sacrifices that are "holy and pleasing to God" (Romans 12:1). The order here is vitally important. One must be declared holy by God as a gift of grace in order to practice holiness as a way of life. If this order is reversed, the practice of holiness becomes spiritually toxic. Legalism will inevitably poison the practice of holiness with self-righteousness.

There is also a qualitative difference between the believer's holy position and the practice of holiness in the Christian life. The holiness that is ours as a result of our position in Christ is Christ's own holiness. It is perfect and cannot be added to or improved upon. On the other hand, the holiness we reflect in daily Christian living is mixed with human weakness and is marred at times by our struggle with the sinful nature (Galatians 5:17). There is always room for improvement when it comes to the practice of holiness. This means that although it is true that those who are in Christ are already holy, there is also a sense in which they are in the process of being made holy. Positional holiness is the work of justification and is immediate. Practical holiness is the work of sanctification and is progressive. The writer of the book of Hebrews referred to both when he said that by the one sacrifice of Christ, God the Father "has made perfect forever those who are being made holy" (Hebrews 10:14).

One of the most surprising aspects of God's holiness that is described in the Bible is what might be called its aesthetic dimension. The Bible teaches that there is beauty in God's holiness. Four references in the Old Testament speak of the "splendor" of God's holiness (1 Chronicles 16:29; 2 Chronicles 20:21; Psalm 29:2; 96:9). The Hebrew noun הָדָר that is used in these verses refers to a particular kind of beauty. This kind of beauty is not merely attractive; it is majestic. In Psalm 93:5 the psalmist declares: "Your statutes stand firm; holiness adorns your house for endless days, O

Lord." The Hebrew term that is translated "adorns" in this verse is נָאֲוָה and is based upon a root that means to be desirable or beautiful. A different term is used in Psalm 27:4, where David wrote that his one desire was to "dwell in the house of the Lord all the days of my life, to gaze upon the beauty of the Lord and to seek him in his temple." In this verse the Hebrew word that speaks of God's beauty is one that refers to something that is pleasant or delightful (נֹעַם). God's beauty is reflected in His people. He "shines forth" from Zion, which is "perfect in beauty" (Psalm 50:2). The term for beauty that appears in this verse is one that is used elsewhere to describe the beauty of a woman (Psalm 45:11; Esther 1:11; cf. Proverbs 6:25; 31:30). It is clear from these passages that, although the popular conception of holiness is rather dreary, true holiness is both attractive and awe inspiring at the same time. If we were to see it in its purest form, its beauty would overwhelm us.

HOLINESS AND JUSTICE

When God's holiness is expressed in actions toward His creatures, those actions are characterized by justice. Theologian Louis Berkhof explained: "Justice manifests itself especially in giving every man his due, in treating him according to his deserts."[13] Simply put, when we say that God is just, we assert that whatever He does is right (Psalm 72:2; Isaiah 5:16). Deuteronomy 32:4 says this of Him: "He is the Rock, his works are perfect, and all his ways are just. A faithful God who does no wrong, upright and just is he." In the Scriptures the biblical term for justice (מִשְׁפָּט) and the biblical term "to judge" (שָׁפַט) are related. God's judgments reflect His justice. He does what is right and expects righteousness from His people. The relationship between justice and righteous can be seen from the fact that the biblical terms for justice in both the Old and New Testaments can also be translated as "righteousness."

Justice is especially important for those who act on God's behalf. Rulers are commanded to govern with justice (Leviticus 19:15; Deuteronomy 16:18–20; Proverbs 16:10; 29:4). In the realm of civil government, those who render judgment and determine punishment for violations of society's laws are said to act on God's behalf. They are God's servants and will themselves be held accountable one day for the decisions they render (Romans 13:4). Indeed, all God's people are commanded to act justly (Micah 6:8). Ultimately we are called to act justly because such behavior is a reflection of God Himself. In simplest terms, acting justly is doing what God would do in any given circumstance.

The biblical idea of justice is a legal concept. God's justice is related to law. Leon Morris pointed out that God is commonly portrayed in the Bible as working through laws. From the natural realm (where creation is said to operate according to the laws set by God), to the Father's special relationship with His people (which is described by the legal term "covenant"), "God is seen to work by the method of law."[14] He sets the standard and holds all of creation accountable to it. This means that one of the expressions of divine justice is the punishment that is assigned to those who violate God's laws. The just God portrayed in the Bible is also the One who has promised, "I will punish the world for its evil, the wicked for their sins. I will put an end to the arrogance of the haughty and will humble the pride of the ruthless" (Isaiah 13:11). As long as we think in purely general terms, these are words of comfort. We like to think that God will punish those we consider to be wicked. The Hitlers and the Stalins of the world clearly deserve the wrath of God. It is much harder to see our friends, family members, and especially ourselves as the objects of this same wrath. We will readily admit that we are not perfect. We will even go so far as to say that we have sinned. We do not believe, however, that God will do much about it.

There are several reasons for this dangerous conviction. For one thing, although we know that we have sinned, we are also sure that everyone else has sinned as well. We feel that there is safety in numbers. After all, if God really were to punish me for my sins, He would also have to punish everyone else. We are like the student who has just flunked an important exam but takes comfort in the knowledge that everyone else in the class flunked it as well. "Surely," the student reasons, "the teacher would not go so far as to flunk the whole class?" In reality, God has already done so. He has already rendered His verdict. All have sinned and all stand condemned (Romans 3:10–12; 5:16, 18; cf. John 3:18).

Second, we do not believe that God will do much about our sin because we do not regard it as very sinful. We recognize that we have done "bad" things, but they do not seem to us to be all that bad. Certainly, they do not seem bad enough to merit some kind of eternal punishment. Some time ago I was discussing the gospel with a woman who seemed quite interested in its message. But when I began to talk about sin and its consequences, she objected. She explained, "I just don't know anyone who has done anything bad enough to deserve hell." I understand her difficulty. It is hard to admit that God will condemn those who are so much like me, because once I do I inevitably condemn myself. Furthermore, my life has been fairly moral. I have not murdered anyone or committed adultery or done any of the kinds of things that might call for eternal punishment. Or have I?

In reality, the difficulty we have in seeing ourselves as the objects of divine wrath is really the result of a downgrading of sin and righteousness. We do not regard our actions as being all that sinful because we ourselves are the measure when evaluating them. Jesus revealed that the Father's evaluation of us is based upon a standard that is far subtler. It is one that takes motivation into account as well as action. He taught that acts like murder and adultery are really only extensions of the secret motives of the heart (Matthew 5:20–22, 27–28). This means that, although I may not have murdered anyone, I have been guilty of murderous intent. If the very attitudes of the heart are enough to condemn me, then I am guilty. I am a thief, an adulterer, a blasphemer, and worse.

Third and most important, we have mistakenly convinced ourselves that God will deal lightly with our sin because we fail to understand the true nature of righteousness. We think of righteousness as though it were a standard that is distinct from God. We imagine it to be a kind of rule book or document like the Constitution. Certainly, it is important to God. He keeps it open before Him and scrutinizes it every so often while observing our behavior. But the standard is something outside of God. Moreover, we know that objective standards like this are often subject to change. We are used to finding loopholes and amendments. So it does not seem so difficult to us that God should "bend" the rules once we have broken them. After all, He is God, and He can do anything! In reality, God cannot ignore sin because He is incapable of acting in a way that is inconsistent with His nature. This does not mean that He is bound by an external law. God does not have a list of rules that He must follow. Rather, He cannot overlook our violation of His laws because they are a reflection of His nature. In order to ignore them He would need to deny Himself. To put it another way, God cannot act in a way that is inconsistent with His nature. He is righteous. He cannot be unrighteous. He cannot overlook sin. This is what Exodus 34:7 means when it says that God does not leave the guilty unpunished.

JUSTICE AND GOODNESS

Fortunately for us, God's justice is tempered by His goodness. In the Old Testament the term good (טוב) is sometimes used in a way that seems synonymous with "righteous." God's people are commanded to turn from evil and do good (Psalm 34:14). The "right way to live" in 1 Kings 8:36 is literally "the good way." Asa and Hezekiah are said to have done what was "good and right" in the eyes of the Lord during their reign as kings (2 Chronicles 14:2; 31:20). Similarly, in the New Testament goodness is listed among the fruit of the Spirit (Galatians 5:22). It is a characteristic of those who live as children of the Light (Ephesians 5:9).

Where God is concerned, however, the quality of goodness not only refers to moral righteousness but to His capacity to do good for His creatures. It is linked with mercy and forgiveness. When Moses asked to see God's glory, the Lord explained that he would not be permitted to see Him face-to-face, explaining that no mortal could see His face and live (Exodus 33:20). Instead, the Lord said: "I will cause all my goodness to pass in front of you, and I will proclaim my name, the Lord, in your presence. I will have mercy on whom I will have mercy, and I will have compassion on whom I will have compassion" (Exodus 33:19). God the Father demonstrates His goodness by showing compassion to those who do not deserve it (Deuteronomy 32:36). Because He is compassionate, He does not rush to execute judgment upon those who deserve it (Psalm 86:15). Instead, He is patient toward them (Romans 2:4).

Although God is faithful to His people even when they are unfaithful, the exercise of His compassion is often contingent upon repentance. He shows compassion when His people return to Him (Nehemiah 9:28; Psalm 51:1). God's ultimate expression of His goodness has come to us through Jesus Christ: "His divine power has given us everything we need for life and godliness through our knowledge of him who called us by his own glory and goodness" (2 Peter 1:3).

GOODNESS AND TRUTH

God the Father is not eager to punish those who sin but would rather see them repent. He expresses this desire in the strongest terms. For example, speaking through the prophet Ezekiel, He stated: "Son of man, say to the house of Israel, 'This is what you are saying: "Our offenses and sins weigh us down, and we are wasting away because of them. How then can we live?"' Say to them, 'As surely as I live, declares the Sovereign Lord, I take no pleasure in the death of the wicked, but rather that they turn from their ways and live. Turn! Turn from your evil ways! Why will you die, O house of Israel?'" (Ezekiel 33:10–11). The apostle Peter expressed a similar sentiment in the New Testament. He noted that what seems to be slowness on God's part in fulfilling His promises regarding Christ's second coming is actually a demonstration of mercy: "The Lord is not slow in keeping his promise, as some understand slowness. He is patient with you, not wanting anyone to perish, but everyone to come to repentance" (2 Peter 3:9).

However, we should not see the Father's unwillingness to hurry in judgment and His goodness in providing those who have sinned an opportunity to repent as indulgence. When the time comes for final judgment and the consignment of those who have not been redeemed by Christ to hell, there will be no hesitation on God's part. Nor, for that matter, will there be any regret. The biblical doctrine of eternal punishment is consistent with the goodness of God because it is a goodness that is consonant with truth. It is the work of Jesus Christ that enables God the Father to express His goodness while remaining true to His nature.

The death of Christ satisfied the Father's demand for justice because it was more than sufficient to cover the debt incurred by the believer's sins. The obedience of Christ satisfied the Father's demand for righteousness and has been credited to the believer's "account." It is the sacrifice of Christ, then, that has reconciled the Father's attribute of justice with that of goodness: "God presented him as a sacrifice of atonement, through faith in his blood. He did this to demonstrate his justice, because in his forbearance he had left the sins committed beforehand unpunished—he did it to demonstrate his justice at the present time, so as to be just and the one who justifies those who have faith in Jesus" (Romans 3:25–26).

QUESTIONS FOR DISCUSSION

1. What do we mean when we say that God is infinite? What is not meant?
2. Describe the positive implications of the Father's eternal nature. What are the negative implications of this attribute?
3. How should we understand those passages that link God to a particular location?
4. How can biblical statements about divine foreknowledge be reconciled with the idea that human beings act as free agents?
5. In what two ways is the Father's omnipotence primarily expressed?
6. What is the relationship between God's holiness and the holiness of the believer?

7. In what sense is the biblical idea of divine justice a legal concept?
8. How are the divine attributes of justice, goodness, and truth reflected in the work of Jesus Christ?

5

THE WORK OF THE FATHER

As a small boy I would hear my father's alarm clock go off every morning at 5:00 A.M. and listen to him as he shuffled into the kitchen to boil the water for his morning coffee. After dressing and having breakfast he steered his big blue Chevy out of the driveway and down the street as he disappeared for the rest of day to that mysterious place we always referred to as "work." I knew where my dad worked. He was employed by General Motors. I even knew his title. He was a "graphic illustrator." But I never really understood what he did. It had something to do with cars and drawing. He didn't design cars. He wasn't a draftsman. He didn't work on the assembly line. To this day I am not entirely sure what my father did when he went to "work" each day.

If this was true of my earthly father, how much more mysterious is the work of our heavenly Father! The God of the Bible is a God who works. The very first description we have of Him is one in which the term "work" is used to characterize His activity. We are told that by the seventh day God "finished the work he had been doing" (Genesis 2:2). What is more, according to Jesus, God the Father continues to work. While arguing with the religious leaders about the proper observance of the Sabbath, "Jesus said to them,

'My Father is always at his work to this very day, and I, too, am working'" (John 5:17). What, then, does the Father do?

THE WORK OF CREATION

The first work attributed to God the Father in the Scriptures is the work of creation. The first verse of the Bible begins with the statement: "In the beginning God created the heavens and the earth" (Genesis 1:1). The Hebrew term that is translated "created" in this verse (בָּרָא) meant to "shape" or "create" and in the Bible is always used of divine activity. This initial act of creation brought the "stuff" of the universe into being. Prior to this it did not exist. The author of Hebrews supports this when he says, "By faith we understand that the universe was formed at God's command, so that what is seen was not made out of what was visible" (Hebrews 11:3). In all, three different Hebrew terms are used in the Genesis account to speak of God's creative work. The term בָּרָא used in Genesis 1:1 means to make something new. A different term is used of the creation of animals in Genesis 1:25. This Hebrew word (עָשָׂה) means "to fashion." Unlike the previous term, this kind of creation involved the shaping of something that already existed. God first brought the universe into being and then used this material to fashion His creatures. A third term is used in Genesis 1:24, which says that the land "produced" (יָצָא) living creatures according to their kinds. This Hebrew word literally means "to cause to come forth."

After its initial creation the earth was "formless and void." Although both terms could be translated "empty," the first term could also be translated "waste" or even "chaos." Some have understood this to be a description of the state of creation following Satan's fall into sin. It is more likely, however, that the phrase underscores God's work of forming the matter that had been brought into existence at creation into the ordered universe in which we now live. After the heavens and earth were created, the Holy Spirit "hovered" over the waters. The same Hebrew term is used in Deuteronomy 32:11 to speak of an eagle who "hovers" over the nest when it stirs up its young. God did not set the universe in motion and then passively sit back and allow natural forces to finish the work on their own. Instead, all the members of the Trinity were directly involved in every aspect of creation.

Some have compared the Genesis account of creation to the Babylonian creation story known as the *Enuma Elish*. When these two are compared, however, the uniqueness of the biblical account is apparent. In the Babylonian account the god of creation is only one among many rival deities. Moreover, the creative activity of the god Marduk, the hero of the *Enuma Elish*, plays a relatively minor role in the story.[1] The Genesis account, on the other hand, focuses on creation to underscore the reality of God's sovereignty and the unique place that humanity holds in created order. When comparing the biblical record with the creation stories of Babylon and Mesopotamia, the simplicity and monotheism of the Genesis description are unmatched.

The first two chapters of Genesis describe a progressive series of creative events culminating in the creation of the first two human beings. Should we take this account literally, or does it use language that is primarily figurative to describe the origin of the human race? There are four primary views concerning the origin of the first humans.

Atheistic Evolutionism

Although he was not the first to propose an evolutionary theory to explain the origin of the human race, Charles Darwin became its most identifiable spokesman. Technically probably a deist, Darwin nevertheless is best known for popularizing a system of evolution that made God unnecessary. In his work entitled *On the Origin of Species by Means of Natural Selection* published in 1859, Darwin argued that random changes over time either strengthen or weaken a species. Changes that enhance a species' ability to survive are reproduced, whereas those that make a species more vulnerable are eliminated when the animals that reflect such changes soon die out. Atheistic evolution asserts that human beings gradually evolved from lower forms of life by means of this process of natural selection. God was not a factor in human creation.

Opponents of atheistic evolution point out that such a process should have left behind fossil records that include a large number of "transitional forms," as changes in species developed over billions of years. Such evidence of natural selection is not to be found. More important, they note that atheistic evolution clearly contradicts the biblical record, which traces the origin of humans and animals alike to the direct creative effort of God.

Theistic Evolution

Some Christians, however, have accepted evolutionary theory as the mechanism used by God in creation. They argue that God often uses natural means to accomplish His purposes and claim that He used the process of natural selection to create the human race. They do not believe that theistic evolution contradicts the Bible because they view the details of the creation account as largely symbolic. Howard J. Van Till, Professor Emeritus of Physics at Calvin College, feels that evolution is consistent with both the biblical account of creation and Christian theism. He notes:

> All Christians are authentic "creationists" in the full *theological* sense of that term. We are all committed to the biblically-informed and historic Christian doctrine of a creation that affirms that everything that is not God is part of a creation that has being only because God has given it being and continues to sustain it. As a creation, the universe is neither a divine being nor a self-existent entity that has its being independent of divine creative action. This theological core of the doctrine of creation sets Judeo-Christian theism in bold distinction from both pantheism (all is God) and naturalism (all is nature).[2]

Van Till argues that Judeo-Christian theists "should be inclined to have exceedingly high expectations regarding the character of creation's formational and functional economies."[3] He compares God's ability to work through the evolutionary process to the kind of divine intervention we expect when we ask God to "bless" the work of a surgical team prior to an operation. God acts but does so through the hospital staff and the normal healing processes of the human body. In such cases God is actively involved, but His presence is not empirically detectable:

> Is God's action of blessing, for instance, empirically detectable as the "effect" of some non-creaturely "cause" that overpowers creatures in such a way that the outcome is clearly beyond the realm of creaturely possibility? I think not. If that were the sort of divine action that we were expecting in response to our pre-surgery prayer, why not skip the surgery and avoid both the pain and the expense? The kind of divine action we pray for is discernable only by those who have eyes (of faith) to see it. The natural sciences have no instruments with which to measure the level of effectiveness of God's blessing.[4]

Christians who reject theistic evolution acknowledge that it is an improvement over atheistic evolution because it allows for the existence of a Creator. However, they counter that it undermines the teaching of Scripture. According to evolution simple life-forms began in the sea and developed into more complex land-based life forms. According to the Genesis account, mankind came into being through a separate creative act and was formed from the dust of the earth.

Opponents of theistic evolution also argue that it undermines the biblical doctrine of sin. According to the apostle Paul, sin entered the world "through one man" (Romans 5:12). This made Adam a "type" or pattern of Christ and prepared the way for salvation to be offered to all as a result of the obedience of Jesus Christ: "For just as through the disobedience of the one man the many were made sinners, so also through the obedience of the one man the many will be made righteous" (Romans 5:19). Paul's argument loses its force if Adam did not really exist. Without Adam, there is no real need for Christ's work.

Progressive Creationism

A third view attempts to do justice to the events described in the book of Genesis while reconciling the scientific evidence that suggests that the earth has existed for billions of years. Progressive creationists believe that the six days of creation were really creative periods that may have lasted for millions or even billions of years. They base this view on a study of the Hebrew word for "day" (יוֹם). Although this term is used most often to refer to a literal twenty-four-hour day, in several places it seems to refer to an indefinite period of time. For example, Zechariah 14:7 speaks of the day of the Lord in a way that implies that it cannot be limited to a twenty-four-hour period. In the creation account itself the term *day* is used in three different senses. In Genesis 1:5 it refers to "light" as opposed to "darkness." Later in the same chapter it refers to the six individual creative periods during which the heavens and earth and all that are in them were made (Genesis 1:5, 8, 13, 19, 23, 31). Third, in Genesis 2:4 the term *day* seems to refer to the entire six-day period of creative activity. In this verse the Hebrew text literally says, "in the day that the Lord God made the heavens and the earth" (cf. KJV).[5]

Progressive creationists also point out that the first creative "day" was finished before the two "great lights" that govern the cycle of day and night (i.e., the sun and moon) were created, thus those days were not timed by one rotation about the sun.[6] They argue that viewing the six days of Genesis as creative epochs enables Christians to reconcile the biblical record with astronomical evidence that indicates that the light from stars that is just now reaching the earth was first emitted billions of years ago. They also contend that this view provides an explanation for fossil evidence that seems to suggest that dinosaurs died out long before man was present on the earth. (Creationists point to contrary evidence that shows dinosaur and human footprints side by side.) Radiometric dating methods that measure the rate of radioactive decay in fossils appear to indicate that some fossils are millions of years old.

Opponents of progressive creationism counter that such a view violates the fundamental rule of interpretation, which says that we should interpret the words of the Bible in their "plain and simple" sense. They contend that in the overwhelming majority of cases the Hebrew word for "day" refers to a twenty-four-hour time period. They also argue that the apparent age of the earth can be explained in other ways. For example, they suggest that, just as Adam and Eve were created as fully developed adults, the earth was also created with the appearance of age. Others ascribe the appearance of age to damage done by the worldwide flood described in Genesis 6–8.

Fiat Creationism

The fourth view of creation is also the most traditional view. It holds that creation took place within a six-day period with each day lasting twenty-four hours. Fiat creationists argue that this view is the most obvious reading of the Genesis text. It is highly unlikely that those to whom the book of Genesis was originally addressed would have understood Moses' words in any other sense. Many who hold that creation took place within six twenty-four-hour days also believe that the age of the earth is relatively young. The evidence of radiometric dating does not bother them, because they feel that its results are largely a matter of conjecture. They explain the appearance of vast age in the geologic record by referring to the biblical account of the flood in Noah's day. This flood wiped out all life— outside the ark—on Earth, including the dinosaurs, and gave the earth the appearance of age. They also suggest that biblical passages that refer to gigantic creatures like Leviathan are actually speaking of dinosaurs (cf. Job 3:8; 41:1; Psalm 74:14; 104:26; Isaiah 27:1). If this is true, it would mean that humans and dinosaurs existed on the earth at the same time.[7]

Nearly half a century ago Old Testament scholar Oswald T. Allis warned interpreters of the Bible to avoid two opposite extremes when dealing with the apparent tension between science and the biblical account of creation. According to Allis the first is the temptation to avoid dealing with the evidence brought forward by scientific study. In their effort to "protect" the Bible, some Christians may be inclined to be hostile toward scientific thought. This is unnecessary. Nor should we minimize scientific discoveries. The Bible has nothing to fear from true science:

> When Kepler said that in studying the heavens he was "thinking God's thoughts after Him", he was simply echoing David's words in Psalms viii and xix. And if the heavens which Kepler viewed through his telescope were far vaster than those which David saw with his naked eye, how vastly great should be the conception of God which is given to us by the amazing discoveries of recent years![8]

The other extreme that must be avoided is the temptation to force the language of the Genesis account to accommodate popular scientific theories: "Science may throw much light on the Bible. It may help us to understand some of its difficult passages. But to allow science to become the interpreter of the Bible and to force upon it meanings which it clearly does not and cannot have is to undermine the supreme authority of the Word of God."[9]

Although Christians do not all agree on the details, at least this much is clear: The Genesis account teaches that the eternal God is Creator and Lord of all things. Interestingly, in recent days an increasing number of scientists have rejected atheistic evolution to embrace what has been called the theory of intelligent design. These scientists believe that the complexity of life on Earth cannot be adequately explained by natural selection. Instead, they are convinced that the universe shows evidence of a plan. In short, they argue that the universe did not come into being of its own accord but was carefully and thoughtfully designed.[10] This is what the church has always believed.

WHAT DOES CREATION TELL US ABOUT OURSELVES?

Two students in a Christian grammar school were embroiled in an argument. "It is so true!" declared one little boy. "It is not!"

replied the other. Finally, one of them went up to the teacher's desk and asked her to resolve the dispute. "Teacher," he asked, "isn't it true that Adam and Eve were the first people who ever lived?" "Why, yes," the teacher replied. "That's what the Bible says." The little boy turned to face his opponent, his eyes shining in triumph. "See!" he said. "I *told* you it wasn't Hansel and Gretel!"

If the biblical account of creation is merely a religious fairy tale, used by a primitive and unscientific society to explain its own existence, it tells us only about one culture's self-perception. If, on the other hand, it is fact, as the Bible purports it to be, it reveals God's view of us and our place in His universe. According to Genesis 2:7, the first human was formed from "the dust of the ground." The Hebrew term used in this verse refers to fine particles of dust. Like the potter who shapes the clay into a work of art, God took the basic elements of the earth and fashioned the first man. Although Adam's physical form was derived from the dust of the earth, God gave him the "breath of life." The Hebrew word that is translated "breath" is used elsewhere as a synonym for life itself (Genesis 7:22).[11] Some have described this as the "kiss of life." It is as if Adam was awakened to life like a child who has been coaxed from sleep by the tender embrace of a loving parent. It was only after God breathed life into Adam that he became a "living being." This same expression is used in Genesis 1:24 of the animals and is translated "living creatures." It shows that humans and animals alike are dependent upon God for their existence.

It is popular today to view humans only as clever animals. Yet we are clearly more than this. Augustine observed that, although mankind shares some characteristics with animals, many traits are unique to humans. Both have the power to take nourishment, grow, and reproduce, as well as the tendency to seek pleasure and avoid pain. Yet only humans seem to have the ability to laugh and tell jokes. He also noted that unlike beasts, mankind possesses a love of praise and glory. However, he warned that unless these desires are controlled by reason, they do not make us any better than the beasts. It was this capacity to reason that Augustine believed truly set mankind apart from the animals.[12] Similarly, the philosopher Blaise Pascal said, "Man is a reed, the most feeble thing in nature, but he is a thinking reed."

The Bible asserts that there is a vast dissimilarity between the Creator and His creatures. It declares, "He who is the Glory of Israel does not lie or change his mind; for he is not a man, that he should change his mind" (1 Samuel 15:29; cf. Numbers 23:19). It points out that God's ways and thoughts are on a different order than our own (Isaiah 55:9). Yet the creation account also emphasizes that it is the distinction of having been created in the image of God that sets mankind apart from the rest of God's creatures (Genesis 1:26).

When the Bible says that we have been created in the image of God, it implies that we are like God in some measure. Theologians have struggled to explain what this means. Some have identified the divine image with the capacity to make moral choices. John Calvin understood the divine image to be Adam's original righteousness. This image was ruined when Adam sinned and is restored through Jesus Christ.[13] Like Augustine, Calvin regarded the mind and the heart as the primary seat of the divine image in man.[14] Others, like Karl Barth, have linked the divine image to the fact that humans were created male and female. A few have even linked it to our physical form, noting that we have been created in an upright position, enabling us to look into the heavens and contemplate eternal matters.[15] This last view, however, seems to be contradicted by the apostle Paul who condemned mankind because it had "exchanged the glory of the immortal God for images made to look like mortal man" (Romans 1:23).

Ultimately, Calvin seems to have had the right idea. The Scriptures do not explicitly define what is meant by the divine image but seem to imply that it is moral and spiritual in nature. Corrupted when Adam sinned, the divine image is being restored to those who have trusted in the Savior. They have "put on the new self, which is being renewed in knowledge in the image of its Creator" (Colossians 3:10; cf. 2 Corinthians 3:18). If we want to know what God's original intent was in creating human beings, we need only look to Christ (Romans 8:29).

Created to Have Purpose

Prior to Adam's creation God had planted a garden east of the land of Eden and placed within it many kinds of trees. God created the garden not only as a dwelling place for Adam but also as a place of service. He placed Adam there "to work it and take care of it" (Genesis 2:15). Adam's responsibilities fell into two main categories. First, he was given the task of tilling the field. This is significant since it indicates that even before Adam's fall into sin, human effort was required in order for the garden to produce food to sustain his life. It establishes that work was part of God's original plan for humanity and not a punishment for sin. Second, Adam was given the responsibility of tending the garden. This Hebrew word literally meant "to guard." Adam's role was primarily that of a caretaker. His work enabled the garden to bear fruit and placed upon him the responsibility of acting as a steward of God's creation. The mandate to "subdue" creation in Genesis 1:28 was not a license to exploit it.

Adam's original calling is proof that we were made for both the sanctuary and the workplace. Someone has said that the thing that most of us don't like about our work is that it is so "daily." Yet it is within the context of this daily routine that we normally experience the Father's activity in our lives. When we work we follow God's own example. Jesus spent the majority of His earthly life laboring as a carpenter. There is no indication that He was serving God less during those years than when He went about preaching and teaching. He also taught that God the Father continues to work (John 5:17). Martin Luther King Jr. once noted that the least glamorous occupation has the potential to bring glory to God. "If you are called to be a street sweeper," he declared, "sweep streets even as Michelangelo painted, or Beethoven composed music, or Shakespeare wrote poetry. Sweep streets so well that all the hosts of heaven and earth will pause to say, here lived a great street sweeper who did his job well."

Created Male and Female

Throughout the creation process God repeatedly evaluated His work and concluded that "it was good" (Genesis 1:4, 10, 12, 18, 21, 25). However, there was a notable departure from this pattern after Adam's creation. Once Adam had begun his work in the garden, the Lord noted that it was "not good for the man to be alone" (Genesis 2:18). This was confirmed as Adam named the animals that God had created and "no suitable helper was found" for him (Genesis 2:20). The Hebrew word that is translated "suitable" literally meant "what is in front of" and conveys the idea of correspondence. It means that in all of creation Adam could find no one who was comparable to himself. Only Eve was suitable for this task. Her equivalence to Adam was reflected in her creation. Although Adam and all other creatures were created from the earth, Eve was taken from Adam himself. Their similarity is also hinted at in the terms used to refer to Eve in the Bible. The name Eve was given to her by Adam after the Fall and signified her role as "the mother of all the living" (Genesis 3:20; 4:1). The term that is translated "woman," however, is simply the feminine form of the Hebrew word for man (Genesis 2:22). Eve was Adam's counterpart in every way.

Although it is true that those who lived in biblical times often regarded women to be inferior to men, the Bible does not sanction this view. Eve was created to be Adam's helper, but nothing in the language suggests that this made her Adam's inferior. On the contrary, the same word is used elsewhere to refer to the kind of help God provides (Psalm 30:10; 121:2). Genesis 1:27 uses the term "man" in a generic sense and explains: "So God created man in his own image, in the image of God he created him; male and female he created them." This same Hebrew word is translated "Adam" elsewhere. Eve differed from Adam, but she was not less than Adam. She was his feminine counterpart and colaborer. The stamp of the divine image was not limited to the male gender. This means that if we want to truly understand what God the Father is like we must consider His "feminine" attributes as well as his "masculine" attributes.

Although used less frequently, feminine images are sometimes used to describe the Father's character and actions, as we saw in chapter 2. The Bible's use of gender-specific language to refer to the Father is intentional. This does not mean, however, that God is male or that men reflect the divine image more clearly than women do. Both genders are necessary to fully reflect the image of God.

Created to Be Creative

Most people recognize that Johann Sebastian Bach was one of the world's greatest composers. Many, however, do not know that he spent most of his career as a church organist. More important, he was a devout Christian who saw his musical ability as a gift that must be dedicated to God. As he composed he often marked his manuscripts with phrases like "Help me Jesus," "in Jesus' name," and "to God alone be the glory." He is just one of many who have used the arts to glorify God. Throughout its history the church has used every major art form in worship. In doing so God's people have simply been following in the footsteps of their heavenly Father. Because we have been made in the divine image we are inveterately creative. This fact means that creative activity has inherent value. Francis Schaeffer explains:

> Being in the image of the Creator, we are called upon to have creativity. In fact, it is part of the image of God to be creative, or to have creativity. We never find an animal, non-man, making a work of art. On the other hand, we never find men anywhere in the world or in any culture in the world who do not produce art. Creativity is a part of the distinction between man and non-man. All people are to some degree creative.[16]

The creative dimension of human nature is reflected in the worship of God. Although the Law of Moses forbade the use of carved images to represent God, artisans and skilled craftsmen were used to build the tabernacle in the wilderness (Exodus 26:1, 31; 35:10). Both men and women employed their artistic abilities to beautify the tent and its furnishings (Exodus 35:25). Skilled craftsmen were also used to make Aaron's high priestly garments (Exodus 28:3, 6, 15). These artisans were led by Bezalel and Oholiab (Exodus 31:2, 6). Their skill was not merely attributed to natural ability but also to the ministry of the Holy Spirit (Exodus 31:3–4).

Other art forms such as music and poetry played an important role in Old Testament worship. During his reign King David organized the priesthood and assigned new responsibilities to the Levites (1 Chronicles 24:3–19). Music played an important part in their new role. "David told the leaders of the Levites to appoint their brothers as singers to sing joyful songs, accompanied by musical instruments: lyres, harps and cymbals" (1 Chronicles 15:16). Although David was himself a musician and a poet, this innovation was not merely a reflection of his own personal artistic bent. Divine revelation played an important part in the change. According to 2 Chronicles 29:25, the organizational structure of Israel's priestly musicians was commanded by God and revealed through the prophets. Music was so important to Israel's worship, in fact, that Levitical musicians were assigned rooms in the temple and were freed from all other duties (1 Chronicles 9:33). In addition to poetry, dance and drama also figured importantly in Israel's religious life.

Created for Dominion

God the Father is the ultimate Ruler of the universe. He is "the great King above all gods" (Psalm 95:3). Because we have been created in His image, however, we also have a responsibility to rule. According to Genesis 1:28, God created mankind to "rule" (KJV: "have dominion") over creation. In its original context, this statement refers to humanity's superiority over the other creatures. Prior to the creation of Adam and Eve, the Lord declared: "Let us make man in our image, in our likeness, and let them rule over the fish of the sea and the birds of the air, over the livestock, over all the earth, and over all the creatures that move along the ground" (Genesis 1:26). After their creation Adam and Eve were commanded: "Be fruitful and increase in number; fill the earth and subdue it. Rule over the fish of the sea and the birds of the air and over every living creature that moves on the ground" (Genesis 1:28). It is important to note, however, that while Adam and Eve were granted authority over creation, they did not exercise absolute dominion. They were to exercise their authority within given limits. In particular, they were commanded not to eat from the tree of the knowledge of good and evil (Genesis 2:16–17). It was Adam's failure to abide by this command that plunged the human race into sin (Romans 5:12).

Adam's sin not only condemned all those who would come after him; it also ruined their nature. When Adam was commanded not to eat of the tree of the knowledge of good and evil, he was as capable of obedience as he was of disobedience. This was not true of humanity after Adam's fall into sin. Our behavior is "skewed" in the direction of disobedience (cf. Romans 7:14–23). This result has produced a tragic irony. Although we were created to rule over all creation, the reality of our own sinfulness means that we cannot even exercise dominion over ourselves. Although we were created to function as vice-regents with the Father, we have been reduced to slavery. Prior to the intervention of Christ we were under the dominion of darkness (Colossians 1:13). We were enslaved to sin (Romans 6:6). Fortunately God had a plan to restore us to our proper place. Even before creation, He purposed to redeem us through Jesus Christ.

THE WORK OF REDEMPTION

The debate between science and theology is important, yet it may actually have caused us to miss the primary theological thrust of the Genesis account. The main focus of the early chapters of Genesis is not upon creation so much as it is upon the fall of that creation into sin. The Genesis story points to the universal nature of sin by tracing its origin to the first human beings that lived.

Moreover, it indicates that God's redemptive plan predated His selection of any family or tribe as His people. The first promise of redemption was addressed to the human race as a whole. Soon after Adam and Eve had sinned, the Lord warned Satan that He would "put enmity between you and the woman, and between your offspring and hers; he will crush your head, and you will strike his heel" (Genesis 3:15). Often described as the protoevangelium, this statement did not describe the future life and ministry of Jesus Christ in detail, but it did briefly foretell the outcome of His work. It promised that Jesus Christ, the offspring of the woman, would be wounded by Satan and as a result would utterly defeat him.

This introduction of the promise of redemption into the creation story helps us to understand several statements in the New Testament that seem to speak of the salvation provided by Jesus Christ in universal terms. John 1:29 refers to Jesus as "the Lamb of God, who takes away the sin of the world." According to 2 Corinthians 5:19, "God was reconciling the world to himself in Christ, not counting men's sins against them." John describes Jesus as "the atoning sacrifice for our sins, and not only for ours but also for the sins of the whole world" (1 John 2:2). In the same way, the writer of Hebrews asserts that Jesus "suffered death, so that by the grace of God he might taste death for everyone" (2:9).

It is clear from many other passages of Scripture that these cannot be taken as promises of universal salvation. Revelation 20:15 indicates that in the final judgment all whose names are not written in the Lamb's Book of Life will be thrown into the lake of fire. Jesus Himself warned of the danger of being thrown into hell (Matthew 5:22–30; 10:28; 18:9; Mark 9:43; Luke 16:23). Rather, these passages describe the implications that Christ's ministry has for all people and point to the universal authority of the gospel. They indicate that the gospel message should be preached to people of all tribes, tongues, and nations.

The call to repent and trust in Christ is more than a promise; it is a universal command. The God of the Bible is not merely the God of Abraham, Isaac, and Jacob. Nor is He only the God of the

Christian church. He is the God of all creation, and all people are accountable to Him for their sins: "In the past God overlooked such ignorance, but now he commands all people everywhere to repent" (Acts 17:30). Jesus Christ alone is the hope of salvation for all the earth, regardless of one's culture or religious heritage. To say that His Son is the Savior of the "world," then, does not mean that He will save all. Rather, it means that there is no other Savior for the world: "Salvation is found in no one else, for there is no other name under heaven given to men by which we must be saved" (Acts 4:12).

The biblical story of the creation serves as the staging ground for the biblical theme of redemption.[17] It establishes the human need for salvation and informs us of God's intent to intervene in the affairs of a broken humanity. It also reminds us that this same God is at work in the world around us. Jesus taught that although God the Father had rested from His creative works on the seventh day, He had not ceased to work. When accused by the religious leaders of violating the Sabbath law by healing, Jesus replied that He was merely following the example of His Father: "Jesus said to them, 'My Father is always at his work to this very day, and I, too, am working'".(John 5:17).

THE WORK OF PROVIDENCE

Many of the roles in which I function are temporary. I am a college professor by day. When I leave the campus, however, few people call me Dr. Koessler. Prior to joining the faculty I was a pastor. Although I am still ordained and continue to preach and teach in churches, nobody uses that title to refer to me. When it comes to my sons, however, I am always a father! When the thunder crashes overhead and shakes our house to its foundation at 2:00 A.M., they tumble downstairs and burst into my bedroom seeking comfort. If I were to say, "Go away, it's after hours. I'm your father only until 10:00 P.M.!" they would only laugh. As far as they are concerned, I am always on duty.

The same is true of our heavenly Father. His divine activity and interest in us did not cease with creation. He continues to uphold and care for all that He has made. This is the work of providence. Theologically speaking, the work of providence is God's work of governing what He has created. He does this, first, by preserving what He has created. We owe more than our creation to God. We also owe our continued existence to Him—even if we do not acknowledge God's authority in our lives. Every breath we take is a gift from God. He supplies our daily food and the strength and ability to work to provide for our own needs. This is graphically described in Job 38–42, which paints picture after picture of God's control and provision for all of His creatures:

> Who endowed the heart with wisdom or gave understanding to the mind? Who has the wisdom to count the clouds? Who can tip over the water jars of the heavens when the dust becomes hard and the clods of earth stick together? Do you hunt the prey for the lioness and satisfy the hunger of the lions when they crouch in their dens or lie in wait in a thicket? Who provides food for the raven when its young cry out to God and wander about for lack of food? (Job 38:36–41)

Second, God governs His creation by directing all the events that take place so that they accomplish His ultimate purpose. The biblical doctrine of providence should be distinguished from the two popular but false views of deism and fatalism. Deism taught that God designed the universe to operate like a machine and then stepped back to let it run its course. The god of deism is impersonal and detached from his creation. The God of the Bible is separate from His creation and distinct from it, but He is also very involved in the outworking of His plan. The pagan view of fatalism teaches that all actions are fixed and that human beings are incapable of acting as free agents. The biblical doctrine of providence recognizes that human beings act as free agents but also teaches that the free acts of men are subordinated to God's ultimate purposes. This doctrine is not intended to relieve us of responsibility for our behavior but to give us confidence in God's ability to work out all things for His glory and for the ultimate good of those who love Him and have been called according to His purpose (Romans 8:28).

Like my earthly father, our heavenly Father goes to work each day. Although God's work is far more mysterious than my earthly father's, in many respects it is more accessible. This is because it is carried out within the context of my own life. I do not need to follow God to His "job" in order to see what He does. I can find evidence of His working in Scripture and in my own life. In so doing, I not only find God, I also find myself. The more I understand God and His work, the easier it is to understand myself.

QUESTIONS FOR DISCUSSION

1. What is the difference between atheistic evolution, theistic evolution, progressive creationism, and fiat creationism?
2. Why might it be said that the Father's work of creation provides a justification for Christian missions?
3. What does the Bible mean when it says that humans have been created in God's "image"?
4. In what way does Adam's role in the Garden help us to understand the spiritual significance of work?
5. How would you respond to someone who said that man was created in the image of God and that women have been created in the image of man?
6. What is implied by the command given to Adam and Eve to "rule" over creation?
7. Where do we experience the Father's work of providence?
8. How does this differ from deism?

6

THE CARE OF THE FATHER

Not all fathers are alike. My boyhood friend Kevin's father was about as different from my own as one could imagine. He was an outdoorsman who loved to hunt and fish. My dad's exposure to the outdoors was limited to the time it took him to walk from the front door to the car. Kevin's father rumbled down the street on a large "hog"—an old Harley Davidson motorcycle that he had restored. It even had a sidecar! My dad drove a large blue Chevy Impala. Kevin's dad was mechanically inclined and liked to work on cars. My dad's intermittent attempts to work on our old Chevy were marked by lost bolts, bruised knuckles, and muffled expletives. Kevin's dad was a welder. My father was an artist and an avid reader. My mental image of him is one in which he is seated on the couch, his face hidden behind a newspaper or a paperback novel. Despite their differences, however, both men had one thing in common: They saw it as their responsibility to care for the needs of their family.

Jesus taught that this is fundamental to the nature of fatherhood. He also taught that this kind of parental care is intrinsic to God the Father: "And when you pray, do not keep on babbling like pagans, for they think they will be heard because of their many words. Do not be like them, for your Father knows what you need before you ask him" (Matthew 6:7–8). The refrain of the old hymn declares, "God will take care of you." But just how do we experience His care?

THE FATHER OF COMPASSION

One of the ways we experience the Father's care is within the context of suffering. Throughout the Scriptures there is a relationship between affliction and divine comfort. We experience God most often, it seems, when we are suffering. Despite this, when we go through affliction we are often plagued by questions about God's love for us. If God truly loved us, we reason, why would He allow such things to happen? All too aware of the advantage he has in such a moment, Satan rushes in and whispers that the answer to our question is that God *doesn't* love us. He paints a picture of an evil god who takes pleasure in tormenting his children. In effect, he portrays God as an abusive and unloving father.

Alistair Begg has observed: "Evangelical Christianity lacks a well-thought-out, Bible-based, clearly articulated theology of suffering."[1] This is somewhat surprising in view of the emphasis this theme receives throughout the Bible. Indeed, one of the Father's titles is "Father of compassion" (KJV: "Father of mercies") because He comforts us "in all our troubles" (2 Corinthians 1:3–4). Paul did not invent this title. Compassion is a characteristic ascribed to God in the Old Testament. Psalm 103:13–14 declares: "As a father has compassion on his children, so the Lord has compassion on those who fear him; for he knows how we are formed, he remembers that we are dust." In Isaiah 51:12 the Lord says, "I, even I, am he who comforts you." In Isaiah 66:13 the Lord promises to comfort His people "as a mother comforts her child."

Two Hebrew terms in particular have been used in contexts that describe the Father's compassion. The first is רָחַם, a word that is commonly associated with parental feeling (Psalm 103:13; Jeremiah 31:20). The other is חָנַן, a word that means to be gracious or show favor. It is a term used by the psalmist in his pleas for God to show mercy: "Turn to me and be gracious to me, for I am lonely and afflicted" (Psalm 25:16). It is also the word Job used when he pleaded: "Have pity on me, my friends, have pity, for the hand of God has struck me" (Job 19:21). The difference between these two terms is that the first seems to focus upon God's feelings for us during the experience of suffering, while the second focuses upon His actions on our behalf. Both are important features of divine compassion.

God has compassion for us because He has the ability to empathize with our experience. God comforts us by sharing our affliction. He feels our sufferings. When we hurt, He hurts. The story is told of a little girl whose best friend died. The girl went to comfort the grieving mother. When her parents learned about it, they were alarmed. They were afraid that the girl had said some childish thing that would have inadvertently intensified the woman's grief. "What did you say?" the girl's mother asked anxiously.

"Nothing," the little girl replied, "I just climbed up on her lap and cried with her."

Well-meaning people often try to help us in our suffering by telling us not to feel bad. They point to the many people who have suffered worse affliction or they point to their own problems and tell us that we don't know what real pain feels like. They don't realize that such comfort hurts more than it helps. In effect, it says that our pain doesn't count. Real comfort comes from those who are willing to suffer along with us. This is what God is like. Isaiah 63:9 describes the Lord's attitude toward His people's sufferings during their sojourn through the wilderness and says: "In all their distress he too was distressed, and the angel of his presence saved them. In his love and mercy he redeemed them; he lifted them up and carried them all the days of old."

What was true for them is also true of us. When we are crushed, God feels the weight of it. However, if His compassion went no farther than this, it could be small comfort. It is nice to know that God empathizes with our suffering, but what we really want is concrete help. Divine compassion does more than merely feel our pain. It intervenes on our behalf. This is especially comforting when we note the context of the suffering described in Isaiah 63:9. It was their own disobedience that compelled God's people to spend forty years in the wilderness prior to entering the land of Canaan. Although they were under divine discipline during this time, God continued to feel compassion for His people and carried them through their most difficult times.

COMFORT AND SUFFERING

Paul indicated that our experience of God's comfort is directly proportional to the degree that we experience the sufferings of Christ: "For just as the sufferings of Christ flow over into our lives, so also through Christ our comfort overflows" (2 Corinthians 1:5). The phrase "the sufferings of Christ" underscores an important fact. Even Jesus experienced suffering. If this was true of Christ, we can hardly expect to be immune.

If we ask the question, "Why do bad things happen to God's people?" the answer must be that it is because they are God's people. Affliction is part of our training—just as it was part of Christ's training as far as His human nature was concerned. Augustine observed, "God had one Son on earth without sin, but never one without suffering." The Scriptures agree with this. Speaking of Jesus, Hebrews 5:8 says: "Although he was a son, he learned obedience from what he suffered." It seems likely that the author of Hebrews had Christ's prayer in the Garden of Gethsemane in mind when he said this. On the night of His betrayal and arrest Jesus pleaded: "Father, if you are willing, take this cup from me; yet not my will, but yours be done" (Luke 22:42). Believers who suffer can take some measure of comfort in knowing that they have not been singled out by the Father for this. Jesus was no less God's Son when He suffered. Neither are we any less the sons and daughters of God when we experience suffering. Indeed, some forms of suffering may actually be a mark of the Father's love (cf. Hebrews 12:7–10).

Suffering is inherent to our Christian experience. Knowing this, however, is of little value unless we understand the Father's intent behind such experiences. When the apostle Paul evaluated his own afflictions, he was able to discern two great purposes behind his suffering. The first was to equip him to be a source of comfort to others: "If we are distressed, it is for your comfort and salvation; if we are comforted, it is for your comfort, which produces in you patient endurance of the same sufferings we suffer" (2 Corinthians 1:6). Paul did not suffer only for his own sake; his suffering benefited others. Certainly it enabled him to understand the circumstances of others. Like Jesus Christ, Paul was better able to sympathize with others because he had gone through similar experiences. More than this, however, Paul's experiences empowered others to carry on in the same kind of suffering. Paul's life was proof that one could endure pain and still flourish.

The other purpose behind Paul's suffering was to teach him to depend upon God. The press of trial was not intended to drive him to absolute despair, only to despair of self-sufficiency: "We do not want you to be uninformed, brothers, about the hardships we suffered in the province of Asia. We were under great pressure, far beyond our ability to endure, so that we despaired even of life. Indeed, in our hearts we felt the sentence of death. But this happened that we might not rely on ourselves but on God, who raises the dead" (2 Corinthians 1:8–9).

George Mueller, known for his life of faith and powerful prayer life, was traveling to Quebec when the steamer he was aboard became engulfed in fog off the coast of Newfoundland. Mueller sought out the captain and expressed his concern. "Captain," he said, "I must be in Quebec on Saturday afternoon."

"That's impossible," replied the captain.

Despite their circumstances, Mueller was not put off by the captain's reply. "I'm helpless!" he explained. "Let's go down to the chart room and pray."

The captain looked skeptically at Mueller. "Do you know how dense this fog is?" he queried.

"No," Mueller answered. "My eye is not on the density of the fog, but on the living God who controls every circumstance of my life." Once they had retreated to the chart room, Mueller dropped to his knees and began to plead with God: "O Lord, if it is consistent with Thy will, please remove this fog in five minutes. Thou knowest the engagement Thou didst make for me in Quebec for Saturday. I believe it is Thy will." In a matter of minutes the fog lifted.

(One of the reasons we find ourselves over our heads in trials is so that we will climb on to God's shoulders and let Him carry us through the raging water.) Paul's experience of divine comfort in the midst of suffering gave him confidence to face the future: "He has delivered us from such a deadly peril, and he will deliver us. On him we have set our hope that he will continue to deliver us, as you help us by your prayers. Then many will give thanks on our behalf for the gracious favor granted us in answer to the prayers of many" (2 Corinthians 1:10–11). It is often true that when we are helpless we are most hopeful in the Christian life. Suffering is not intended to drive us to despair but to give us confidence in God.

The experience of God's comfort in affliction brings an obligation with it. Those who are comforted by the Father have a responsibility to share that same comfort with others. One of the ways we do this is through prayer. The biblical teaching regarding affliction is not fatalism. Paul did not tell his readers to resign themselves to suffering as though nothing can be done about it. Whether it is our own suffering or that of another, we can at least do one thing. We can pray. In 2 Corinthians 1:11 Paul drew a direct line from his own experience of God's comfort in the midst of affliction to the prayers of others on his behalf.

It is not always easy to know how to help those who are suffering. The Old Testament patriarch Job is a good example. After Job had listened to his three friends lecture him about the cause of his affliction, Job angrily said, "I have heard many things like these; miserable comforters are you all!" (Job 16:2). The irony of this is that their sole purpose for visiting Job was "to go and sympathize with him and comfort him" (2:11). Yet somewhere along the way they changed their agenda. Instead of offering comfort, they felt a need to defend God. They tried to explain why such terrible things had happened to Job. Unfortunately for Job, the only explanation they could arrive at was that Job must have deserved his suffering. Ultimately, God has not called us to answer the question: "Why do bad things happen to God's people?" He has, however, called us to comfort those who are suffering by joining in with them during their experiences and by praying for God to relieve them.

FATHER TO THE FATHERLESS

Throughout the Bible, God the Father expresses an interest in the fatherless and promises to protect them. Deuteronomy 10:18 states: "He defends the cause of the fatherless and the widow, and loves the alien, giving him food and clothing." In the Mosaic Law He commanded that a portion of Israel's tithes be set aside to provide for the fatherless (Deuteronomy 14:29; 16:11, 14; 26:12). Judges were reminded of their responsibility to protect the interests of the fatherless (Deuteronomy 24:17; 27:19). A portion of the field was to be left unharvested so that they would have food (Deuteronomy 24:19–21). In the Psalms God is called "helper of the fatherless" (Psalm 10:14). These verses originally focused upon the needs of the orphan. Today, however, their message is made especially poignant in view of the widespread collapse of families. Although many sociological and psychological remedies have been proposed, Myron Chartier, a professor of ministry at Eastern Baptist Theological Seminary, believes that the ultimate solution is theological:

> Theologically, human parenting has its antecedent in the biblical concept of the Fatherhood of God. As human parents, we stand in relation to our children in a way analogous to the way in which God is related to his people as a Father. Both parents, the mother and father, bear equal responsibility for fulfilling, by analogy, that which is represented by the Fatherhood of God.[2]

According to Chartier, God is our ultimate model when it comes to parental care. If we are to follow this example, we must first know how God cares for us. Chartier identifies seven key attributes of divine "parenting."[3] Among them are the following attributes:

God the Father Cares for His Children

The apostle Peter urged the readers of his first epistle to cast their anxieties upon God "because he cares for you" (1 Peter 5:7). Commenting on this verse, Robert Leighton, who served as archbishop of Glasgow during the seventeenth century, urged his readers: "Entertain no care at all but such as thou mayest put into God's hands, and make his on thy behalf; such as he will take off thy hand, and undertake for thee."[4] A parent identifies with the needs of his or her child. God the Father does the same for us. He makes our concerns His. If God, then, urges me to leave the worrying to Him, why should I worry myself—especially in view of the fact that God cannot really be anxious about anything? I have no concern that is greater than His power to deal with it.

God the Father Responds to His Children

Genuine love is responsive. Just as the other strings on a musical instrument resonate when one string is plucked, God's own heart resonates with us in our circumstances, Chartier explained:

> The Eternal is something other than impersonal, creative energy behind and within the structures and processes of the universe. The Creator is something other than the Great Clockmaker, who resides in some remote part of the universe. Indeed, Yahweh is a living God (Judg. 8:19; 1 Kings 17:1), an extraordinarily active presence, who is intensely personal in that this God emotes divine anger as well as divine tenderness. Such a God is not a static being behind the universe, but rather a dynamic, responsive, personal being who acts redemptively in human history.[5]

He feels our anxiety, rejoices in our happiness, is angered when we are treated unjustly and jealous when the love that is due Him is given to another. It is noteworthy that a large range of "human" emotions is ascribed to God throughout the Scriptures. As we have already noted, however, the distinguishing mark of divine compassion is not merely seen in the fact that God feels for us, but is reflected in His willingness to intervene on our behalf. He responds in deed. This response is informed by His understanding of what we need. As Jesus pointed out, God the Father will not give His children a stone when they are in need of bread (Matthew 7:9). God the Father is responsive to us, but He is not indulgent.

God the Father Disciplines His Children

The exercise of discipline is fundamental to the parental role. It is an experience common to all children. The author of Hebrews uses this argument to urge his readers not to be discouraged when they are disciplined by their heavenly Father: "Endure hardship as discipline; God is treating you as sons. For what son is not disciplined by his father?" (Hebrews 12:7). Although there may be an element of punishment in divine discipline, it is never vindictive. God's discipline is nurturing. It produces "a harvest of righteousness and peace" (Hebrews 12:11). It has the added advantage of being guided by God's perfect knowledge of our nature and personal need. No human discipline can make the same claim: "Our fathers disciplined us for a little while as they thought best; but God disciplines us for our good, that we may share in his holiness" (Hebrews 12:10). The fact that God's aim in discipline is our holiness means that the Father's discipline is ultimately redemptive in nature. We may not enjoy it, but we will survive it and be better off as a result. Perhaps more important, the author of Hebrews stresses that the experience of discipline should not hinder our ability to love and revere God the Father. He argues from our experience with our earthly parents to prove his point: "Moreover, we have all had human fathers who disciplined us and we respected them for it. How much more should we submit to the Father of our spirits and live!" (Hebrews 12:9).

Divine discipline provides a threefold warning. First, it serves as a warning to the individual believer. Those who are disciplined by God are expected to change. The book of Proverbs warns: "He who ignores discipline despises himself, but whoever heeds correction gains understanding" (Proverbs 15:32). Rejecting divine discipline is a self-destructive act. Second, the Father's discipline provides a warning to the church at large. This is reflected in the church's practice of discipline. When congregational discipline is practiced, the church's leaders function as God's representatives. It is exercised "in the name of our Lord Jesus" and in "the power of our Lord Jesus" (1 Corinthians 5:4). In some cases a public rebuke is issued "so that the others may take warning" (1 Timothy 5:20). Third, divine discipline serves an evangelistic purpose. It provides a warning to the unbelieving world that a final day of judgment looms on their horizon: "However, if you suffer as a Christian, do not be ashamed, but praise God that you bear that name. For it is time for judgment to begin with the family of God; and if it begins with us, what will the outcome be for those who do not obey the gospel of God?" (1 Peter 4:16–17).

What form does discipline take? The term that is translated "punish" in Hebrews 12:6 literally means to "scourge." Puritan John Owen noted of this term: "The word 'scourgeth' argues a peculiar degree and measure in chastisement above that which is ordinary, and is never used but to express a high degree of suffering."[6] In the context of the book of Hebrews, this discipline seems to have taken the form of persecution. The experience of the Hebrews is compared to that of Jesus, "who endured such opposition from sinful men" (Hebrews 12:3). Elsewhere, the apostle Peter also linked the church's experience of persecution, described as suffering "as a Christian," with divine discipline or judgment (1 Peter 4:16; cf. 4:12–14). Peter warns, however, that some forms of suffering are self-inflicted: "For it is commendable if a man bears up under the pain of unjust suffering because he is conscious of God. But how is it to your credit if you receive a beating for doing wrong and endure it? But if you suffer for doing good and you endure it, this is commendable before God" (1 Peter 2:19–20; cf. 3:17; 4:15). The fact that things go right is not always a guarantee that we are experiencing God's favor, nor does the fact that things go wrong necessarily show that He is against us. Sometimes it's possible to do the right thing and suffer for it, as when a person's integrity means he forfeits his chance at a promotion.

Divine discipline may also come in the form of a rebuke. In Proverbs 3:11, the passage upon which Hebrews 12:1–11 is based, the terms "discipline" and "rebuke" are virtually synonymous. If unheeded, the Father's verbal rebuke, which is usually conveyed through the Scriptures, may lead to severer forms of discipline. In the end, however, all of the believer's life experiences are a form of discipline in the sense that they are the tools the heavenly Father uses to train us in godliness.

God the Father Gives Himself to His Children

A popular proverb says that it "takes a village to raise a child." Although it is appealing, this sentiment is sadly misleading. It is true that there is a community dimension to child rearing. However, the "village" tends to intervene only when a child's behavior threatens the interests of the community at large. In other words, community parenting is primarily reactive rather than proactive. One of the marks of true parental love, on the other hand, is its willingness to take the initiative. It anticipates the need of a child and makes provision in advance. In the same way, God the Father takes the initiative in His relationship with His children. We love Him because He first loved us (1 John 4:19). His design for us to be holy and blameless in Christ was fixed before the creation of the world (Ephesians 1:4). He sent His Son to suffer the penalty for our sin long before we were in position to respond to Him and made us alive in Christ when we were helplessly dead in sin (Ephesians 2:1–5).

It is this divine initiative that the apostle Paul set forward as the ultimate evidence of God's care for us: "You see, at just the right time, when we were still powerless, Christ died for the ungodly. Very rarely will anyone die for a righteous man, though for a good man someone might possibly dare to die. But God demonstrates his own love for us in this: While we were still sinners, Christ died for us" (Romans 5:6–8).

Paul's reasoning is that we can be supremely confident of God's love for us in the future because He has already removed the greatest obstacle that might have hindered it. Commentator C. E. B. Cranfield explains: "The point made is that, since God has already done the really difficult thing, that is, justified impious sinners, we may be absolutely confident that He will do what is by comparison very easy, namely, save from His wrath at the last those who are already righteous in His sight."[7] Later in the epistle to the Romans, Paul used a similar argument to prove that we can be confident of God's care for us, regardless of the condition of our daily circumstances: "What, then, shall we say in response to this? If God is for us, who can be against us? He who did not spare his own Son, but gave him up for us all—how will he not also, along with him, graciously give us all things?" (Romans 8:31–32).

HUSBAND TO THE WIDOW

Unlike the deities worshiped by their neighbors, Israel's God did not have a wife or consort. He is a Father but not a husband. However, many of the same passages that emphasize God's interest in the fatherless also stress the importance of looking out for the interest of the widow (Deuteronomy 24:17, 19–21; 26:12–13; 27:19; Isaiah 1:17; Jeremiah 7:6–7; 22:3; Zechariah 7:10). This priority reflects God's own interest: "He defends the cause of the fatherless and the widow, and loves the alien, giving him food and clothing" (Deuteronomy 10:18). He watches over the alien and sustains the fatherless and widow (Psalm 146:9). The fatherless and the widow are linked in these passages not only because they were both among the most vulnerable classes in the ancient world, but also because their lots were often cast together. The woman who had lost her husband was often a mother.

Widows in Bible Times

A "social net" of sorts was available to help those who were widowed. One element of this was the practice known as Levirate marriage. The term "Levirate" comes from a Latin word that means "brother-in-law." A woman whose husband died before the couple could produce offspring was required to marry her husband's brother (Deuteronomy 25:5). The practice of Levirate marriage was primarily designed for the husband's benefit, to ensure that his family name would be carried on.

Levirate marriage was not compulsory for the man. The surviving brother-in-law had the right of refusal. The widow, however, seems to have been bound by family ties to marry her husband's brother as long as he was willing. In addition, Deuteronomy 25:5 stipulates that Levirate marriage was allowable because both brothers were living together. According to J. Barton Payne it served an economic as well as a social purpose: "In other words, there was not simply the humanitarian purpose of caring for the widow, there existed also the economic necessity of maintaining the unity and the normal functioning of a mutually dependent household group."[8] In addition to Levirate marriage, widows were granted a portion of Israel's tithes (Deuteronomy 26:12). They were also permitted to pick up what was left behind after the harvesters went through the field (Deuteronomy 24:20–21). Both practices are reflected in the book of Ruth. Ruth supported herself and her widowed mother-in-law by gleaning barley that had been dropped in the field by Boaz's harvesters. Eventually Boaz, a relative of Ruth's late husband, married her according to the law of Levirate marriage.

God's concern for the widow is further indicated in the Old Testament story of the prophet Elijah. While fleeing from King Ahab, Elijah's life was preserved by the miraculous provision of food that God supplied to a widow of Zarephath (1 Kings 17:7–16). Later, when the widow's son died, Elijah restored him to life (vv. 17–24). This same concern for widows was reflected in the life and ministry of Jesus. He criticized the teachers of the Law because "they devour widows' houses and for a show make lengthy prayers. Such men will be punished most severely" (Mark 12:40; cf. Luke 20:47). The phrase "devour widows' houses" probably refers to their habit of taking financial advantage of the widows who supported them.[9] Jesus publicly praised a poor widow for the small offering she brought to the temple because it represented all she had to live on (Mark 12:43; Luke 21:2–3). Luke 7:13 says that when Jesus saw the funeral procession of a widow whose only son had died "his heart went out to her." He urged her not to cry and raised the widow's son.

Widows played an important role in the early church. One of the first social crises faced by the New Testament believers concerned the daily distribution of food to widows (Acts 6:1). This practice was probably adapted from the Old Testament laws that commanded Israel to make provision for its widows. Paul's first epistle to Timothy speaks of a "list" of widows who were to be supported by the church. Those who were placed on this list had to meet certain criteria first. The qualifications combined physical, family, and spiritual factors (1 Timothy 5:9–11). Some of the church's widows may even have been organized into a kind of religious order devoted to prayer, the ministry of service, and the training of young women (1 Timothy 5:10; cf. Luke 2:37; Titus 2:4).[10] The church's responsibility to the fatherless and widows was so great, in fact, that James labeled it as one of the identifying marks of true spirituality: "If anyone considers himself religious and yet does not keep a tight rein on his tongue, he deceives himself and his religion is worthless. Religion that God our Father accepts as pure and faultless is this: to look after orphans and widows in their distress and to keep oneself from being polluted by the world" (James 1:26–27).

A New Class of Orphans and Widows

Although in Western society the civil government has taken over many of the social responsibilities once considered to be the province of the church, the biblical command to look out for the interests of the fatherless and widows is still extremely relevant. Divorce, abandonment, and changing views about sexual behavior have created what might be described as a "new" class of widows and orphans. One demographic analyst predicts that if current divorce rates continue, a majority of children will spend a portion of their childhood in single-parent homes.[11] According to the U.S. Census bureau nearly one quarter of children aged seventeen or younger are growing up in a single-parent home. These families often face significant financial and emotional challenges.

Although the problems created by absent parents are challenging, they are not insurmountable. The same God who has promised to defend the cause of the fatherless and the widow can provide the love and comfort that is lost when a parent is gone. The psalmist wrote: "Though my father and mother forsake me, the Lord will receive me" (Psalm 27:10). The psalm writer does not say this because he assumes that being forsaken by one's parents is a common occurrence. Rather, he focuses on it because it is the most extreme case that he can imagine (cf. Isaiah 49:15). Charles Spurgeon explains: "These dear relations will be the last to desert me, but if the milk of human kindness should dry up even from their breasts, there is a Father who never forgets. Some of the greatest of the saints have been cast out by their families, and persecuted for righteousness' sake."[12] The church can also play an important role by following the example of the New Testament church and making the needs of the widows and fatherless in its midst a priority. Its members can function as surrogate parents to children who need parental role models. A renewed vision for the New Testament pattern of older men and women mentoring those who are younger can help to change some of the social dynamics that created the problem in the first place.

SUSTAINER OF THE POOR AND OPPRESSED

Many of the passages that speak of the Father's interest in orphans and widows also refer to His concern for the poor (Psalm 82:3; Isaiah 10:2; Jeremiah 5:28; Zechariah 7:10). The Lord promised to bless Israel to such an extent that poverty would not be necessary in the Land of Promise: "However, there should be no poor among you, for in the land the Lord your God is giving you to possess as your inheritance, he will richly bless you, if only you fully obey the Lord your God and are careful to follow all these commands I am giving you today" (Deuteronomy 15:4–5). However, this was a conditional promise and not a guarantee. It merely stated what could be possible as a result of God's blessing and Israel's obedience. A more realistic picture was given a few verses later: "There will always be poor people in the land. Therefore I command you to be openhanded toward your brothers and toward the poor and needy in your land" (v. 11).

Some of the same provisions made for the widow and orphan were available to the poor. They were permitted to follow harvesters and glean in the fields after them (Leviticus 19:10; 23:22). Those who were so poor that the only collateral they had for debt was their own cloak were entitled to take possession of it at night so that it might keep them warm while they slept (Exodus 22:25–27; Deuteronomy 24:12–13). When the lender came to collect the collateral, he was not permitted to enter the house of the borrower. Instead, he had to wait outside until the cloak was brought to him (Deuteronomy 24:10–11). Poor laborers were to be paid on a daily basis (vv. 14–15). Every seven years the land was to be left unused. During this year the poor were allowed to eat freely from all that grew of its own accord (Exodus 23:11). During the seventh year, known as the Year of Jubilee, all debts were canceled. Moreover, loans could not be withheld from the poor in the year prior to the Year of Jubilee, even though they would be canceled the following year (Deuteronomy 15:1, 9).

One of the more drastic remedies for poverty in ancient Israel was the practice of indentured servitude. Poverty-stricken Israelites could sell themselves into the service of other Israelites. In the book of Leviticus this was differentiated from slavery: "If one of your countrymen becomes poor among you and sells himself to you, do not make him work as a slave" (Leviticus 25:39). This condition was temporary. In the Year of Jubilee indentured servants were to go free along with their families (Exodus 21:2; Leviticus 25:41). In addition, the servant's master was responsible for providing for the servant upon his release: "If a fellow Hebrew, a man or a woman, sells himself to you and serves you six years, in the seventh year you must let him go free. And when you release him, do not send him away empty-handed. Supply him liberally from your flock, your threshing floor and your winepress. Give to him as the Lord your God has blessed you" (Deuteronomy 15:12–14). R. K. Harrison noted that these laws served a twofold purpose. They preserved the dignity of the poor while allowing them to maintain their social responsibilities.[13]

The New Testament echoes the Law's concern for the poor. For a very brief time the early church seems even to have achieved the state that God promised to Israel: "There were no needy persons among them. For from time to time those who owned lands or houses sold them, brought the money from the sales and put it at the apostles' feet, and it was distributed to anyone as he had need" (Acts 4:34–35). Jesus, however, affirmed what the Law of Moses had also warned, that the plight of the poor would be a continual concern for God's people (John 12:8). He was Himself poor and pronounced a blessing on the poor in the beatitudes (Luke 6:20). At the inauguration of His ministry, He announced that He had come to proclaim the gospel to the poor (Luke 4:18; cf. Luke 7:22). Jesus gave general guidelines for giving to the poor in the Sermon on the Mount and urged one of His would-be followers to sell all that he had and give it to the poor (Luke 18:22; see Matthew 6:2–4).[14]

The apostle Paul regularly taught new converts to provide for the needs of the poor. When he visited the apostles in Jerusalem to compare his gospel to theirs, this was the one practice that they urged him to emphasize to the Gentiles (Galatians 2:9–10). Some years later Paul organized a relief project among several of the Gentile churches and carried their gifts to the famine-stricken church in Jerusalem (1 Corinthians 16:1–2; 2 Corinthians 8:4). He taught the participating churches that those who gave generously would "reap generously" (2 Corinthians 9:6). In his epistle, James cited a lack of generosity to the poor when one has the resources to meet the need as an example of faith without works (James 2:15–16). There does seem to have been an order of priority for the New Testament church in this area. The pattern appears to have been one in which the needs of poor believers were given attention first: "Therefore, as we have opportunity, let us do good to all people, especially to those who belong to the family of believers" (Galatians 6:10). Paul's effort to provide famine relief was focused upon the Jewish church.

FOLLOWING THE BIBLICAL EXAMPLE

In the community where I formerly served as pastor, several of the churches participated in a local food pantry. It was located in a low, flat building in the center of town that doubled as a polling place. The food was placed in cupboards that lined the walls and was administrated by a few elderly women who sat at tables near the front door. The clients who came through the door were understandably self-conscious. First, they had to demonstrate that they were poor enough to merit receiving food from the pantry. Then, they often had to endure the stares and sometimes the disapproving comments of those who were seated at the tables.

Many in today's affluent culture feel that society has a responsibility toward the poor but feel that such help should be limited to the "deserving" poor. There is often a lurking suspicion that poverty is really the result of laziness. When help is made available, it is offered in a condescending manner.

What is the Father's disposition towards the poor? The biblical data paints a portrait that is significantly different. God's laws regarding the poor reflect several important assumptions:

The poor should be treated with respect. When the Bible talks about the poor, it repeatedly emphasizes that they are our brothers and sisters. The kind of concern that it calls for is not a civil obedience that is given grudgingly "for the sake of society" but the kind of concern we would show toward a member of the family.

The poor need to be protected. Old Testament laws in particular are intended to ensure that the poor receive justice. In biblical times, as is in our own, an abundance of privilege brought with it a monopoly on power. The Law of Moses warns God's people not to deny the poor justice (Exodus 23:6). Interestingly, it also warns against the opposite extreme. God's people were not to show favoritism to the poor (Exodus 23:3). Others were not to be robbed of justice in order to create a "level playing field."

The poor should be understood. The rationale behind Old Testament commands to protect the interests of the poor point to Israel's experience in Egypt. God's people were to deal sympathetically with the poor because as a nation they had once been poor themselves (cf. Deuteronomy 24:21–22). True compassion grows out of shared experience. We are more likely to be sensitive to the needs of the poor when we understand their circumstances.

The needs of the poor are the responsibility of the community at large. The philosophy of an individualistic society says that the helping hand you are looking for is found at the end of your own arm. There is a widespread conviction among many affluent believers that those who are poor got themselves into trouble and should get themselves out of it. The Bible does not sanction this "every man for himself" kind of philosophy. In Israel's theocracy and later in the church, the needs of the poor were the responsibility of the community at large.

Help for the poor should provide for basic needs. Biblical commands regarding the poor reflect an interest in meeting basic needs. The prohibition against keeping a poor man's cloak as collateral after the sun goes down shows a remarkable sensitivity to personal comfort. If God is concerned about such a small detail, should not His people reflect a similar sensitivity?

Our goal in helping the poor should be to enable them to improve their conditions. Old Testament laws that limited indentured servants to a term no longer than six years and urged masters to be generous with them when their time was up indicate that God's desire is for the poor to improve their condition. God's goal was not to keep them living at a mere subsistence level. This may involve more than money. Friends of mine once "rescued" a man they found sleeping in a doorway in downtown Detroit. They brought him back to their church in the suburbs, found him an apartment, bought him a new wardrobe, and helped him enroll for public assistance. He remained in the apartment for about two weeks and then returned to his life on the street. They were well intentioned in their effort, but the changes they had made in his life were mostly cosmetic. Until his addiction problem was dealt with it was unlikely that any amount of money they had given him would have helped. The factors that contribute to a lifestyle are complex and may involve spiritual, educational, social, and psychological aspects.

When we ignore the needs of the poor, we hurt ourselves. It is often self-interest that keeps us from providing for the poor. Ironically, the Bible indicates that this kind of selfishness is also self-destructive. God warned His Old Testament people that they would be judged if they ignored the plight of the poor: "Do not take advantage of a hired man who is poor and needy, whether he is a brother Israelite or an alien living in one of your towns. Pay him his wages each day before sunset, because he is poor and is counting on it. Otherwise he may cry to the Lord against you, and you will be guilty of sin" (Deuteronomy 24:14–15).

Generosity toward the poor must be offered willingly. Paul's directions to the church of Corinth regarding the collection for the poverty-stricken believers in Jerusalem emphasize the importance of a willing spirit: "Remember this: Whoever sows sparingly will also reap sparingly, and whoever sows generously will also reap generously. Each man should give what he has decided in his heart to give, not reluctantly or under compulsion, for God loves a cheerful giver" (2 Corinthians 9:6–7). The manner of our obedience in this area is as important as our method. In the end, the goal is not merely to do the same things that our heavenly Father does but to do them with the same attitude of heart.

QUESTIONS FOR DISCUSSION

1. If the Father is compassionate by nature, why does He allow us to suffer?
2. How does God show that He is a "Father to the fatherless"?
3. What are the advantages of being disciplined by the heavenly Father?
4. What forms does divine discipline take in the Christian life?
5. What made the widow so vulnerable in the biblical world? What provisions did God make to address this need?
6. In view of the many social programs provided by civil government today, why is there still a need for believers to show concern for the fatherless and widows?
7. How should we treat the poor?
8. What should our attitude be like as we help the poor?

7

THE BLESSINGS OF THE FATHER

When I was about seven years old I saw a toy stagecoach during one of our family's visits to the local department store and decided that it had to be mine. When I asked my father to buy it for me, he said no. "It isn't your birthday," he explained.

Undaunted, I began to wheedle him, playing on his sense of guilt. "Why is it that you only give me presents on my birthday?" I whined. "Why can't I get a present just to get a present?" When my nagging seemed to have little effect, I began to cry. With large crocodile tears rolling down my face, I wailed, "You don't love me."

Although such tactics usually did not change my father's mind, this time it seemed to work. With a snort of disgust he grabbed the toy off the shelf and headed for the checkout. I had gotten what I wanted, or at least it appeared that I had. Later, however, when I played with my new toy, it gave me little joy. Every time I looked at it only seemed to remind me of the tantrum I had thrown in the store. I was embarrassed and ashamed. What made it worse was the knowledge that, although my father had done as I had asked, he had acted against his will. He hadn't really wanted me to have the toy. He had only purchased it to silence me. My father had given me what I had asked for, but it was not a gift freely given.

Fortunately for us, our heavenly Father cannot be so easily manipulated. We can be certain that the good gifts we receive from Him are given with a joyful heart (Luke 12:32).

GOOD AND PERFECT GIFTS

Although it is true that not everyone who gives a gift does so with a willing heart, it is also true that a gift that is given willingly is not automatically a "good" gift. I know a woman who is a compulsive giver of useless gifts. One room in her small condominium is literally piled to the ceiling with items purchased at garage sales, flea markets, and discount stores to be used as gifts. Over the years her family members have collected an assortment of back-scratchers, heart-shaped pillows, and cheap boxes of chocolate large enough to fill a room of their own.

The gifts we receive from the Father are quite different. According to James 1:17: "Every good and perfect gift is from above, coming down from the Father of the heavenly lights, who does not change like shifting shadows." It is significant that this statement comes within a context that deals with temptation. It follows immediately upon the heels of James's warning that no one should say that God is the source of his temptation (James 1:13–14). It contrasts both the nature and the source of the gifts that come from God with the false promises of temptation. The lure of temptation seems good at the time but springs from the root of evil desire. It offers the promise of satisfaction but in the end produces only death: "Then, after desire has conceived, it gives birth to sin; and sin, when it is full-grown, gives birth to death" (James 1:15). The gifts that God gives, on the other hand, are "good." When we enjoy them, they produce results that work in the best interests of those who receive them. Sin may be temporarily enjoyable, but it ultimately exacts a price from those who indulge in its pleasures (Romans 6:23; Hebrews 11:25). The gifts of God are also "perfect." The biblical concept of perfection often refers to that which is "complete." When compared to all that God provides, sin's promises of fulfillment are empty. They leave those who have been victimized by them hungering for more.

A French actress who was dining at the home of a wealthy count admired the silver centerpiece that graced the table. In a grand gesture, the count said that he would be happy to give it to her. After she said she would accept the gift, however, the actress became nervous that the count would change his mind before the expensive item could be delivered to her. She explained to her host that she had come in a cab, hoping he would offer her a ride home in his personal carriage. When he did, the actress happily accepted. "Indeed," the actress replied, "that will suit me very well, as there will then be no danger of my being robbed of your gift, which I had better take with me."

"With pleasure," said the count as he bowed, "but you *will* send my carriage back, won't you?" If we can be confident about the nature of the gifts that come to us from God, we can be even more certain of His motives. He gives without regret. He does not "change like shifting shadows." Elsewhere the Bible contrasts the Father's faithfulness with human inconstancy (1 Samuel 15:29; Jeremiah 4:28). This assertion reaches a peak in Romans 11:29, which states that God's gifts and His call are "irrevocable." The order of the words in Greek text places emphasis on this term.[1]

THE BLESSING OF GRACE

Grace is the foundation of all the Father's blessings. If faith is the door through which we must enter in order to have a relationship with the Father, grace is the hinge upon which it is hung. In Ephesians 2:8–9 grace and faith are inseparably linked: "For it is by grace you have been saved, through faith—and this not from yourselves, it is the gift of God—not by works, so that no one can boast." In ancient Greek the term that is translated "grace" in the New Testament was often used to speak of the favor of the gods. In later Greek it was used to refer to a ruler's demonstration of favor or a gift.[2]

The Old Testament language of grace revolves around a cluster of words that refer to mercy, help to the needy, and the favorable disposition of a superior to an inferior (cf. Genesis 6:8; 19:19; Exodus 33:19; Psalm 103:13; etc.). Lewis Sperry Chafer noted that "the one thought which is almost exclusively expressed in the New Testament by the word *grace,* is, in the Old Testament, almost exclusively expressed by the word *favor.*"[3] When I ask someone for a favor I want him to do something that he would not otherwise be obligated to do. Grace, then, is God's unmerited favor. This favor is an outgrowth of His mercy. He shows kindness to those who do not deserve it. The Father's bestowal of grace is free; it is not extended to anyone as a result of obligation. However, once God's grace has been extended, it guarantees its benefits to all those who receive it. Although God was not obligated to show grace to anyone, once He chose to extend His grace He obligated Himself to fulfill what He had promised.[4]

Grace is first and foremost an attribute of God. He is "the compassionate and gracious God" (Exodus 34:6; cf. 2 Chronicles 30:9; Nehemiah 9:17, 31; Psalm 86:15; 103:8; 111:4; 116:5; 145:8; Joel 2:13; Jonah 4:2). In most of these passages God's grace is linked with His compassion or mercy. The Father is compassionate by nature and demonstrates that compassion by showing mercy. He is slow to anger, and when He forgives, He does so with love. His grace is reflected in His faithfulness. Although His people have often forsaken Him, He will never desert them. God is ultimately the source of all human compassion, even when it is expressed by those who do not acknowledge Him (cf. 1 Kings 8:50).

Grace is also a matter of relationship. When God shows grace to believers, He accepts them. The relational dimension of the grace of God is reflected in the language of Romans 5:1–2: "Therefore, since we have been justified through faith, we have peace with God through our Lord Jesus Christ, through whom we have gained access by faith into this grace in which we now stand. And we rejoice in the hope of the glory of God." Those who are the objects of God's grace "stand" in that grace.

As a result of the work of Jesus Christ, the believer is in a new position with respect to God. Prior to Christ this relationship was adversarial. We were God's enemies as long as we were separated from Christ and were alienated from God in thought and deed (Romans 5:10; Colossians 1:21). By placing our faith in Christ, we have entered into a state in which we have been declared righteous (i.e., justified) by God and are at peace with Him. He is no longer our adversary and we are no longer His enemies. Because Jesus Christ has satisfied the demands of God's law and has paid the penalty for our sin, all the obstacles that once stood in the way of a relationship with Him have been removed. He can look favorably upon us without being unjust. This is reflected in Paul's frequent use of the formula "Grace and peace to you from God our Father" in His epistles (Romans 1:7; 1 Corinthians 1:3; 2 Corinthians 1:2; Galatians 1:3; Ephesians 1:2; Philippians 1:2; Colossians 1:2; 2 Thessalonians 1:2; cf. 1 Thessalonians 1:1; 1 Timothy 1:2; 2 Timothy 1:2; Titus 1:4; Philemon 3). Since this is all the work of God, initiated by the Father, executed by the Son, and applied to us by the Holy Spirit, we are secure in our position.[5] The things that the heavenly Father gives to His children are not given grudgingly.

Theologians use two categories to describe the primary types of grace: "common" or "general" grace and "efficacious" or "special" grace. These types of grace differ in their objects and their effects. Common grace refers to the benefits bestowed by God upon all of humanity. Efficacious grace refers to the benefits that are bestowed upon the believer as a result of the work of Jesus Christ. All people experience a form of God's grace by virtue of His role as the Creator and sustainer of the universe (Psalm 147:8; 2 Corinthians 9:10). They also have access to the revelation of His "eternal power and divine nature" demonstrated through creation (Romans 1:20; cf. Psalm 19:1–6). God's provision for those whom He has created serves as a universal testimony to His kindness (Acts 14:17). Humanity in general has experienced God's grace in the form of divine patience. Although all have sinned against Him, God the Father has been patient with mankind, providing an opportunity for repentance (Acts 17:30). However, His ultimate demonstration of grace to all was by providing a Savior: "For the grace of God that brings salvation has appeared to all men" (Titus 2:11).

Efficacious grace is sometimes referred to as "saving" grace. It is the experience of grace that leads its recipient to saving faith in Jesus Christ. Charles Hodge described it as the efficacious influence of the Spirit secured "for all who have been given to the Son as an inheritance."[6] Included in efficacious grace are God's effectual call and the believer's subsequent conversion and regeneration. God's "effectual call" differs from the general call issued through the gospel. The gospel message issues a general call to all who hear it to believe in Christ as God's Son and their Savior. However, only some will actually understand its significance and turn to Jesus Christ. It is God's effectual call that enables those who do believe to respond. Their response is known as "conversion." The apostle Paul described conversion in his sermon to the Ephesian elders in Acts 20:21: "I have declared to both Jews and Greeks that they must turn to God in repentance and have faith in our Lord Jesus." This is also the work of God. He is said to "give" repentance (Acts 5:31). There are, however, both active and passive dimensions to the experience of conversion.

The Puritan Richard Baxter observed that conversion affects the believer in four primary areas. There is a change of mind, heart, affections, and life. He described conversion as the work of God by which He causes man's will to turn itself:

> So that conversion, taken actively, as it is the work of the Holy Ghost, is a work of the Spirit of Christ, by the doctrine of Christ, by which he effectually changes men's minds and heart and life from the creature to God in Christ: and conversion, as it is our work, is the work of man, wherein, by the effectual grace of the Holy Spirit, he turns his mind and heart and life from the creature to God in Christ. And conversion, as taken passively, is the sincere change of a man's mind, heart and life from the creature to God in Christ, which is wrought by the Holy Spirit, through the doctrine of Christ, and by himself thus moved by the Holy Ghost.[7]

The term "regeneration" refers to the new life experienced by the believer as a consequence of the work of Christ. Those who place their trust in Jesus Christ are "born again" (John 3:3, 7; 1 Peter 1:23). As a result of what Christ has done they are a new creation (2 Corinthians 5:17). The biblical teaching about regeneration reveals that this blessing of grace is dynamic rather than static in nature. On several occasions the apostle Paul described grace as an empowering force in his life. He stated that he had been able to lay the foundation of his ministry "by the grace God has given me" (1 Corinthians 3:10). He attributed his successes in ministry to God's grace and said that it was "not without effect" (1 Corinthians 15:10). He taught that those who believe had been enabled to do so "by grace" (Acts 18:27; Ephesians 2:8).

The entire Trinity is involved in all three of these effects (1 Peter 1:2). It is the Father who draws us to Christ, but it is the Spirit who illuminates the understanding of those who are called so that they understand and believe the gospel (John 6:37; 1 Corinthians 2:14).[8] Jesus pronounced Peter blessed because the Father had revealed the true nature of Christ to Him (Matthew 16:17). Yet He also said: "All things have been committed to me by my Father. No one knows who the Son is except the Father, and no one knows who the Father is except the Son and those to whom the Son chooses to reveal him" (Luke 10:22). Those who have come to Christ are "born of God" and "born of the Spirit" (John 1:13; 3:8). Just as Jesus Christ was raised from the dead through the glory of the Father, we have been buried with Christ through baptism so that "we too may live a new life" (Romans 6:4).

THE INSTRUMENTS OF GRACE

I was not raised in a Christian home. My family attended church only when the occasional wedding or funeral demanded our presence. I did have an opportunity to hear the gospel, however, at the children's club sponsored by a neighborhood church. On a muggy Wednesday night, I sat on the edge of a metal folding chair and listened intently as the group's leader spoke of the torments of hell. I had always been terrified of death, and his words seemed to confirm my worst fears. As I listened further, however, I discovered that a loving Father had provided a way for me to escape the punishment he described. Using the Bible to support all that he said, he assured us that those who placed their faith in Jesus Christ would be given the gift of eternal life. At the end of the message I prayed and asked God to forgive me and give me that gift.

Although I went home with a lighter heart that evening, my life changed very little. I had no encouragement from my parents to continue in the faith, did not attend church, and never read my Bible. Things were very different a decade later. At that time I was active in lay ministry, had changed my morals, my habits, and even my language. What made the difference? The turning point came when I decided to begin reading the Bible. While working alone on the midnight shift at a local fast-food restaurant I carried a small pocket Bible with me and read it during my breaks. Before long I had recommitted my life to Jesus Christ, was baptized, and had begun attending church. From that point on my spiritual growth seemed to accelerate.

God's Word and Prayer

Although God alone is the source of grace, He often works through secondary means to enable us to experience it. Instruments of grace are those practices used by God to bring us into a right relationship with Him and to enable us to grow in that relationship. Some of the instruments of grace are obvious. Prayer is one. Those who pray in faith to God for salvation experience His saving grace. "Everyone who calls on the name of the Lord will be saved" (Romans 10:13). God also enables us to understand His Word, gives us success in our ministry endeavors, and supplies us with the ability to preach the gospel clearly in answer to prayer (Romans 10:1; 2 Corinthians 1:11; Ephesians 1:18; Colossians 4:3–4; 2 Thessalonians 3:1). B. B. Warfield has said: "In its very nature, prayer is a confession of weakness, a confession of need, of dependence, a cry for help, a reaching out for something stronger, better, more stable and trustworthy than ourselves, on which to rest and depend and draw."[9] The practice of prayer can be linked to nearly every spiritual blessing we experience in Christ.

The Scriptures are another important instrument of grace. God's Word has the power to disclose the deepest thoughts and attitudes of the heart (Hebrews 4:12). It is the means by which God brings those who hear it to new birth in Christ (James 1:18). Once they have trusted in Christ, the Scriptures are used by God to equip believers for service. In 2 Timothy 3:16–17 the apostle Paul describes the four primary functions of God's Word:

God uses His Word to instruct us. The New Testament term that is translated "teaching" in 2 Timothy 3:16 is often used in pastoral epistles to mean "doctrine." This term focuses on the content of biblical instruction. In the Christian life spiritual growth and knowledge are linked. The Scriptures are the foundation upon which all of the church's teaching should be based. Biblical teaching, however, is not an end in itself. The ultimate aim of instruction is application. Paul linked doctrine to practice when he urged Timothy: "Watch your life and doctrine closely. Persevere in them, because if you do, you will save both yourself and your hearers" (1 Timothy 4:16).

God uses His Word to rebuke us. In addition to teaching, 2 Timothy 3:16 states that Scripture is useful for rebuking. One of the functions of God's Word is to enable us to see where we are wrong. The book of Proverbs warns against two dangerous extremes when responding to rebuke. One is to disregard or "scorn" it. This is how the fool responds (Proverbs 1:30; 13:1; 23:9). The other extreme is to become discouraged by it. Proverbs 3:11–12 warns: "My son, do not despise the Lord's discipline and do not resent his rebuke, because the Lord disciplines those he loves, as a father the son he delights in." We should not despair when our heavenly Father rebukes us through His Word. Rebuke is one of the strongest manifestations of His love.

God uses His Word to correct us. God's Word does not merely diagnose our problem, but it also prescribes a remedy. One of the functions of the Scriptures is to "correct" those who have been exposed to its rebuke. The nature of correction is restorative. The Greek term that is translated "correct" in 2 Timothy 3:16 literally meant to "set up again." The sword of God's Word has the power both to wound and to heal.

God uses His Word to train us. The changes called for by God's Word do not always come easily or immediately. The correction we receive from the Father through the Scriptures is one aspect of the believer's ongoing process of sanctification. The ultimate objective of the training that comes through the Bible is "righteousness." We are already righteous in position, having been declared righteous by faith in Christ (Romans 3:22–24). However, as we study God's Word, we learn what our heavenly Father expects from those who have been redeemed by His love and also of the provision He has made through Christ that will enable us to meet those expectations. God uses the Word as a tool to ensure that our practice in the Christian life accurately reflects our position in Christ.

The Sacraments

The Book of Common Prayer defines a sacrament as an "outward visible sign of an inward spiritual grace." This statement reflects the church's view that the sacraments hold a significant place among the tools that God uses to foster spiritual growth in our lives. The term *sacrament* comes from the Latin word *sacramentum,* a word that was employed by the Romans to refer to a military oath of allegiance, and was used in the Latin translation of the Bible known as the Vulgate to translate the Greek word for mystery. Donald Whitney uses the term "ordinance" to refer to the same thing and defines an ordinance as "a ceremony that the Lord Jesus Christ has commanded to be permanently practiced by the church."[10] Theologian Louis Berkhof uses both terms when he defines a sacrament as "a holy ordinance instituted by Christ."[11]

Israel was obligated to observe a host of ceremonies as part of its worship. The church, however, has been commanded to practice only two: the Lord's supper and baptism. The ordinance of baptism is significant because it is associated with the believer's entrance into spiritual life in Christ: "You are all sons of God through faith in Christ Jesus, for all of you who were baptized into Christ have clothed yourselves with Christ" (Galatians 3:26–27). It should be noted, however, that the Bible does not assign a mechanical relationship between baptism and new life in Christ. Baptism is a symbol of the believer's union with Christ in death and resurrection and is not the actual cause of that union.[12] The apostle Peter characterizes baptism as "the pledge of a good conscience toward God" (1 Peter 3:21). Baptism is both a confession of faith and an act of commitment.

The church's practice of observing the Lord's Supper is based upon Christ's command during His last Passover meal with the disciples that they "do this in remembrance of me" (Luke 22:19; cf. 1 Corinthians 11:24). In 1 Corinthians 10:16 the Lord's Supper is described as a "participation" in the body and blood of Christ. Elsewhere in the New Testament this same word is also translated "fellowship" or "sharing." Donald Whitney explains:

> Participation in the Lord's Supper allows us an experience with Christ that cannot be enjoyed in any other manner. Neither prayer, the preaching of God's Word, public or private worship, nor any other means of encounter with the Lord can bring us into the presence of Jesus Christ in exactly the same way. God has given to His children several means of communion with His Son, but one is unique to the Lord's Supper. Further, this communion is spiritual— that is, it does not occur merely by eating the bread and drinking from the cup, but by faith. And even though the bread and the cup do not contain the physical body and blood of Jesus, nor are they changed into them, they really do minister Christ to those who believe.[13]

The spiritual benefit that comes as a result of observing the Lord's Supper is not automatic. J. C. Ryle warns: "There is such a thing as fitness and preparedness for the ordinance. It does not work like a medicine, independently of the state of mind of those who receive it."[14] The first step in preparation is the practice of self-examination: "A man ought to examine himself before he eats of the bread and drinks of the cup" (1 Corinthians 11:28). The goal in self-examination is not to become morbidly introspective but to "[recognize] the body of the Lord" (1 Corinthians 11:29). The term "body" in this verse does not refer to the physical body of Jesus somehow manifested in the elements of Communion, but to the nature of the church as the body of Christ.[15]

One of the ways regular observance of the Lord's Supper promotes spiritual health is by giving us an opportunity to examine our relationship with the Father and with other members of the church. It is a time for repentance and confession of sin but also for boldly claiming the Father's offer of forgiveness through the work of His Son Jesus Christ. Observing communion in a "worthy" manner (cf. 1 Corinthians 11:27) demands that we be aware of our mutual need for God's grace and of the new position that is ours now that we are in Christ. It does not mean that we must come to a state of moral perfection before we are able to partake. The proper attitude is exemplified in the story of the Scottish minister who noticed the hesitation of one of his church members before accepting the elements of Communion in the service. It was plain to see that she wanted to participate but was afraid that she was not worthy. As she wavered, about to draw back her hand from the elements that had been offered to her, the pastor smiled and gently said, "Take it, Lass. It's for sinners!"

The Blessing of Wisdom

Wisdom is another of the blessings that comes from the Father. God's wisdom differs significantly from the kind of wisdom that the apostle Paul describes as "human" or "worldly" wisdom (1 Corinthians 1:17, 20). Both employ the same basic tools of words and ideas. But the words of human wisdom are devoid of divine power. Worldly wisdom is centered on man rather than God. It is more concerned with style than with substance and is overly dependent upon human skill. In the Corinthian church this was reflected in an excessive love of rhetorical style and an unhealthy attachment to some of the church's prominent leaders at the expense of corporate unity. This kind of wisdom gives rise to conceit and creates an environment in which those who embrace it "take pride in one man over against another" (1 Corinthians 4:6). Ultimately it is as self-destructive as it is self-absorbed.

God's wisdom seems like foolishness to those who value the wisdom of the world because it underscores human weakness. Nowhere is this more evident than in the message of the gospel (1 Corinthians 1:18). With its focus on the cross of Christ, the gospel message deals a deathblow to human self-sufficiency. The gospel says that human effort and wisdom are unable to lead those who use them to a true knowledge of God. It removes all ground for boasting because its benefits come as a gift of grace rather than as a result of personal achievement (1 Corinthians 1:21; 4:7). Paul deliberately avoided using "words of human wisdom" in his preaching, because he did not want the message of the cross to be obscured (1 Corinthians 1:17).

Human wisdom is rooted in human intellect and philosophy. As a result, it is restricted to those who possess a natural capacity for it. This is why it tends to generate pride in those who possess it (1 Corinthians 8:1). It allows them to boast in the fact that they possess what most others cannot have. Those who seek God's wisdom, on the other hand, can boast in the fact that they know and understand the Lord but cannot take credit for such knowledge (Jeremiah 9:24). Unlike human wisdom, God's wisdom is available to all who ask for it, because the Father "gives generously to all without finding fault" (James 1:5). The blessing of wisdom is a gift the Father gives without hesitation or regret, but it is not without important conditions. The first of these is the condition of faith. Those who ask for the blessing of wisdom must believe that God is willing to grant their request (James 1:6–7). Faith is a necessary precondition to obtaining wisdom because it reflects an attitude of dependence upon God. Those who have faith must first believe that God exists and be convinced that He will respond to those who seek Him (Hebrews 11:6).

The Disciplines of Wisdom

The fact that James described wisdom as a gift should not lead us to conclude that it comes without effort. When Proverbs 2:4 compares the pursuit of wisdom to the search for hidden treasure, it implies that divine wisdom is accessible only after an expenditure of time and energy. Yet if this is true, how can wisdom still be regarded as a gift?

Apart from God's grace any effort to obtain divine wisdom would be useless: "The man without the Spirit does not accept the things that come from the Spirit of God, for they are foolishness to him, and he cannot understand them, because they are spiritually discerned" (1 Corinthians 2:14). Before we can lay hold of the blessing of wisdom, we must first enter into a relationship with Jesus Christ and be illuminated by the Holy Spirit. This means that there is a supernatural dimension to the quest for wisdom.[16] Yet just as the Father uses secondary means to impart the blessing of grace, He has also chosen to link the gift of wisdom to certain practices. First among these is the practice of prayer. Wisdom is a gift from the Father, but to obtain it we must ask for it (James 1:5–6). We must "call out for insight and cry aloud for understanding" (Proverbs 2:3). These prayers should be coupled with the study of God's Word. According to 2 Timothy 3:15, the Scriptures are able to make one "wise for salvation through faith in Christ Jesus." Once we have entered into a relationship with Jesus Christ, God's Word ensures that we will be "thoroughly equipped for every good work" (2 Timothy 3:17).

In his autobiography, Augustine tells how he had been taught about Jesus Christ "with my mother's milk." His personal conversion, however, did not come until many years later. One afternoon while meditating he heard a child's voice from a nearby house chanting repeatedly, "Take and read. Take and read." He took this to be a divine command. He found a Bible, immediately opened it, and read the first chapter his eyes fell upon. The passage he had turned to was Romans 13:13–14: "Let us behave decently, as in the day-time, not in orgies and drunkenness, not in sexual immorality and debauchery, not in dissension and jealousy. Rather, clothe yourselves with the Lord Jesus Christ, and do not think about how to gratify the desires of the sinful nature." The result was instantaneous. It was as if someone had drawn back a heavy curtain from the window of his soul so that light and peace could flood his entire being. "No further would I read," Augustine later wrote, "nor needed I: for instantly at the end of this sentence, by a light as it were of serenity infused into my heart, all the darkness of doubt vanished away."[17]

Yet despite this remarkable experience, Augustine still felt that it was necessary to study in order to understand God's truth. In his treatise entitled *On Christian Doctrine,* Augustine wrote: "There are two things necessary to the treatment of the Scriptures: a way of dis-covering those things which are to be understood, and a way of teaching what we have learned."[18] According to Augustine each of these is "a great and arduous work."[19] Wisdom, like grace, cannot be earned or deserved. But we should not conclude that because it is free it is always easy. Wisdom comes as a result of careful study. In order to benefit from our study, we must be consistent. Consistency, in turn, usually requires a method. Although no single method is the best, every effective plan of study has similar characteristics. Effective methods of Bible study are simple, comprehensive, and practical. Our plan of study should be simple enough to incorporate into our daily schedule, comprehensive enough to cover the entire Bible over time, and practical enough to enable us to implement what we have learned in daily living.

Personal study is not the only way we grow in wisdom. God has also provided the church with gifted individuals whose ministry of preaching and teaching can enable us to grow in wisdom (Ephesians 4:11–12). They are used by the Holy Spirit to enable us to understand and apply God's Word, sometimes with striking results. Martyn Lloyd-Jones wrote of a man from South Wales who had been a Christian for some time but had fallen into sin. He had abandoned his wife and children for another woman. After he had squandered his money, the woman deserted him. In despair he decided to commit suicide by leaping from the Westminster Bridge into the Thames. When he arrived at the bridge, however, Big Ben struck six-thirty, and he realized that the service at Westminster Chapel would just be beginning. The man decided that he would listen to Lloyd-Jones one more time and then commit suicide. Just as the man entered the gallery, he heard Lloyd-Jones utter these words: "God have mercy on the backslider." Lloyd-Jones wrote: "Everything was put right immediately, and he was not only restored but became an elder in a church in a suburb of London and rendered excellent service for a number of years."[20]

Although our experience may not be as dramatic, the benefit we receive from listening to others explain and apply God's Word is just as important. One of the reasons the early church grew at such a phenomenal rate was that they devoted themselves to the teaching of God's Word (Acts 2:42; 11:26; 15:35; 20:20).

Wisdom is the fruit that springs from God's Word when it is implanted in our hearts. We are to "let the word of Christ dwell in you richly as you teach and admonish one another with all wisdom, and as you sing psalms, hymns and spiritual songs with gratitude in your hearts to God" (Colossians 3:16). The ultimate goal, however, in studying God's Word is to apply what is learned. James warns that those who merely listen to the Word are self-deceived (James 1:22–25). Consequently, God uses our daily experience as one of the disciplines of wisdom. Daily life is the laboratory in which the truth of all that the Bible teaches is proved. It is also the crucible that God uses to transform our character. Scottish pastor and hymn writer Horatius Bonar noted that the true character of a believer's life is usually measured in the small things of the day: "It is the little things of the hour, and not the great things of the age, that fill up a life like that of Paul and John, like that of Rutherford, or Brainerd, or Martyn. Little words, not eloquent speeches or sermons, little deeds, not miracles, nor battles, nor one great heroic act of mighty martyrdom, make up the true Christian life."[21]

THE FIVE PILLARS OF BLESSING

Ultimately, the list of blessings enjoyed by those who belong to the Father is endless. According to Ephesians 1:3 we have been blessed "with every spiritual blessing in Christ." In a letter to a friend, John Newton, the author of the hymn "Amazing Grace," identified five primary areas where these blessings are experienced. The first and most foundational area is in the realm of assurance. Those who have trusted in Christ are entitled to the assurance that they have been accepted by the Father. This assurance is based upon the Father's blessing of grace. Since our salvation is entirely the work of God, its successful completion does not depend upon us. It is begun by God and will be completed by Him (Ephesians 1:5–6; Philippians 1:6). The subjective evidence that our salvation has been guaranteed comes from another of the Father's gifts to us. It is a ministry of the Holy Spirit (2 Corinthians 1:22; 5:5; Ephesians 1:14). The objective proof of our assurance is found in the Scriptures (1 John 5:13). God's Word assures us that nothing can separate us from the love of God (Romans 8:38–39).

Newton assigned assurance first place among the believer's blessings and noted that "we cannot be said to enjoy blessedness without it."[22] Second, Newton pointed out that we experience God's blessing when we experience communion with Him. One of the ways this is achieved is through the means of grace.[23] This experience is really just a foretaste of the blessing to come when believers experience God's presence (Revelation 21:3). It is this that makes heaven a place of blessing. Jesus described heaven as "my Father's house" (John 14:2). Third, Newton pointed out that believers experience God's blessing when they depend upon the Father for guidance and protection.[24]

Divine wisdom teaches us to trust in the Lord more than in our own understanding. Our dependence upon a loving Father for daily needs like food and clothing is a practical reminder that we are just as reliant upon Him for our eternal needs. This is why Jesus told His disciples not to be concerned about things like food or clothing—not because these things are unimportant but as a way of training our faith. The same Father who provides daily bread is just as pleased to give us the kingdom (Luke 12:32). Fourth in Newton's list, the Father's authority and loving provision teach us to submit to His will.[25] The access that we have to the Father's grace gives us reason to rejoice in the worst of circumstances. Although we may not enjoy the problems we face, we can still rejoice while going through them because we know that God will use them to prove His love to us. Newton captured this hope in one of his lesser-known hymns entitled "The Lord Will Provide":

> Though troubles assail us and dangers affright,
> Though friends should all fail us and foes all unite,
> Yet one thing secures us, whatever betide,
> The promise assures us, "The Lord will provide."

> The birds, without garner or storehouse, are fed;
> From them let us learn to trust God for our bread.
> His saints what is fitting shall ne'er be denied
> So long as 'tis written, "The Lord will provide."

> When Satan assails us to stop up our path,
> And courage all fails us, we triumph by faith.
> He cannot take from us, though oft he has tried,
> His heart cheering promise, "The Lord will provide."

> No strength of our own and no goodness we claim;
> Yet since we have known of the Savior's great Name,
> In this our strong tower for safety we hide:
> The Lord is our power, "The Lord will provide."

Finally, Newton pointed out that we experience God's blessing as we serve Him.[26] We are not merely the recipients of the Father's blessings. By serving Him we also become channels through which those same blessings are dispensed to others (1 Peter 4:10). The Father's blessings are like the manna that the Lord provided during Israel's journey through the wilderness. Like the manna, a fresh supply of blessing is provided for us each day from the Father's inexhaustible supply. We never have to worry about depleting it. If anything, we tend to be satisfied with too little. However, it is also true that, like the manna in the wilderness, the Father's blessings tend to spoil when they are hoarded. Like our spiritual ancestor Abraham, we have been blessed in order to be a blessing to others (Genesis 12:3; Galatians 3:8). If we keep God's blessings for ourselves, they will grow old and our spiritual lives will become stagnant. When we share them by serving others, we will find both our blessings and ourselves renewed.

QUESTIONS FOR DISCUSSION

1. What is the relationship between grace and faith? What is the relationship between grace and mercy?
2. Why is grace a matter of relationship?
3. What is the difference between common grace and special grace?
4. How does God use the Scriptures in the life of the believer?
5. What is a sacrament?
6. Why are baptism and the Lord's Supper important?

8

PRAYING TO THE FATHER

It is difficult to know how to talk to some people. Early in my marriage I had trouble deciding how to address my wife's mother. At first I felt funny about calling her "Mom." I knew that I didn't want to refer to her as "Mother-in-law," and I was sure that she wouldn't like it if I called her "Mrs. Goulait." But calling her by her first name didn't seem right either. For a long time I didn't call her anything. When I wanted to talk to her I would position myself directly in front of her and just begin speaking. As our relationship grew, however, I was finally able to call her "Mom."

Should Christians find it that difficult to communicate with God the Father? Someone has said that prayer should be as natural as breathing. Experience, on the other hand, teaches otherwise. Most of us feel that our prayer life could be improved. This was true even of Jesus' disciples. According to Luke 11:1: "One day Jesus was praying in a certain place. When he finished, one of his disciples said to him, 'Lord, teach us to pray, just as John taught his disciples.'" The prayer Jesus gave as a result was the most famous prayer ever prayed. Known as the "Lord's Prayer," Jesus' words provide a model that we can use in our own prayer life.

PRAYER AS PERFORMANCE

Matthew's version of the Lord's prayer begins with instructions that focus on motivation rather than methodology. From God's point of view, why I pray is more important than how I pray. In particular, Jesus warned of the danger of praying to be heard by others: "Be careful not to do your 'acts of righteousness' before men, to be seen by them. If you do, you will have no reward from your Father in heaven" (Matthew 6:1). In Jesus' day, like today, some prayers were really offered for public display. Jesus spoke of the "hypocrites" who loved to pray on street corners to be seen of men (Matthew 6:5). Jesus did not intend to condemn public prayer with these words. Public prayers were a common feature of Old Testament worship, and the plural form of address in the Lord's Prayer ("our Father," "our daily bread," "our debts," etc.) suggests that it was designed for use in public worship.

The problem with the hypocrites was that their primary focus in prayer was not upon God but upon themselves. They were addressing God in their prayers but were really hoping to be seen and heard by men. In many respects they were like the bodybuilder who appeared on a popular television show. The host admired the bodybuilder's physique and asked, "Why do you develop those particular muscles?" In response the bodybuilder stepped forward and flexed. "What do you use those muscles for?" the host asked. The bodybuilder flexed his muscles again. The host persisted. "But what do you *use* all those muscles for?" This time the bodybuilder's response was merely a confused smile. He had already answered the host's question. He had developed his muscles for the sole purpose of being seen and admired by others.

When the hypocrites prayed for the sole purpose of being heard by others, they distorted the true nature of prayer. The spiritual purpose of prayer, to commune with God, was not important to them. They weren't even concerned with the functional purpose of prayer, to obtain answers from God. Their interest was in the prayer itself and in the human audience that might hear it. If God were deaf, their prayers would have been the same. Ironically, the human listener probably found their prayers quite impressive. To the searching eye of God, however, who evaluates prayer on the basis of the motives of the heart, they were empty words. Prayer that is merely performance for others is really a kind of self-worship. In theory I am worshiping God, when all the while I am really concentrating on myself. *How do I look and sound to others? What will they think of me?* When we pray, we must make certain that we are truly addressing God.

Jesus' solution to this problem is to develop a habit of secrecy: "But when you pray, go into your room, close the door and pray to your Father, who is unseen. Then your Father, who sees what is done in secret, will reward you" (Matthew 6:6). The test of secrecy asks: "Would I pray differently if I were alone?" Some, whose devotional life is confined to occasions of public worship, might ask further: "Would I even be praying if I were alone?" There is certainly a place for public prayer in the Christian life, but these two spheres, the public and the private, must both be in agreement. The foundational arena for prayer is the private sphere. When I am by myself I am more likely to be myself.

Television journalist Bill Moyers formerly served as press secretary for President Lyndon Baines Johnson. On one occasion when the two men were at lunch together, Moyers began the meal by quietly giving thanks for his food. The president interrupted him. "Speak up," Johnson shouted. "I can't hear a thing you are saying." Moyers finished his prayer and then gently replied, "I wasn't addressing you, Mr. President." Prayer is not a performance. Whether it is offered in public or in private, it is intended for an audience of One.

PRAYER AS MANIPULATION

Another pitfall Jesus warned of in His instructions regarding prayer was the danger of attempting to use our words to manipulate God: "And when you pray, do not keep on babbling like pagans, for they think they will be heard because of their many words" (Matthew 6:7). According to commentator David Hill, the term "babbling" in this verse is probably related to an Aramaic word that meant "idle" or "useless": "The idea behind the verse is that of the long prayers made by heathen people who believe that, in order to be sure of addressing the right god by the right name, all the gods and their titles have to be named."[1] The pagan view of prayer saw it as a form of word magic. Prayer was an attempt to control God. When prayer is approached in this manner, it turns what was intended to be meaningful conversation into meaningless repetition. In some religious traditions prayer is actually an incantation. The same words or phrases are spoken over and over again in the hope that if they are repeated enough or in the right order God will do something. In time it becomes possible to pray without thinking at all about what is said.

Another variation of this error approaches prayer as if it were a form of verbal "blackmail." This approach turns prayer into nagging. It is true that Jesus taught His disciples to be persistent when praying. In the parable of the unjust judge He told the story of a woman whose continual appeals convinced a judge to grant her requests. His purpose in telling the parable was "to show them that they should always pray and not give up" (Luke 18:1). A similar parable told the story of a friend who had received an unexpected visitor at midnight and begged his next-door neighbor to loan him three loaves of bread. In His application Jesus noted: "I tell you, though he will not get up and give him the bread because he is his friend, yet because of the man's boldness he will get up and give him as much as he needs" (Luke 11:8). Both parables teach something about God by way of negation. God is not like the unjust judge or the unwilling neighbor. He is eager to hear and respond to our prayers. On the surface it may appear as if Jesus is encouraging the very thing He condemns in Matthew 6:7. However, the difference between the kind of persistent prayer that Jesus encourages and the nagging prayer that He condemns is rooted in the view of God that lies behind it. Nagging prayer assumes that God is grudging in His response to our requests and must be bullied into answering.

Is it wrong, then, to use repetition in prayer? Most of us have certain forms or models that we use when we pray. We begin and end our prayers with similar phrases. Our requests often concentrate on the same areas prayer after prayer. We may even use a prayer book like *The Book of Common Prayer* and repeat specific prayers on certain occasions. Repetition is not in itself a bad thing. In the book of Psalms, for example, the psalmist often repeated certain themes and phrases in his prayers. The apostle Paul made the same request three times until he was told to stop (2 Corinthians 12:7–8). Even Jesus used repetition in His prayers. On the night of His betrayal and arrest, He prayed for the same request three times, apparently using the same words each time (Matthew 26:39–44). Jesus' criticism in Matthew 6:7 is not against repetition but is against *meaningless* repetition.

A business executive was called into the office of the CEO of a large automobile company to answer some questions. In the ensuing conversation the CEO asked several questions but then went on to answer them as well. What was supposed to be a conversation quickly turned into a long lecture. We have all had the unfortunate experience of being forced to listen to someone who was carrying on a similar one-sided conversation. The kind of meaningless repetition that Jesus criticizes is even worse. At least in a lecture the one doing the speaking has a point to get across. Prayer that hopes to be heard because of its many words is more interested in counting than in content. Our prayers should not be occasions in which we storm heaven's gates with a barrage of words in the hope that we will prevail by sheer volume. God's answers are not determined by weight. Furthermore, if prayer is a conversation, there must be listening as well as speaking. Eugene Peterson points out: "Prayer is answering speech; it is not primarily 'address' but 'response.'"[2]

That prayer should include listening as well as speaking sounds easy, but in reality it is quite difficult. One reason for this is that our attention in prayer is usually focused upon the answers we are seeking. This was certainly the aim of the Gentiles that Jesus condemns in Matthew 6:7. They used many words because they "think they will be heard." They wanted God to do something for them. Their focus was on the requests that they hoped to manipulate God into granting. But is this such an unreasonable objective? When I pray, I want God to grant my requests too. If I knew that God would never respond to any of the things I asked for in prayer, it is likely that I would cease praying, even if I was certain He was listening to me. What would be the point in continuing? Jesus, on the other hand, takes pains to remind us that God is listening to our prayers and will be responsive to our requests. This is, in fact, the basis for His argument that we should not pray like the pagans: "Do not be like them, for your Father knows what you need before you ask him" (Matthew 6:8). In saying this Jesus implies that this one aspect that is so significant to us—the request itself—is in some respects the least important element in prayer. This is not because our requests are unimportant to God. To the contrary, God knows what we need. He knows our requests before the words ever pass from our lips (cf. Isaiah 65:24). Indeed, He knows them even before we know them ourselves. That is why God always answers the believer's prayer but does not always grant the believer's requests.

The critical factor in prayer is the relationship. This is what is missing in the prayer of the hypocrite and the pagan. The hypocrite wants honor from men. The pagan wants results. But what does God want? This is the ultimate question we must ask when we pray, and the fundamental answer is that what God wants is us. He wants our hearts and our lives. This is the starting point for prayer.

APPROACHING THE FATHER

In view of this, it is significant to note how Jesus teaches us to address God in the Lord's Prayer. Unlike that of the hypocrite who is more interested in the crowd and the pagan who is only interested in results, the prayer of the believer is marked by intimacy: "This, then, is how you should pray: 'Our Father in heaven . . .'" (Matthew 6:9). Elsewhere Jesus used the term "Abba" to refer to the Father, a practice that was followed by the early church (Mark 14:36;

Romans 8:15; Galatians 4:6). Although this word was originally a childish form of address, perhaps equivalent to "Daddy" or even "Da Da," by Jesus' day it was commonly used by people of all ages. This universal use, however, does not detract from its intimacy. Nor does the term somehow make God smaller or more under our control, since a child has the biggest concept of his father and of God. The more accurate translation of "my Father" may lack the charm that "Daddy" has for some, but it still points to a special relationship. Willem A. VanGemeren argues that Jesus' use of this term was based upon Old Testament precedent, but that the Savior employed it in a way that restored God's people's awareness of the Father's loving concern for His children and expanded the biblical teaching about the potential for intimacy with Him:

> Jesus' distinctive contribution does not lie in the newness of his reve-lation of God as 'Abbâ. Rather, Jesus restored the OT teaching of Yahweh's love, forgiveness, readiness to listen to prayer, and fatherly concern. Jesus intensified this relationship in that he, as the Son, lived among us and taught more about the uniqueness and the glory of our relationship with our heavenly Father. Appreciation for the continuity between OT and NT also requires recognition of the dis-continuity. In the OT Yahweh relates to his people in a paternalistic way. He is like a patriarch as he defines his relationship with, and the freedom of, his people through Moses and the prophets. In the min-istry of His Son he emancipates his children while requiring them to walk in the footsteps of His Son. In the Son he gives them the Spirit of freedom. Instead of being the *paterfamilias* [head of the house-hold], he establishes a *familia Dei* [family of God] in Christ.[3]

When my children were first learning to talk they called me "Daddy." It didn't take them long, however, to notice that my wife, Jane, used a different name for me. Since she calls me "John," my boys also started to call me "John." Whenever this happened I inter-rupted and told them that I wanted them to call me "Daddy." When they asked me why, I explained that "Daddy" was their spe-cial name for me. Of all the people in the world, they were the only ones who had the right to call me by that name. The same is true of us when we address God as Father. It is His family name. When we begin our prayers by calling upon "Our Father in heaven" we acknowledge that we have entered into a unique relationship with the God of the universe.

What, then, are we saying about God when we address Him as Father? First, we are affirming our confidence in His provision for us. Before we articulate our needs, we address Him by the title that lays claim to His paternal care. It is the child's right to expect care from the father. If this is true on an earthly level, how much more will it be true of our heavenly Father (Matthew 7:9–11)? The Scriptures repeatedly remind us that it is the Father's nature to give. The same God who provided for His people during their trek through the wilderness will continue to provide for us today (Deuteronomy 29:4–5). Jesus assured us that it pleases the Father to provide for our needs (Luke 12:32–34). When we come to Him in prayer, we should approach Him expectantly.

Second, when we address God as Father we acknowledge that He is the source of our physical and spiritual life. There is a sense in which it can be said that He is our Father because He is our Creator (Acts 17:25–26). For those who know Christ, however, He is a Father in a special sense. Those who have trusted in Christ are not merely God's creatures—they are His children. This is a special relationship, limited to those who are in Christ: "Yet to all who received him, to those who believed in his name, he gave the right to become children of God—children born not of natural descent, nor of human decision or a husband's will, but born of God" (John 1:12–13). This means that when we address God as Father we are also affirming something about ourselves. We are confessing that we have entered into a relationship with the Father through faith in His Son Jesus Christ. We are sons and daughters of God by faith in Jesus Christ.

When we name God as our Father, we are also admitting that He has authority over our lives and that we owe Him reverence. In Malachi 1:6 the Lord asks the question: "'A son honors his father, and a servant his master. If I am a father, where is the honor due me? If I am a master, where is the respect due me?' says the Lord Almighty." Intimacy of address does not give us the right to be irreverent. The writer of Ecclesiastes reminded us that there is still an important distance between us and the heavenly Father that should be respected in prayer: "Do not be quick with your mouth, do not be hasty in your heart to utter anything before God. God is in heaven and you are on earth, so let your words be few" (Ecclesiastes 5:2).

In a sermon on the Lord's Prayer, Dr. Haddon Robinson described a game he often played with his children when they were young. He would take some coins in his fist, and they would sit on his lap and attempt to pry his fingers open. Once they succeeded, they grabbed the pennies and ran away laughing with glee. Robinson observed that when God answers our prayers, we often respond in a similar way: "We reach for the pennies. When God grants the request, we push the hand away. More important than the pennies in God's hand is the hand of God himself. That's what prayer is about. When you go to God in prayer, the name that should come easily to your lips is Father."

A Focus on God

This God-centered focus is evident in the first request of the Lord's Prayer, which asks that the Lord's name be "hallowed" (Matthew 6:9). This word means to "set apart as holy." Throughout the Bible, and especially in the Old Testament, God's name is a reflection of His character and authority (Exodus 34:5–7). The term "name" itself is sometimes used in a way that seems synonymous with "reputation." In the Shepherd's Psalm, for example, David said that the Lord will guide him in paths of righteousness "for his name's sake" (Psalm 23:3; cf. Psalm 109:21; 143:11). In Isaiah 48:9 the Lord promises: "For my own name's sake I delay my wrath; for the sake of my praise I hold it back from you, so as not to cut you off."

Much of God's treatment of His people, especially His faithfulness in the face of their continuing disobedience, can be traced to His own regard for His name's sake (Ezekiel 20:44). One of the foundational commandments in God's Law warned against the misuse of God's name (Exodus 20:7). However, dishonoring God's name includes more than merely taking it upon our lips in a careless manner. Certainly, using the name of God as a curse is forbidden by the third commandment. But God's name can also be dishonored by our actions. In Romans 2:19–22 the apostle Paul criticized those who boasted in their knowledge of God and yet violated the principles of His law. He concluded by saying: "You who brag about the law, do you dishonor God by breaking the law? As it is written: 'God's name is blasphemed among the Gentiles because of you'" (Romans 2:23–24). This condemnation is ironic, in view of the reverence the people of Israel traditionally paid to God's name. This was especially true of the name revealed to them by Moses that is often translated as "Jehovah" or "Yahweh" (Exodus 3:13–14). This term eventually became so revered by the Israelites that they refused to pronounce it. In some cases, when the scribes copied the Scriptures, they even refused to write it and put three small dots in its place. As commendable as the motivation behind such practices may have been, the practical result was to reduce reverence for God's name to the level of superstition.

How, then, do we hallow God's name? One way is by telling others what the Lord has done. The psalmist declared: "I will extol the Lord at all times; his praise will always be on my lips. My soul will boast in the Lord; let the afflicted hear and rejoice. Glorify the Lord with me; let us exalt his name together" (Psalm 34:1–3). According to this Psalm, to exalt the name of the Lord is to "boast" in Him. We usually think of boasting as a form of exaggeration. In this case, however, it signified an attitude of deep gratitude and sincere appreciation. We treat God's name as holy whenever we give Him the credit that belongs to Him for all that He has done. We may do this directly, by expressing our praise and thanksgiving to God in worship. Or we may do it indirectly, by telling others what God has done for us. Another way that we hallow God's name is by walking in the truth. Psalm 86:11 says: "Teach me your way, O Lord, and I will walk in your truth; give me an undivided heart, that I may fear your name." In a sense, when we pray for God's name to be hallowed, we are also praying for ourselves. God's reputation is linked with ours because we are called by His name.

In addition to a concern for God's name, Jesus taught us to pray "your kingdom come, your will be done on earth as it is in heaven" (Matthew 6:10). Behind this petition is the recognition that a day is coming when the kingdom of God will literally be established upon Earth. After His second coming, Jesus Christ will rule from Jerusalem over a worldwide kingdom for a thousand years (Revelation 20:4). The essence of the kingdom is expressed in the phrase "your will be done on earth as it is in heaven."

In its ultimate fulfillment the kingdom of God is something that can only come into being when Jesus Christ directly intervenes in the affairs of humanity. We can wait for it and look forward to it. Yet the Bible also teaches that there is a sense in which we can actually "speed" the arrival of the kingdom (2 Peter 3:12). Jesus' inclusion of this petition in the Lord's Prayer implies that our prayers will contribute to the consummation of Christ's kingdom. Although God Himself has already set the time of its fulfillment, the arrival of the kingdom is linked to the spread of the gospel (Mark 13:10). Prayer does not affect God's decision about the timing, but it does aid in the extension of the message of Christ (2 Corinthians 1:10–11). We can also speed the day of Christ by acting as Christ's ambassadors and allowing ourselves to be used as His instruments in proclaiming the gospel message (2 Corinthians 5:20).

Many countries establish embassies in other parts of the world. People who serve in them have been assigned the important task of representing the nations that appointed them. In all that they do they must constantly ask themselves what bearing their actions will have on the interests of the country they represent. Those who know Jesus Christ have a similar responsibility. In a sense, the Christian's life is an embassy for the kingdom of God. We cannot change our status as members of Christ's kingdom because it is the gift of grace if we have trusted in Christ. But if our lives reflect only the values of the world around us and not those of Christ's kingdom, we have taken territory that belongs to the King and have placed it at the disposal of the Enemy. Those who look forward to the day when Jesus Christ will rule the world from Jerusalem should be the first to demonstrate the reality of that rule in their own lives. Now that we have experienced the grace of Christ, we are no longer to allow sin to reign over us (Romans 6:12). We should think of the believer's life as the advance guard of the kingdom of God.

A Focus on Our Material Needs

After focusing on the Father's interests, the Lord's Prayer moves on to the kind of request with which most of our prayers begin. He teaches us to pray: "Give us today our daily bread" (Matthew 6:11). The Greek term that is translated "daily" is found only in the Lord's prayer (cf. Luke 11:3). New Testament scholars have suggested several possible meanings. It may mean something like "necessary" and be translated "the bread necessary for our existence." It could refer to bread for "today." Another suggestion is that it means "bread for the coming day." If the prayer was prayed in the morning, the "coming day" would be the present day. On the other hand, if the prayer was prayed in the evening, the "coming day" would refer to tomorrow. If this is the sense the meaning might be something like: "Give us the bread we need for today and tomorrow." It has also been suggested that the phrase focuses only on the day at hand and should be translated as: "Give us today the bread that comes to it."[4]

Some scholars believe that the term has eschatological significance and points to the bread that will be provided at the future messianic banquet.[5] Whichever view is correct, each of these possibilities emphasizes the fact that we are dependent upon God each day to provide for our most basic needs, whether they are spiritual or material. As I. Howard Marshall observed: "The food which God provides is food for body and soul; he gives men what they need and he gives them a foretaste of the rich provision available in the kingdom of God—and he does so each and every day in answer to their prayers."[6]

This petition is significant in view of Jesus' assurance that the Father knows our needs even before we ask Him (Matthew 6:8). If our heavenly Father is already aware of these things, do we really need to ask Him for them? The answer is yes. According to Jesus we ought to bring our most basic needs to Him in prayer.

Early in my Christian experience I learned the importance of thanking God at the beginning of my meals. However, since my parents were not believers and it was not their custom, I usually bowed my head for a few moments and said a silent prayer at the family dinner table. One day my father noticed what I was doing and became angry. "What are you thanking God for?" he stormed. "My money paid for this food. Your mother cooked it. You ought to thank us!"

There was a degree of truth in what he said. He did deserve my appreciation for providing for our family. He was also right in noting that there was an element of human effort involved in that provision. The food did not magically appear on the table already cooked and ready to eat. Someone had to work in order to purchase it. Someone had to prepare it. These plain facts of common sense are recognized by Scripture as a part of the natural order established by God. The general rule laid down in 2 Thessalonians 3:10 is this: "If a man will not work, he shall not eat." Jesus' petition does not allow us to use faith as a masquerade for irresponsibility. Yet even when we work for our food, it is God who provides the ability and opportunity to do so. One person may earn a large salary and have no financial worries. Another literally lives from hand to mouth. Yet both are equally dependent upon God for their needs.

In our culture of fast-food restaurants, refrigerators, and grocery stores, it is easy to lose sight of our dependence upon God for these things. It is important that we grasp the immediacy of Jesus' request. In effect, He teaches us to pray: "Give us something to eat today." This third petition also provides us with a needed reality check in our consumer-oriented culture. It is a request for daily bread, daily necessities. Although I want many things, the things that I truly need are much fewer. In our modern culture we have been taught to strive for our wants. Jesus, on the other hand, teaches us to focus on what we truly need and then entrust ourselves to the God who knows what we need before we ask Him. Those who live this kind of lifestyle will find God at the center when their lives are whittled down to the bare essence.

A Focus on Our Spiritual Needs

God's concern for us extends beyond the material needs we face on a day-to-day basis. In the fourth petition of the Lord's Prayer, Jesus teaches us to pray for the needs of the spirit. In particular, He tells us to focus on our need for forgiveness: "Forgive us our debts, as we also have forgiven our debtors" (Matthew 6:12). It may appear at first as if this request is out of place. In view of its importance, we might expect it to be at the top of Christ's list. However, if we consider the progression of thought in these petitions, the logic of its position becomes evident. The movement is from God's glory to God's will to our sin. This is the normal progression. An awareness of God's glory always brings with it a corresponding consciousness of our own sinfulness. Jesus uses the metaphor of indebtedness to bring home to us the reality of our spiritual need in this area. To speak of sin as an unpaid debt is a reminder that we owe something to God that we have not paid. The specific request that Jesus teaches us to make is that this debt be forgiven.

The term that is translated "forgive" means to "let go" or "release." It is a prayer for the cancellation of the debt. In human experience there are two primary ways a debt can be canceled. One method is for the debt to be erased from the books while it is still unpaid. This is what happens when someone declares bankruptcy. The other method is for the debt to be canceled because it has been paid in full. When it comes to those whose debt of sin has been forgiven in Christ, both analogies apply.

Those who have trusted in the Savior can claim God's forgiveness because Jesus Christ paid the debt with His own blood. He was a "sacrifice of atonement" (Romans 3:25; cf. 1 John 2:2; 4:10). His death satisfied the Law's demand for punishment for sin, and His obedience on our behalf satisfied its requirement for righteousness. This is described as substitutionary or vicarious atonement. A substitute is required because the debt of sin is so great that no human being, apart from Christ Himself, has sufficient righteousness to satisfy the Law's obligation. Charles Ryrie explains:

> Man could atone for his sins personally only if he could suffer eternally the penalty that sin incurred. Man, of course, could never do this, so in His love and compassion, God stepped into a hopeless situation and provided a Vicar in Jesus Christ who did provide an eternal satisfaction for sin.[7]

Our inability to repay the debt ourselves places us in the same position as one whose debt has been canceled through bankruptcy. Jesus made this evident through the parable of the unforgiving servant (Matthew 18:23–35). In this parable Jesus told the story of a servant who owed ten thousand talents to a king. Despite the fact that this amount was so great that it was humanly impossible to repay it, the servant pleaded with the king for more time. Instead, the king graciously canceled the debt. After the servant left the king's presence, he found a fellow servant who owed him a fraction of the amount that the king had forgiven. Instead of following the king's example, the unforgiving servant choked the man and demanded immediate repayment. When the king learned of this, he was furious. He called for the servant and said: "Shouldn't you have had mercy on your fellow servant just as I had on you?" (Matthew 18:33). This is the same thought that undergirds the petition for forgiveness in the Lord's Prayer. It is a request linked with an important condition. It asks that forgiveness be granted to the same degree that we also have forgiven our debtors (Matthew 6:12).

A man whose family had a history of colon cancer was urged by his doctor to submit to an uncomfortable examination. "Do I have to?" he asked the doctor.

"Well, that depends," the doctor replied. "Do you want to live or do you want to die?" Put in that perspective, the exam didn't seem so bad.

In a similar way, when I am struggling with the thought of forgiving someone else, this portion of the Lord's Prayer helps me to keep the actions of others in perspective. As I weigh the choice of whether to forgive, the prayer provides me with a blunt ultimatum. Do I want to experience God's forgiveness? This is further strengthened by the warning Jesus gave in Matthew 6:14–15: "For if you forgive men when they sin against you, your heavenly Father will also forgive you. But if you do not forgive men their sins, your Father will not forgive your sins."

It could be said that this petition is more a request for the grace to forgive than it is a prayer for forgiveness. If prayed daily, it serves as a constant reminder that I am in the same position as the unforgiving servant. I have already been forgiven an insurmountable debt that could never be repaid. In light of what I owe God, what others owe me is insignificant. It is important to note, however, that before there can be true forgiveness, there must first be a true reckoning. If I minimize what others have done, I do not really forgive them. This was God's pattern with us. In order to forgive us He first had to hold us accountable for our actions:

> There can be no forgiving in the dark. God will forgive; but He will have the sinner to know what and how much he is forgiven; there must be first a "Come now, and let us reason together", before the scarlet can be made white as snow (Isaiah 1:18). The sinner must know his sins for what they are, a mountain of transgression, before ever they can be cast into the deep sea of God's mercy; he must first have the sentence of death in himself, ere the words of life will have any abiding worth for him.[8]

It is no accident that the parable of the unforgiving servant appears in Matthew's Gospel in a context that deals with confrontation and accountability (Matthew 18:15–17). The request to be forgiven in the Lord's Prayer enables us to hold ourselves accountable for our own actions, toward God and man, as we reflect upon the treatment we have experienced at the hands of others.

The other spiritual concern addressed in this portion of the Lord's Prayer focuses on the need for spiritual protection: "And lead us not into temptation, but deliver us from the evil one" (Matthew 6:13). At first glance this request might seem to contradict James 1:13–14: "When tempted, no one should say, 'God is tempting me.' For God cannot be tempted by evil, nor does he tempt anyone; but each one is tempted when, by his own evil desire, he is dragged away and enticed." However, there is really no conflict between these two statements. Jesus' request is not to be delivered from temptation from God but for deliverance from "the evil one." It is not God who poses the danger but Satan. God, on the other hand, has the power to protect us so that we are not brought into circumstances where we are likely to fall.

Every Christian must learn to stand against temptation. Some temptations, however, are more dangerous than others. On the night of His arrest Jesus warned the disciples: "Watch and pray so that you will not fall into temptation. The spirit is willing, but the body is weak" (Matthew 26:41). Instead, the disciples slept. When the temptation came, despite their sincere faith and good intentions, they all deserted Him. Christ's warning coupled with this petition show that there are certain paths in life that have dangers known to God alone. Jesus taught us to pray for God's protection so that we would never have to tread those dark places.

Taken together, these requests provide a kind of spiritual road map that can guide us in our prayer life. It is a map that has three major landmarks. It begins with God. Before we think of others, ourselves, or the multitude of requests that press upon our minds, we put God in first place. The second landmark focuses on the mundane necessities of life such as daily bread. The third marks those equally necessary but easily forgotten needs of the spirit: the need to forgive and be forgiven and the need to be protected from spiritual danger. Although the church has a rich tradition of praying the Lord's Prayer verbatim, there is no magic in its words. It is the One to whom it is addressed that gives it its power.

CONDITIONS FOR ANSWERED PRAYER

A pastoral colleague of mine was once notified that two members of his congregation had rushed to the hospital with a very sick child. When my friend arrived at the hospital, the doctor came to him with a grave look on his face and gave him terrible news. "You had better go in there and talk to the parents," he said. "There really isn't anything else we can do."

"It was bad," my friend later explained to me. "The parents were beside themselves with grief. The doctors had given up hope. But the parents pleaded with me saying, 'You've got to do something!' But what could I do? All I knew to do was to pray."

My friend went over to the bed and placed his hands on the child. Out of his own desperation he said, "God, You've got to heal this baby."

A few minutes later the doctor came in for a last check—a formality really—because he expected the child to be dead by that time. Instead, he gasped in amazement. "Wait a minute," he exclaimed. "Something has happened!" The child's vital signs had suddenly improved. Because this pastor had prayed a desperate prayer of last resort, the child made a complete recovery. This pastor's story is an important reminder that the power of prayer is unlimited because God's power is unlimited. But it is equally important to remember that its effects are not automatic. There are important conditions that must be met before the believer's prayers can be answered.

Faith is a precondition to answered prayer. The first condition that must be met is that of faith. When His disciples expressed amazement at one of His miracles, Jesus promised: "If you believe, you will receive whatever you ask for in prayer" (Matthew 21:22). This is not positive thinking or generalized faith but faith that focuses on the person of Christ: "Until now you have not asked for anything in my name. Ask and you will receive, and your joy will be complete" (John 16:24). When we pray to the Father, we do so in the name or authority of Jesus. It is Jesus who has earned us the right to approach God as sons and daughters and boldly make our requests.

Disobedience will short-circuit answers to prayer. Jesus promised His disciples: "If you remain in me and my words remain in you, ask whatever you wish, and it will be given you" (John 15:7). Inherent to the concept of abiding is the idea of obedience. Likewise, the psalmist declared: "If I had cherished sin in my heart, the Lord would not have listened; but God has surely listened and heard my voice in prayer" (Psalm 66:18–19). Similarly the apostle Peter warns: "Husbands, in the same way be considerate as you live with your wives, and treat them with respect as the weaker partner and as heirs with you of the gracious gift of life, so that nothing will hinder your prayers" (1 Peter 3:7). The way I treat others will impact the effectiveness of my prayer life.

Answers to prayer must come in God's time. God's actions reflect a sense of timing (John 7:6, 8; Romans 5:6). We are so concerned about the small details of our daily lives that we often forget that we are also part of a larger plan. When the Father delays in answering our prayers, we do not need to be afraid that ours is lost somewhere beneath the pile on His desk. God's answers to our prayers are subordinated to His greater purpose for our good and His glory. He will answer, but He will do so in His own time.

To be answered, the things we ask for must be in accordance with God's will. We must not confuse prayer with the wishes that were granted to Aladdin from the genie of the lamp. In the Aladdin story the genie was not Aladdin's master but his slave. The genie was compelled to grant whatever Aladdin asked. This is not the case with the Father. No matter how fervent the language or pious the life, we do not command Him to grant our requests. God will never move in a way that is contrary to His will (1 John 5:14–15). Even Jesus' requests were subject to this limitation (Luke 22:42). A study of the godly who have had to accept an answer of no yields an impressive list. Moses, David, Elijah, Paul, and even Christ all made requests that were denied by the Father.

STRENGTHENING YOUR PRAYER LIFE

Most of us feel that our prayer life could be improved. Can we take any practical steps to improve this dimension of our relationship with our heavenly Father? Three strategies will help. First, we need to develop a habit of prayer. Jesus modeled this during His earthly ministry by regularly setting aside time to pray (Matthew 14:23; Luke 6:12; 9:28). The best way to do this is to make it a part of our daily schedule. When we try to squeeze prayer into the many things we do during the day, it often becomes a casualty of our busy lives. Yet we manage to find time to exercise, watch our favorite television program, eat our meals, and do many other things in the course of the day. One reason is that we have blocked off time in our schedule for these other activities. When we try to "fit" prayer into our day, we are saying that it belongs only on the periphery of our lives. Instead, make it a priority item on your calendar each day—as important as the three meals you eat. When scheduling your prayer time, however, plan it for a time when you are at your best. It is true that the Scriptures often speak of seeking God in the morning (Psalm 5:3). But the afternoon and evening are also suitable times for scheduling prayer (Psalm 55:17; Daniel 6:10, 13).

Second, when you pray, do all you can to remove any distractions that might interrupt you. Like Jesus, you may want to find a location that is secluded. Do not take other work with you when you pray. Unplug the television and take the phone off the hook. If music helps to set the mood, make sure it is not the type that will distract you from the task at hand. Choose a comfortable setting for prayer, but not so comfortable that you will fall asleep!

Finally, do not limit your prayer life to those times you have scheduled. Cultivate the art of "practicing the presence" of God at all times. Nicholas Herman, a former soldier and footman who lived during the seventeenth century, entered the Carmelite order in Paris and served there as a lay brother. Known as "Brother Lawrence," he was assigned to the kitchen, a task for which he later said he had a "natural aversion." While there, however, he determined to do all his daily tasks, no matter how mundane, for the love of God and with prayer. He soon discovered that he could experience God's presence as much while cleaning the pots and pans as in the formal times of worship. In fact, Brother Lawrence felt that as far as his experience of God's presence was concerned, set times of prayer were no different than any other time. No matter how busy he became, he did not feel that busyness had to divert him from God. In his Fourth Conversation, he wrote: "The time of business does not with me differ from the time of prayer, and in the noise and clatter of my kitchen, while several persons are at the same time calling for different things, I possess God in as great tranquillity as if I were upon my knees at the Blessed Sacrament." Brother Lawrence's approach to prayer was very practical. He counseled others not to be discouraged by wandering thoughts but to "quietly and gently" recall their minds to Him. He believed that prayers should be short and to the point. Long prayers, he noted, were often a cause for wandering thoughts.

Our problem is not that we do not know how to pray. It is that we do not know when to pray. For those who know their need, prayer is simple. J. C. Ryle noted: "It is useless to say you do not know how to pray. Prayer is the simplest act in all religion. It is simply speaking to God. It needs neither learning, nor wisdom, nor book-knowledge to begin it. It needs nothing but heart and will. The weakest infant can cry when he is hungry. The poorest beggar can hold out his hand for alms, and does not wait to find words. The most ignorant man will find something to say to God, if he has only a mind."[9]

GETTING OVER OUR DISCOMFORT

Today it feels natural for me to refer to my mother-in-law as "Mom." My earlier struggle now seems rather silly. What changed between us? As the years have passed our relationship with each other has deepened. We know each other better today than we did in the early days of my marriage. Most important, I have come to understand how deep her love is for me. The same must be true of our relationship with God. In the end, the secret to a successful prayer life is not a matter of methodology. Prayer is an outgrowth of relationship. The more that we know of God's love for us, the more we will want to experience His presence.

QUESTIONS FOR DISCUSSION

1. How would you characterize the faulty approaches to prayer that Jesus describes in Matthew 6:1–7?
2. What is the "spiritual purpose" for prayer? What is the "functional purpose" for prayer?
3. What do we imply about God when we address Him as "Father" in prayer? What do we imply about our relationship to Him?
4. How do we "hallow" God's name?
5. Why should we pray for the coming of the kingdom? Can our prayers make it come any sooner?
6. When Jesus taught us to ask for our daily bread, He instructed us to pray for daily necessities. What might be included in such a request? What would not be included? Why?
7. Jesus singled out two areas of spiritual concern in the Lord's Prayer. Why do you think He chose these and not others?
8. What conditions must be fulfilled before a prayer can be answered?

9

WORSHIPING THE FATHER

Worship is like art. We all have our own opinions about it. What one person loves, another person hates. For Jim worship is synonymous with the ruby glow of the stained glass images he meditates upon during the service and the comfortingly familiar cadence of the liturgy. For Mary it is captured in the simple worship choruses she learned in the campus group she attended in college. Tom would be happy to skip the musical "preliminaries" of the first half hour of the church service and arrive just in time for the sermon—as far as he is concerned, it's the only thing that really counts anyway.

I learned very early in my Christian experience that not everyone views worship the same way. What moved me to tears seemed to have no effect on others. I would leave some services bored and unaffected and notice that the person seated next to me glowed as if he or she had seen God in the burning bush. Some people lifted their hands and prayed openly; others stood with their hands at their side and never uttered a word. Many of these differences, of course, are largely a matter of taste or personality. They are a reflection of how the worship experience has affected the worshiper. In fact, our evaluation of what constitutes "good" worship and "bad" worship is almost entirely subjective. We judge worship on the basis of how it makes us feel. When it comes to worship, however, we are not the primary focus. How does God evaluate worship?

GOD THE FATHER
IS SEEKING WORSHIPERS

God the Father is deeply interested in worship. Although He is entirely self-sufficient and needs nothing from us, the Father is seeking a certain kind of worshiper. In His conversation with the Samaritan woman about the location of worship, Jesus explained: "Yet a time is coming and has now come when the true worshipers will worship the Father in spirit and truth, for they are the kind of worshipers the Father seeks" (John 4:23). The phrase "in spirit and truth" not only describes the type of worshiper the Father is seeking, but it also characterizes the only kind of worship that He accepts: "God is spirit, and his worshipers must worship in spirit and in truth" (v. 24).

These words, both profound and simple, are doubly important because they occur within the context of a conversation about worship. When the woman of Samaria perceived that she was talking with someone who had spiritual insight, she raised a subject that had been a bone of contention between her people and the Jews for some time: "'Sir,' the woman said, 'I can see that you are a prophet. Our fathers worshiped on this mountain, but you Jews claim that the place where we must worship is in Jerusalem'" (John 4:19–20). The Jews worshiped at the temple in Jerusalem. The Samaritans worshiped on Mount Gerizim. Which was the right location? The Jews argued that Jerusalem had been sanctioned by God. Its priority was clearly taught in the historical books of Samuel, Kings, Chronicles, Ezra, and Nehemiah. The Samaritans, on the other hand, only accepted the Torah, the first five books of the Old Testament. They noted that in the book of Genesis Mount Gerizim was identified as the location where the patriarchs Abraham and Jacob had worshiped (Genesis 12:7; 33:20). According to Deuteronomy it was the mountain from which blessings were pronounced upon Israel (Deuteronomy 11:29; 27:12). The Samaritan

Bible had even been changed to include a command that God must be worshiped on Mount Gerizim. Leon Morris explains:

> With this way of reading the Bible, Mount Gerizim became a most significant and historical spot. The Samaritans thought that almost every important happening in the days of the great patriarchs took place on or near Mount Gerizim. They accordingly had strong feelings about their beloved holy mountain. This is illustrated in a story that was told about a Samaritan who got into a conversation with a traveler, evidently a Jew. The traveler said that he was going up to Jerusalem to pray. The Samaritan replied, "Would it not be better for you to pray in this blessed mountain rather than in that dunghill?"[1]

Before considering what Jesus meant by His reply to the woman's statement, it might be instructive to ask ourselves how we might answer her today. I am convinced that many would say, "What does it matter whether you worship on Gerizim or in Jerusalem, as long as you worship God somewhere and do it with sincerity?" At first glance, it may appear as if this is precisely what Jesus was saying. After all, Jesus emphasized the importance of worship in the spirit. True worship is not a matter of externals. It is what is inside that really counts. What is more, Jesus taught that acceptable worship was not limited to a single geographic area. In John 4:21 Jesus declared, "Believe me, woman, a time is coming when you will worship the Father neither on this mountain nor in Jerusalem." However, Jesus also offered a blunt assessment of the Samaritans' system of worship: "You Samaritans worship what you do not know; we worship what we do know, for salvation is from the Jews" (v. 22). In effect, Jesus said: "You Samaritans are worshiping in ignorance." Sincerity is vital to worship, but it is not enough to guarantee that our worship will be acceptable to the Father. True worship must be offered in truth as well as in spirit.

IS ALL WORSHIP ACCEPTABLE TO GOD?
The first instance of worship ever recorded is found in Genesis

4:1–8, which records the story of Cain and Abel. This does not mean that this is the first time humans ever worshiped. We can assume that Adam and Eve also worshiped. The account of Cain and Abel is particularly significant because it provides us with the first record of a person approaching God with an offering: "In the course of time Cain brought some of the fruits of the soil as an offering to the Lord. But Abel brought fat portions from some of the firstborn of his flock. The Lord looked with favor on Abel and his offering, but on Cain and his offering he did not look with favor. So Cain was very angry, and his face was downcast" (vv. 3–5). The text does not say why Cain and Abel brought these offerings, but it does tell us how God evaluated them. He accepted Abel's offering and rejected Cain's.

The Bible, then, begins its teaching on worship with a very basic lesson: Not all worship is the same. There was a fundamental difference in the quality of what Abel offered when it was compared to Cain's offering. Perhaps more important, the rejection of Cain's offering indicates that the worshiper is not the one who determines the true quality of worship. God determines what is acceptable and what is not. Cain was satisfied with His offering. He found the worship experience meaningful. In fact, he was so satisfied with what he had done that he became angry that God had rejected his offering and he murdered his brother (Genesis 4:8).

The worship of the church in our age is primarily self-centered. We evaluate worship on the basis of what it does for us. Is it lively and interesting? Is the music enjoyable? Do I leave the service feeling "pumped up"? If so, then it has been "good" worship. Donald McCullough notes that true worship is marked by a reverent awareness of God's presence and asks:

> Why, then, can you enter many a sanctuary on Sunday morning— formal or informal, liberal or evangelical—and find very little reverence? Respectable reserve may be there, but little, if any, flat-on-your-face awe; self-conscious dignity may hang in the air like incense after high mass, but nothing unsettling, nothing disorienting, noth-

ing to strip away your certainties until your soul lies prostrate in naked embarrassment. You may find much good, such as vibrant fellowship or inspirational teaching or emotional music, but too much of it happens on the horizontal plane, with only a courteous nod toward the vertical. Chatty friendliness moves from the narthex into the sanctuary, intruding on preparation for worship. The purpose of the whole enterprise, it seems, is to guarantee that everyone feel comfortable and entertained.[2]

We offer our worship in a way that assumes that God should be satisfied merely with our presence. To ask anything more of us would be unreasonable. Yet God does have a standard. What does the Father want from us in worship, beyond our mere bodily presence?

Acceptable worship is marked by faith. Faith is at the heart of the Christian life. It is the engine that drives all that we do for God. Worship is no exception. Anything that is done apart from faith is unacceptable to the Father: "And without faith it is impossible to please God, because anyone who comes to him must believe that he exists and that he rewards those who earnestly seek him" (Hebrews 11:6). This statement by the author of Hebrews is helpful, because it shows us that there is nothing wrong in enjoying our worship. To say that much of today's worship is too self-centered does not mean that our worship would be better if the experience made us miserable. It is appropriate to approach God with an expectation that He will bless us.

Acceptable worship is Christ-centered. Any worship that is offered to the Father must be based upon the finished work of Christ. This is what Jesus was alluding to when He told the woman of Samaria that a massive change in worship was about to take place. Up until the coming of Christ, true worship had been centered in Jerusalem and was based upon the system of offerings described in the Law of Moses. The purpose of these offerings was to foreshadow the work that Christ would accomplish and make the worshiper aware of his need for God's gift of forgiveness. The New Testament uses the metaphor of a supervisor (the KJV says "schoolmaster," but the Greek term refers to someone who functioned as a personal attendant and disciplinarian) whose purpose was to lead us to Christ (Galatians 3:24–25).

When we worship the Father, we approach Him on the basis of Christ's finished work. We pray to Him in Jesus' name. This is what makes the worship of the synagogue or the Buddhist priest invalid. Despite their sincerity and the beauty of form that they may employ, those who worship God apart from Jesus Christ have no grounds for approaching Him. It is to Jesus alone that the Father has given the name that is above every other name: "That at the name of Jesus every knee should bow, in heaven and on earth and under the earth, and every tongue confess that Jesus Christ is Lord, to the glory of God the Father" (Philippians 2:10–11).

To celebrate the work of Christ when we worship God the Father is entirely appropriate. This was certainly the pattern of the early church. In a letter addressed to the Roman Emperor Trajan in A.D. 111–12, Pliny, the governor of Pontus and Bithynia, described the worship practices of the Christians in his district. His description was based upon the account of eyewitnesses who said that it was their custom on a fixed day to meet before dawn and to sing an antiphonal hymn to Christ as to a god.[3] We would not know nor could we approach the Father apart from Christ.

Acceptable worship is Spirit-driven. The Holy Spirit also plays an important role in the worship of the Father. The apostle Paul describes Christians as those who "worship by the Spirit of God, who glory in Christ Jesus, and who put no confidence in the flesh" (Philippians 3:3). It is the Spirit who prompts us to call out to the Father (Romans 8:15; Galatians 4:6). Robert G. Rayburn points out that the early church was aware of the importance of the Spirit's ministry in their worship. He notes that as early as the second century they used a prayer of invocation called the *epiklesis* to the Holy Spirit.[4] The fact that true worship is Christ centered and Spirit-driven means that any acceptable worship of the Father must ultimately be Trinitarian in nature.

Acceptable worship is participatory. One of the criticisms leveled against churches that practice some forms of "contemporary" worship, especially those that describe themselves as "seeker sensitive," is that those who attend function largely as spectators.[5] Lack of involvement, however, is not really a result of worship style; it is a function of ministry philosophy. Many churches that practice traditional or classical forms of worship are just as passive. Robert E. Webber, Professor of Theology at Wheaton College, describes worship as a form of communication. In worship God speaks to us and we respond to God and to each other.[6] We see a reflection of this pattern in Paul's description of worship in the Corinthian church: "What then shall we say, brothers? When you come together, everyone has a hymn, or a word of instruction, a revelation, a tongue or an interpretation. All of these must be done for the strengthening of the church" (1 Corinthians 14:26). It is true that Paul's tone is corrective in this verse. The problem in Corinth was, however, more a matter of motive than practice.[7] Paul did not criticize the Corinthian believers for their participation in the service but emphasized that everything must be done with the intent of building up the church.

Acceptable worship is a lifestyle. A habit of compartmentalizing the Christian life can cause us to view worship as a single event. We worship on Sunday and go to work on Monday. One church service is designated for worship and another for business. The philosophy of worship depicted in Romans 12:1 is much broader: "Therefore, I urge you, brothers, in view of God's mercy, to offer your bodies as living sacrifices, holy and pleasing to God—this is your spiritual act of worship."

Many of the great cathedrals of Europe are decorated with carvings of gargoyles and other hideous creatures. A man who asked about this custom was told that the builders wanted these figures to represent the worshiper's carnal appetites. They were placed on the cathedrals to remind those who came to worship that they should leave such things outside the sanctuary if they hoped to receive God's blessing. The problem with this perspective is that it implies that we can pick them up again once we are outside the door! If I am to offer my entire self to God, then there is a dimension of worship in every aspect of my life.

G. Campbell Morgan said: "It is true 'they also serve who only stand and wait.' But it is equally true that they also worship who serve, and serve perpetually. And it is in the service of a life, not specific acts done as apart from life, not because I teach in Sunday school, or preach here, that I worship."[8]

In order to understand the New Testament concept of worship we must begin with the Old Testament. This is the foundation upon which the New Testament church's view of worship was built. Three major themes resound in Old Testament worship. These are the themes of sacrifice, celebration, and Sabbath.

The Importance of Sacrifice

The important place of sacrifice in the worship of God's people has already been seen in the account of Cain and Abel. Both offered a sacrifice to God, but only Abel's was accepted. Many believe that the reason Cain's offering was rejected was that it was not a blood offering but was made up of the "fruits of the soil." Abel's sacrifice came from fat portions from some of the firstborn of his flock (Genesis 4:3–4). Cain's angry response when God rejected his offering reveals another major flaw. The context of Genesis 4:5–6 suggests that this response occurred while Cain was worshiping. As soon as he realized that God was going to disregard his offering, his pious facade disappeared. Instead of repenting and offering what was acceptable, he flew into a rage directed at the One he was supposed to be worshiping.

Apparently Cain had expected something in return for His offering and felt that God wasn't fulfilling His end of the bargain. This means that Cain viewed his sacrifice as an act of merit. He had come with an offering, but it lacked the primary ingredient that would have rendered it acceptable. It was an offering made without faith: "By faith Abel offered God a better sacrifice than Cain did. By faith he was commended as a righteous man, when God spoke well of his offerings. And by faith he still speaks, even though he is dead" (Hebrews 11:4).

The account of Cain and Abel is important because it indicates that sacrifice was an element of worship even before the Law of Moses was given. This is also reflected in the Flood account. According to Genesis 8:20, one of the first things Noah did after the flood was to offer a sacrifice. God had told Noah to take seven of each kind of "clean" animal on board, so apparently some guidelines for sacrifice had already been given. It was not until the time of Moses, however, that we see the stipulations for sacrifice spelled out in detail.

The first six chapters of the book of Leviticus describe five kinds of sacrifices in two general categories. Sweet savor offerings included the burnt offering, the meal offering, and the peace offering. The burnt offering was completely consumed on the altar. The meal offering was an offering of grain and meal and it usually accompanied blood sacrifices. The peace offering was a sacrifice that was eaten by the worshiper in a communal meal before the Lord. Guilt offerings included the sin offering and the trespass offering. The sin offering was a sacrifice made for specific sins. The trespass offering was like the sin offering but also required that restitution be paid to the offended party.

These Old Testament sacrifices symbolized the work of Jesus Christ and its consequences in the life of the believer. For example, Jesus is described as a sweet savor offering in Ephesians 5:2, which says, "Christ loved us and gave himself up for us as a fragrant offering and sacrifice to God." He is our peace and has removed the barrier that separated Jew and Gentile from God and from each other (Ephesians 2:14). Like the sin offering and the trespass offering, Jesus died for our trespasses (Romans 5:15, 17–18, 20). As a result of what Jesus has done we now have fellowship with the Father (1 John 1:3).

It is important to recognize that although these sacrifices were prescribed by God, they did not have the power to take away sin. In fact, instead of alleviating the worshipers' guilt, they actually made them more aware of their guilt. The writer of the book of Hebrews describes them as only a "shadow" of the good things to come (i.e., Christ's sacrifice) and notes that they could not make perfect those who drew near to God by them: "If it could, would they not have stopped being offered? For the worshipers would have been cleansed once for all, and would no longer have felt guilty for their sins. But those sacrifices are an annual reminder of sins, because it is impossible for the blood of bulls and goats to take away sins" (Hebrews 10:2–4).

The effect of the once-and-for-all sacrifice of Jesus Christ is radically different. By His one sacrifice He has "made perfect forever those who are being made holy" (Hebrews 10:14). There is a wonderful tension in this verse. It says, on the one hand, that as a result of what Jesus Christ has done for us we have been made perfect forever. This means that, as far as our position in Christ is concerned, we are already perfect. Donald Guthrie captures the sense of the verse well when he says, "In himself Christ gathered up all those whom he represents to share with them his perfection."9 Yet this same verse also asserts that in terms of our daily experience we are still undergoing the process of sanctification. Therefore, we who are perfect in Christ are now in the process of "being made holy."

If these Old Testament sacrifices did not have the power to take away sin, what good were they? We might describe them as tangible sermons that could be seen, touched, and even smelled by the worshiper. They declared a three-point message to the one who offered them. The first point was negative. They were "an annual reminder of sins" (Hebrews 10:3). The bloody nature of these sacrifices was a solemn reminder that the wages of sin is death (Romans 6:23). The second point was positive. They indicated that there is a remedy for sin and symbolized the fact that God would provide a substitute. The third point was prophetic. They predicted that Jesus Christ would come and serve as the one Sacrifice that would be acceptable to God as a payment for sin.

Because Jesus offered the only sacrifice that could take away sin and the one sacrifice that all those in the Law of Moses foreshadowed, the elaborate system of offerings described in the Old Testament has now passed away. Despite this, those who are in Christ can still offer sacrifices to God. Like the Old Testament, the New Testament has its own prescribed offerings. We have already noted that Romans 12:1 tells us to offer our bodies as living sacrifices. Hebrews 13:15 calls for "a sacrifice of praise," which is further described as "the fruit of lips that confess his name." According to 1 Peter 2:5 we are to offer "spiritual sacrifices." The gift of money that the Philippian church sent to the apostle Paul was called "a fragrant offering, an acceptable sacrifice, pleasing to God" (Philippians 4:18). Other offerings mentioned in the New Testament include the conversion of the Gentiles, the offering of Paul's life in martyrdom, and doing good to others (Romans 15:16; Philippians 2:17; Hebrews 13:16). The sacrifice that the Father desires from the believer today is the one described by Christina Rossetti in her hymn entitled "In the Bleak Midwinter":

> What can I give him, poor as I am?
> If I were a shepherd, I would bring a lamb;
> if I were a Wise Man, I would do my part;
> yet what I can I give him: give my heart.

The Importance of Celebration

Robert Webber has pointed out that celebration is a common occurrence in our lives. In addition to Christmas, we celebrate birthdays, anniversaries, and civil holidays such as Memorial Day, Labor Day, and Thanksgiving. These occasions are eagerly anticipated and are often observed with large gatherings of family and friends, feasts, and parties. Yet all too often when God's people gather, the event is "dull, intellectual, cold, formal, and alienating; or it has become, consciously or unconsciously, a form of emotional exercise which ultimately has little effect on what goes on in a person's life during the rest of the week."[10] What the church desperately needs today is a recovery of the biblical perspective on celebration.

Worship under the Law of Moses was never meant to be a dull, lifeless affair. It was often an occasion of lively celebration. One of the ways that God taught His people to celebrate was by commanding them to assemble regularly for festivals of worship: "Speak to the Israelites and say to them: 'These are my appointed feasts, the appointed feasts of the Lord, which you are to proclaim as sacred assemblies'" (Leviticus 23:2). Israel's feasts were appointments that provided His people with an opportunity to commune with God in worship and were often announced with the blast of a trumpet (Leviticus 23:24).

Israel celebrated several feasts each year. Three of these— Passover, Pentecost, and the Feast of Tabernacles—required every adult male to make a pilgrimage to the sanctuary. Passover commemorated Israel's deliverance from slavery in Egypt. Pentecost and the Feast of Tabernacles, also known as the Feast of Weeks, were harvest celebrations. The Day of Atonement was one of Israel's most solemn occasions and served as a day of national repentance. The Feast of Trumpets was a kind of New Year's celebration.

The purpose of these feasts was threefold. First, they often commemorated the mighty works that God had done on behalf of His people. The celebration of Passover and the Feast of Tabernacles reminded Israel of the way God had miraculously rescued them from the Egyptians and then provided for them during their journey through the wilderness. Second, these five feasts reminded the people of Israel of the Father's provision for them. The Feast of Pentecost, with its offering of loaves to God, was a reminder that the Father would provide for their daily needs (Leviticus 23:17). The Day of Atonement was a solemn reminder of the need for forgiveness but also of God's promise to provide a Redeemer. Third, these feasts contained a promise of things that God would do in the future for His people. Passover and the Day of Atonement looked forward to the sacrifice of Christ. The Feast of Trumpets anticipated the day when the Father will gather His people to Himself.

It should be noted that some of these celebrations, most notably the Day of Atonement and to a lesser extent the Feast of

Passover, were marked by an air of solemnity. This serves as an important reminder that our celebration of God should be somber at times. This truth is a valuable corrective in an age when the church is often more interested in a pep rally than a worship service. We want upbeat music, entertaining sermons, and an experience that will leave us feeling good. Yet if worship is ultimately an encounter with the living God, then there must be times when we will sense God's presence, and God's presence is not always a comfortable thing. Glorious, yes. Awesome, certainly. It is a majestic and overwhelming experience. But it is not usually comfortable.

An interesting account in Genesis 35 tells how God commanded the patriarch Jacob to travel to Bethel and build an altar. Jacob ordered his household to get rid of all their idols and then set out for Bethel. Genesis 35:5 says that as they traveled, "the terror of God fell upon the towns all around them so that no one pursued them." Obviously, God did this to protect Jacob and his family during their journey. But it is also a common theme in those biblical passages that describe a man's encounter with God. Those who encounter God tremble and fall on their faces (Exodus 19:16; Hebrews 12:21; Revelation 1:17). They are rendered speechless (Acts 9:7). The presence of God can be unsettling, even for His own people. I am not suggesting that we haven't really worshiped until we have felt like crawling underneath a pew and hiding. Nor am I saying that we should sing funeral dirges or kneel on a bed of stones in order to guarantee that we feel a measure of discomfort. There should be times, however, when we experience a deep sense of reverence and even fear in God's presence. There is a place for mourning over our sins in worship. There should be times when we plead with God for mercy and grace. Charles Spurgeon observed: "If the very angels veil their faces when they come near Him, we must humbly bow before Him when we come to worship in His house. He is in heaven and we are upon earth. He is our Father, but He is also our Father who is in Heaven; and we poor sinful creatures can never come into the light of His presence without perceiving that we are full of sin."

There are no official Christian feast days, at least not the same kind of obligatory feasts that we see in the Old Testament. The New Testament teaches that Christians can exercise liberty in this area: "One man considers one day more sacred than another; another man considers every day alike. Each one should be fully convinced in his own mind" (Romans 14:5). It also warns of the danger of slipping back into Judaism by legalistically observing special days and months and seasons and years (Galatians 4:10). Many Christians, however, have found it valuable to order their worship celebrations around a calendar of dates that celebrate the main events in the life of Christ and of the church. The cornerstone of the Christian calendar is the celebration of Christ's resurrection at Easter. Some prepare for this celebration by observing Lent, which is usually a time of repentance and fasting. The church also celebrates the birth of Christ at Christmas. Some believers prepare for this event by observing a season of Advent. The birth of the church is celebrated at Pentecost. A number of lesser holidays and feast days are recognized by various groups. One proponent of using such an approach in worship describes its value this way:

> In briefest terms, the church's year of grace functions to show forth Jesus Christ until he comes again and to testify to the Holy Spirit indwelling the church in the meantime. The church year is both proclamation and thanksgiving. In much the same way as Jewish and Christian prayer recites what we give thanks for, so the Christian year proclaims and thanks God for God's marvelous actions. Christians and Jews praise God, not in abstract terms, but by reciting the marvelous works of God. It is a think-thank process by which we glorify God through recalling what God has done.[11]

Celebration should not be limited to the church's holy days and weekly services. Dallas Willard encourages believers to practice it as one of the spiritual disciplines. When we practice celebration as a discipline, "we enjoy ourselves, our life, our world, in conjunction with our faith and confidence in God's greatness, beauty, and goodness. We concentrate on *our* life and world as God's work and as

God's gift to us."[12] Willard warns that it is not possible to have a healthy faith without heartfelt celebration. He warns further that by failing to celebrate what God has done, we may actually be dishonoring God: "Certainly this will seem far too hedonistic to many of us. But we dishonor God as much by fearing and avoiding pleasure as we do by dependence upon it or living for it."[13]

The Importance of Sabbath

The first one to observe a Sabbath was not man but God. On the seventh day of creation God rested from all His works (Genesis 2:1–2). Later the practice of observing the seventh day (the term Sabbath comes from the Hebrew word for seven) was commanded in the Mosaic Law, and a connection was made between God's example and Israel's observance of the Sabbath (Exodus 20:8–11). The connection between these two seems to be one of example. God set the example at the time of creation for the Law that He would later give to His people. In Leviticus 23:3 it is referred to as a Sabbath "to the Lord." This is an indication of the priority it was to be given, but it also raises a question. Why was the Sabbath important to God? Obviously, when the book of Genesis says that God rested from all His works, it does not mean that He was so exhausted that He needed to take a break. This statement points to the completion of God's creative activity rather than to inactivity. God's observance of the Sabbath was meant to be an example to man. It was so important that He commanded that it be observed weekly. He also demanded that it be observed entirely; it was a day of rest when no work could be done (Leviticus 23:3). Instead of fitting the Sabbath into their schedule, God's people framed their schedule around the Sabbath. No work could be done. Slaves, foreigners, and even animals had to rest on that day. Although Israel's practice of the Sabbath eventually became so encumbered with human traditions that it was more of a burden than a blessing, Jesus clarified God's original intent when he said that the Sabbath was made for man, not man for the Sabbath (Mark 2:27).

The goal of the Sabbath was to teach God's people of their

need for rest and especially for the true rest that can only be found in God's grace. This is pictured in the Sabbath observance but is ultimately found only in Christ: "There remains, then, a Sabbath-rest for the people of God; for anyone who enters God's rest also rests from his own work, just as God did from his. Let us, therefore, make every effort to enter that rest, so that no one will fall by following their example of disobedience" (Hebrews 4:9–11). Some groups claim that Christians should still observe the Jewish Sabbath law and meet on Saturday. Others feel that the Sabbath law is still valid but that the day in which it is to be observed has been changed from Saturday to Sunday. Yet Paul warns in Colossians 2:16–17: "Therefore do not let anyone judge you by what you eat or drink, or with regard to a religious festival, a New Moon celebration or a Sabbath day. These are a shadow of the things that were to come; the reality, however, is found in Christ."

Although we are no longer bound by the Sabbath law, it is interesting to note that the New Testament church seems to have practiced the Sabbath principle. Out of the seven days of the week, one day in particular became identified with congregational worship. In Acts 20:7, Luke describes how the New Testament church came together on the first day of the week to observe the Lord's Supper. Paul gave directions to the Corinthian church for the collection to be taken on the first day of the week (1 Corinthians 16:2). Furthermore, in Revelation 1:10 the apostle John says that he was in the Spirit "on the Lord's Day," a phrase many believe refers to Sunday. According to Leon Morris, Sunday worship served as a weekly reminder of Christ's resurrection.[14]

Israel's practice of the Sabbath taught the church that when it worshiped the Father, it must cease from its own works, both sinful and self-righteous, and rest in the finished work of Christ. It provided a weekly reminder that all of life is an act of worship by showing that the culmination of all the week's activities was to be found in the presence of God. Because it was a convocation, the Sabbath taught the church that it was important to gather together on a regular basis and worship as a congregation.

NEW TESTAMENT WORSHIP

Although many spiritual truths were taught by Old Testament worship, God's people sometimes missed the point because they were distracted by the form in which it was expressed. Their practice eventually deviated so far from God's intention that He said: "I hate, I despise your religious feasts; I cannot stand your assemblies" (Amos 5:21). This statement is sobering when we consider that these were the same feasts and assemblies that He had Himself commanded.

As important as sacrifice, celebration, and Sabbath were to the spiritual life of Israel, they could not substitute for genuine faith. When God's people lost sight of the spiritual truths being taught by Old Testament practices, they mistakenly concluded that form alone mattered. Jesus condemned this sort of thinking when He criticized the religious leaders of His day for their meticulous attention to the minute details of the Law, while ignoring the more important matters of justice, mercy, and faithfulness (Matthew 23:23–24).

In His discussion with the woman of Samaria, He identified spirit and truth as the two terminal points that were to determine the axis of true worship for the church. When Jesus said that the true worshipers would worship the Father in spirit, He meant that their worship would involve more than a coating of ritualistic veneer. Those who worship in spirit do not ignore matters of form and ritual, but they give equal attention to the attitude of the heart. Worship in spirit, however, is not enough. It is just as important for the church's worship to be directed by truth. When spirit is separated from truth, worship is always deficient. At best, it manifests itself as emotionalism—worship that is all heat and no light. At its worst it degenerates into error and becomes worship that is based upon false principles. Jesus' words to the Samaritan woman indicate that in order to worship God acceptably, we must worship what we know. Sound doctrine is the engine that drives true worship and the fence that protects it. It ensures that we will worship with knowledge.

Does worship in "truth" mean, then, that we should worship exactly as the New Testament church worshiped? As appealing as such a conclusion is, the Bible provides us with only a broad outline of the church's practice. In Acts 2:42 Luke marks off the four corners that defined the landscape of congregational life in the New Testament era: "They devoted themselves to the apostles' teaching and to the fellowship, to the breaking of bread and to prayer." These four principles directed their worship. As clear as this is, it does not say exactly what form these four principles took when they were carried out. For example, we know that they met in homes for worship. Does this mean that church buildings are wrong? Probably not. The early church also gathered at the temple (Acts 2:46). The absence of church buildings in the New Testament era may have been more a result of the church's legal status than any theological conviction about where the church should worship. One of the first things the church did after it was legally recognized by the Roman Empire was to begin constructing places of worship.

We know generally that the New Testament church observed the Lord's Supper, listened to teaching, and shared with one another. Paul's first letter to the Corinthians indicates that they exercised spiritual gifts and took up a collection. But there is much more that we do not know. What was the order of service? What role did music play in their meetings? That they sang hymns seems clear. We may even have traces of such hymnody in the New Testament. But what was their music like? Did they sing before the sermon, after the sermon, or both? What was the ratio of singing when compared to teaching? How long did the sermons last? Most of the sermons recorded in the New Testament are fairly short. Yet Acts 20:9 tells of a time when Paul preached late into the night. What was the seating arrangement like? Men and women were separated in the synagogue, but the worship of the church of Corinth involved women who prayed and exercised the gift of prophecy.

The congregation that says that its worship is patterned after that of the New Testament church can mean this only in terms of the broad principles that guide its worship practices. To say that today's church worships exactly like the apostolic church is an overstatement at best, if not outright arrogance. We do not know enough about the fine details of the early church's practice to make such a claim. We should also consider the likelihood that the form that the church's worship took among the Gentiles differed somewhat from that of Jewish believers. It is certainly true that worship forms became more elaborate as the church aged and its place in society became more secure. The fully developed church calendar that guides some congregations in worship today was clearly not a feature of worship in the first century:

> Although early Christian worship was deeply indebted to Jewish worship, much was simply abandoned. Why were only two of the Jewish festivals (Passover and Pentecost) taken over and adapted by Christians? In modern times many Christians have rediscovered the value of linking worship to the rhythms of the seasons. In the first and second centuries, however, Christians were more coy about adapting the religious festivals of their rivals. The only two which were "Christianised" could be associated readily with the "story" of Jesus Christ. Since the others could not, they were abandoned.[15]

In view of this, we must ask why this area of worship has become such a battleground for the church. More often than not, when there is contention about worship, these conflicts focus on form rather than principle. Unfortunately, such conflicts are usually expressed in the language of moral absolutes. One style or methodology is branded as the "right" way to worship, while another is labeled as the "wrong" way. In reality, ministry forms are more often a reflection of culture. Musical style, the use of physical space, the amount of time devoted to the service, the nature in which the congregation expresses itself during the service, and many other factors that shape worship behavior are all reflections of core cultural values. This is often why our debate about them becomes so heated. Of course, core cultural values can be antithetical to worship.

Core cultural values are those fundamental assumptions we hold about the way life is supposed to work. They provide us with a road map or rule book that we can use to guide our behavior. When core values are challenged we become uncomfortable. The first violation will provoke nervous laughter. After a second or third violation we become embarrassed. Repeated challenges produce anger. When these clashing cultural preferences are expressed in moral terms, the result is holy war. In reality, we are fighting to protect our own selfish interests and personal tastes. In a culturally diverse world God does not intend for every believer to worship the same way. It is only reasonable that the style of worship employed by a small tribe in South America differ from that of a church in the suburban Chicago area. One of the keys to the successful spread of Christianity to every tribe, tongue, and nation is its ability to speak to every culture, although forms may differ. As long as our differing cultural expressions are guided by the fixed points of spirit and truth, God is pleased.

Donald McCullough tells of the time that he and his wife were invited to hear Italian tenor Luciano Pavorotti sing. At the conclusion of the concert the entire audience leapt to its feet and roared its appreciation. "We *had* to respond," McCullough explained. "We jumped to our feet and clapped, hooted, and whistled. We did not stop, not for a long time. Wave after wave of grateful applause was sent up to the platform, calling forth encore after encore." During the long applause, McCullough thought to himself, "This is deeply satisfying, a profound joy."[16] Many of us have had a similar experience while watching our favorite team play. We happily express our appreciation with wild and satisfying abandon. Should we settle for less when we express our appreciation to God?

QUESTIONS FOR DISCUSSION

1. Why isn't all worship acceptable to God? What differentiates acceptable worship from unacceptable worship?
2. List the five characteristics of acceptable worship.
3. What was the relationship between the sacrifices commanded by the Law of Moses and the sacrifice of Jesus Christ on the cross?
4. In what way is sacrifice an element of Christian worship?
5. Why should celebration and solemnity both play a role in the believer's worship? How?

6. What do you think it means to worship in spirit and truth?
7. How can the New Testament serve as a guide to the church's worship practices? What are its limitations in such a use?
8. Why do you think worship style is such a battleground for the church today?

10

GLORIFYING THE FATHER

In one of his sermons pastor and author John Piper told of the time he and his wife were deciding where to send their thirteen-year-old daughter to school. At one Christian school they visited, Piper asked two of the faculty members what they thought ought to be the ultimate goal of education. They answered without hesitation: "Our goal in this institution is to train minds of young people so that they will think critically and become fully human." When Piper seemed disappointed by their reply, they looked at him questioningly. Piper said, "I thought maybe the mission statement of a Christian school would be different than an atheistic school." When they seemed shocked at this, Piper went on to explain, "I just thought you'd say, 'To glorify God and enjoy him forever,' or something like that."

CAN WE GLORIFY GOD AND
ENJOY HIM AT THE SAME TIME?

Piper's response was, of course, based upon the first question of the Westminster Larger Catechism, which asks: "What is the chief and highest end of man?" The catechism answers by saying, "Man's chief and highest end is to glorify God, and fully to enjoy Him for-

ever." At first glance the pairing of these two concepts by the
Westminster divines may seem odd. What does the one have to do
with the other? We can understand our responsibility to glorify
God, but to *enjoy* Him? Doesn't that seem a little selfish? It would
make more sense if they had used the language of duty or effort or
suffering. If asked to frame our own response to this question we
would be inclined to say something like, "The chief end of man is
to glorify God and to do your best." We suspect that these two concepts of glorifying God and enjoying Him at the same time are fundamentally incompatible, and we harbor a sneaking suspicion that
one must be uncomfortable in order to glorify God. Athletes who
are in training have a saying, "No pain, no gain; no guts, no glory."
This is our philosophy when it comes to glorifying God. Given an
array of options from which to choose, we often believe that the
least attractive one must be the one that brings God the most glory.

It is true that suffering, self-denial, and duty are common
aspects of the Christian life. Jesus warned that those who would follow Him as disciples must also bear the cross (Matthew 10:37–39;
Luke 9:23; 14:27). Acts 14:22 tells us that "We must go through
many hardships to enter the kingdom of God." We are even told
that we must hate our own life if we are to be Christ's disciples
(Luke 14:26). This, however, is only half the story. The Bible also
talks about the enjoyment of God.

Discovering Our Wrong Motives

The psalmist declared: "Whom have I in heaven but you? And
earth has nothing I desire besides you" (Psalm 73:25). The Hebrew
verb in this verse means to "take pleasure" or "delight" in something.
It is a word that is used in contexts that speak of emotion and is the
language of intense enjoyment. David used language that is even
more graphic in Psalm 63:1: "O God, you are my God, earnestly I
seek you; my soul thirsts for you, my body longs for you, in a dry
and weary land where there is no water." Duty, effort, and suffering
are often paths that must be taken in one's effort to glorify God, but

they are unlikely choices for those who have never learned to enjoy Him first. Augustine said, "You awaken us to delight in your praise; for you have made us for yourself, and our hearts are restless until they rest in you." Yet if the experience of God is the one thing for which our souls long, why does it seem so difficult to enjoy Him? Several factors make it hard for us to enjoy our heavenly Father:

We may be doing the right thing for the wrong reason. When our effort to glorify God becomes a path of drudgery, we can be certain that something is wrong. We see this reflected in the attitude of God's people during the time of the prophet Micah. They had accused God of burdening them with an intolerable load of commands (cf. Micah 6:3). Their unspoken feelings were articulated for them by the Lord in Micah 6:6–7: "With what shall I come before the Lord and bow down before the exalted God? Shall I come before him with burnt offerings, with calves a year old? Will the Lord be pleased with thousands of rams, with ten thousand rivers of oil? Shall I offer my firstborn for my transgression, the fruit of my body for the sin of my soul?" These questions indicate that their worship was carried out with a calculating spirit and betray an attitude that assumed that if they gave God what He wanted, He would give them what they wanted. The questions themselves reveal the weakness of such thinking. If we approach God with a calculating spirit we will always be disappointed, because we will be plagued by the knowledge that no matter how much we have given to God it is never enough.

God's people in Micah's day had asked the wrong question. They had asked "What does God want from me?" without first asking "What has God done for me?" Both questions are important in the Christian life, but they must be asked in the right order. A life of obedience, duty, and suffering that brings glory to the Father is acceptable only when it is offered out of gratitude for what God has done by making us His own. The proper order is love first and then obedience. If we reverse this order, our devotion to God, no matter how strong, will eventually degenerate into drudgery. Jesus linked obedience to discipleship but also to friendship. He told His disciples: "You are my friends if you do what I command. I no longer call you servants, because a servant does not know his master's business. Instead, I have called you friends, for everything that I learned from my Father I have made known to you. You did not choose me, but I chose you and appointed you to go and bear fruit—fruit that will last. Then the Father will give you whatever you ask in my name" (John 15:14–16).

Whether Israel's questions in Micah 6:6–7 were sincere or just a cynical complaint, God gave an answer through the prophet that was simple and to the point. In Micah 6:8 He responded: "He has showed you, O man, what is good. And what does the Lord require of you? To act justly and to love mercy and to walk humbly with your God." This three-point directive commanded God's people first to "act justly." In simplest terms to do justice means to do what God would do in any given situation. What God would do was spelled out in the second directive "to love mercy." The biblical concept of mercy has two primary thrusts. One of them is to show kindness to the undeserving. This is what God the Father has shown us by sending His Son to die in our place (Titus 3:3–6). The second dimension to mercy is that of loyalty. Mercy is action with commitment to the one on whose behalf we are acting. This is reflected in the command to "love" mercy. We might expect Micah 6:8 to say that we should act justly and "show" mercy. However, it is possible to show mercy without loving it. When we do not love those to whom mercy is shown, we fall short of what God requires. The third thing that God lists is to "walk humbly with your God." The Hebrew means to walk with awareness. It is important to remember that we serve within the context of a relationship. The things that we do to bring glory to the Father are not done "for" God so much as they are done "with" God. We are God's fellow workers and must serve with an awareness of His presence (1 Corinthians 3:9).

We may be doing the wrong things for the right reason. When Jesus was in Bethany, He often stayed at the home of his friends Martha, Mary, and Lazarus. Hospitality was important to Martha. Whenever Jesus and His disciples were in town, she was a blur of carrying, cutting, chopping, and cooking. One particular day, as she bustled about the house preparing a large meal, she noticed that her sister, Mary, was seated at Jesus' feet listening to Him teach. When Martha saw her sister quite at ease and not at all concerned about the work that was left to be done, she could not contain herself: "Lord, don't you care that my sister has left me to do the work by myself? Tell her to help me!" (Luke 10:40). Instead of offering sympathy, Jesus gently rebuked her: "'Martha, Martha,' the Lord answered, 'you are worried and upset about many things, but only one thing is needed. Mary has chosen what is better, and it will not be taken away from her'" (Luke 10:41–42).

I believe that Martha had good motives, but Mary's choice was the better of the two. Jesus' loving rebuke is a valuable reminder that opportunity does not always imply obligation and that activity is not always the best way to glorify God. Martha made a second mistake by serving with an eye on her sister. Since not everyone in the body of Christ has been gifted to do the same thing, my service for God should be consistent with His design for me (1 Corinthians 12:1–30). If God has created me to be an "eye," then I should function as an eye. I should not try to do what the foot does. However, it is equally important not to expect one who has been designed to function as the "foot" to serve God in the same way that I do. We are often tempted to respond to God's individual purpose for us in the way that Peter did when Jesus informed him that he would eventually give his life for the sake of the gospel. When Peter saw the apostle John standing nearby, he asked, "Lord, what about him?" Jesus answered: "If I want him to remain alive until I return, what is that to you? You must follow me" (John 21:22).

We may be plagued by the memory of past sins. A woman who had become deeply embittered toward her sister once told me that she kept a written record of every mean thing that her sister had ever done. "I keep it locked in my safety deposit box," she explained, "with instructions that it is to be given to my sister when I die." Her intent was plain to see. She wanted her sister to feel guilty. Her plan to wait until death before making the list known was calculated to maximize her sister's suffering, since it would ensure that no reconciliation could take place between them. Her plan underscores the tremendous power of guilt.

In itself guilt is not a bad thing. Like physical pain, it serves an important diagnostic function and acts as a signal from our conscience that something is wrong. However, if its ultimate cause is not dealt with, it will turn a once flourishing life into a desert (Psalm 32:3–4). God's Word promises that if we turn to Jesus Christ in faith, the Father will forgive us. But what can we do when we have difficulty accepting Christ's forgiveness? When this happens, past sins loom so large in our memory that they block out the rays of the Father's smile. We know that the Bible says that we are forgiven; we just don't feel forgiven. The key to recovery is to shift the focus of our attention from ourselves to the Father. As much as our sinful past says about us, it also tells us much about God: "But God demonstrates his own love for us in this: While we were still sinners, Christ died for us" (Romans 5:8). Our past shows the Father's compassion in bold relief and puts His love beyond a shadow of a doubt. If He loved us then, how much more can we be certain of His love for us now?

We may be suffering from a distorted view of God. The complaint of God's people that is implied in Micah 6:3, 6–7 indicates that they suffered from a distorted perception of the Father. They viewed Him as a harsh and demanding tyrant whose chief pleasure was to exhaust them with unrealistic demands. In reality, it was not God who had worn them down. They were stumbling under a burden of their own making. The prophecy of Isaiah, a contemporary of Micah, uses similar language: "You have not brought me sheep for burnt offerings, nor honored me with your sacrifices. I have not burdened you with grain offerings nor wearied you with demands for incense. You have not bought any fragrant calamus for me, or lavished on me the fat of your sacrifices. But you have burdened me with your sins and wearied me with your offenses" (Isaiah 43:23–24).[1] J. Alec Motyer notes that at first glance the prophet's words seem to imply that God's people had not been sacrificing at all. He points out that this cannot have been the case, in view of what other biblical passages reveal about this period in Israel's history. Motyer explains: "The emphasis in verse 22 requires a translation like 'Not me did you call.' This repeats the accusation of 1:10ff., not that prayer and ritual had ceased, but that though abundant both were failing to reach and satisfy God."[2] We may first need to recapture a true vision of the Father before we can enjoy serving Him, otherwise we are liable to simply "go through the motions" of worship and service or attempt to manipulate Him by our efforts.

Recapturing Our Joy

What should we do, then, if we find that we no longer enjoy God? Martyn Lloyd-Jones counseled: "Whatever you may feel about it do not consider the suggestion that comes to you from all directions—not so much from people, but from within yourself, the voices that seem to be speaking around and about you—do not listen to them when they suggest that you should give up, give way, or give in."[3] Lloyd-Jones warned that there are three primary dangers for one who is in such a condition. The first is that he will simply give up on the Christian life. When some abandoned Christ because they were offended by His teaching, Jesus turned to the disciples and asked, "You do not want to leave too, do you?" Simon Peter replied: "Lord, to whom shall we go? You have the words of eternal life. We believe and know that you are the Holy One of God" (John 6:68–69).

When we find ourselves contemplating such a course of action, we would do well to consider that there is no viable alternative. We must go on. Such a decision, however, may cause us to fall prey to the second danger mentioned by Lloyd-Jones. That is the danger that we will resign ourselves to our misery and go on out of sheer duty. This is particularly a temptation for Christian workers. Lloyd-Jones warns: "The danger of the majority at this point is just to resign themselves to it and to lose heart and to lose hope. They will go on, but they go on in this hopeless dragging condition."[4] Although such a course of action doesn't make us feel any better, it does feed the ego. We can compare ourselves favorably to others who have dropped out along the way. They are gone, but we are still trudging along. God, of course, takes little pleasure in such obedience. Although we may feel that what we are doing is a noble thing and worthy of the admiration of others, in reality it is likely to bring God more reproach than glory. When others who do not know Christ see our joyless Christianity, they wonder why anyone would find such a drab faith appealing. If that is the best you can do, they reason, then you may keep your Christianity.

The third danger that Lloyd-Jones warns of is that of resorting to artificial stimulants in a misguided attempt to kick-start our enthusiasm.[5] These stimulants can take several forms. Many turn to substitutes like drugs, alcohol, sex, food, or recreation to re-create the thrill that has been lost. Others take on an additional load of work, hoping that by exerting more effort they will recapture the excitement they felt when they began to serve God at first. A more subtle danger is the temptation to turn to false teaching that promises a quick fix or spiritual rush. Although these practices might seem to be unrelated to one another, the objective is the same with each. The goal is to mask the discomfort we presently feel. Depending upon artificial stimulants only provides a temporary solution because it treats the symptom and not the root cause. This actually contributes to the problem because it deadens our awareness of the very joy we seek.

We do not necessarily need to change our circumstances to recapture our joy. Biblical joy is often linked to suffering. Jesus told His disciples to rejoice when they were persecuted for the sake of righteousness. He did not mean that they would enjoy the experience of persecution, but that they should be joyful because of what such persecution implied: "Rejoice and be glad, because great is your reward in heaven, for in the same way they persecuted the prophets who were before you" (Matthew 5:12). Similarly, Peter told suffering believers to rejoice during painful trials because it meant that they were sharing in the same kind of experiences suffered by Christ and would be "overjoyed when his glory is revealed" (1 Peter 4:13). The apostle Paul noted that it was still possible to "rejoice in the hope of the glory of God" while in the midst of suffering (Romans 5:2).

Two things are clear from these verses. First, biblical joy is not determined by one's environment. Indeed, Peter speaks of the possibility of experiencing joy and grief simultaneously (1 Peter 1:6). Second, the joy spoken of in these verses is linked to the believer's future hope. The old cliché says that some people are so heavenly minded that they are no earthly good. In reality, it is more likely that we are not heavenly minded enough. In his classic work entitled *The Saints' Everlasting Rest,* Puritan pastor Richard Baxter said that "a heavenly mind is a joyful mind and the truest way to live a life of comfort." When Baxter speaks of comfort, he speaks not of earthly comfort but of that which comes from God Himself. According to J. I. Packer, this was a lesson that Baxter had learned from personal experience. Broken in health and considered to be near death by his own doctors, Baxter began to record his personal meditations on the believer's hope of eternal life. Packer noted:

> It was Baxter's habit of holding heaven at the forefront of his thoughts and desires that goes furthest to explain why, "when he spoke of weighty Soul-concerns, you might find his very Spirit Drench'd therein," and whence over the years, pain-racked bag of bones that he was, he drew the motivation and mental energy that sustained his ministry. The hope of heaven brought him joy, and joy brought him strength, and so, like John Calvin before him and George Whitefield after him (two verifiable examples) and, it would seem, like the apostle Paul himself (see 1 Co. 15:10; 2 Co. 11:23–30; Col. 1:29), he was astoundingly enabled to labor on, accomplishing more than would ever have seemed possible in a single lifetime.[6]

The Westminster divines were right. The glorification and enjoyment of God belong together. If we do not enjoy God, it is highly unlikely that our lives will bring Him much glory. Instead, they will be marked by a certain drab obedience that is as unremarkable as it is unattractive. At the same time, it is also clear that those who do not seek to glorify God do not derive much enjoyment from Him. Instead they waste themselves on other things. Such people make the same mistake that God's Old Testament people made: "My people have committed two sins: They have forsaken me, the spring of living water, and have dug their own cisterns, broken cisterns that cannot hold water" (Jeremiah 2:13).

WHAT DOES IT MEAN TO GLORIFY GOD?

Glory is both an attribute of God and something that is ascribed to Him. Moses asked to see God's glory (Exodus 33:18). Similarly, the Israelites saw the glory of God settle upon Mount Sinai (Exodus 24:16; cf. 16:7, 10).[7] Yet glory was also something that the Lord said that He would gain through the defeat of Pharaoh and his army. The Lord promised: "I will gain glory for myself through Pharaoh and all his army, and the Egyptians will know that I am the Lord" (Exodus 14:4). Glorifying God involves the recognition of His attributes and worth. Not surprisingly, then, many of the biblical texts that speak of glorifying God occur in a context that deals with praise. Those who glorify God "exalt" His name and "boast" of all that He has done (Psalm 34:2–3). They glorify God by speaking of Him, either in worship or to others (Psalm 63:3–5). They glorify God in song (Psalm 69:30).

However, we should not think that all it takes to glorify God is to speak well of Him. Isaiah 29:13 complains: "The Lord says: 'These people come near to me with their mouth and honor me with their lips, but their hearts are far from me. Their worship of me is made up only of rules taught by men'" (Isaiah 29:13). Jesus said that this was also a characteristic of God's people in His day (Matthew 15:8; Mark 7:6). God is not pleased by lip service alone but by praise that issues from the heart. The apostle Paul prayed that God would grant the believers in Rome a spirit of unity: "So that with one heart and mouth you may glorify the God and Father of our Lord Jesus Christ" (Romans 15:6).

To truly glorify God we must acknowledge His authority in our lives. This is underscored in the sobering account of Achan's sin after the battle of Jericho. When it was discovered that Achan was the source of Israel's defeat at the battle of Ai because he had taken some of the plunder of Jericho after God had commanded that it should be destroyed, Joshua told him to "give glory to the Lord, the God of Israel, and give him the praise. Tell me what you have done; do not hide it from me" (Joshua 7:19). Achan "gave glory" to God by admitting his crime. His confession is described as a form of "praise." The term that is translated "praise" in Joshua 7:19 is rendered "confession" in Ezra 10:11: "Now make confession to the Lord, the God of your fathers, and do his will." We glorify God when we do His will, regardless of what it may cost us. Even though Achan confessed, he was still executed. This is a solemn reminder that God's authority over us is absolute.

In several biblical passages the terms "glory" and "honor" are linked (1 Timothy 1:17; Revelation 4:9, 11; cf. Hebrews 2:7, 9; 1 Peter 1:7; 2 Peter 1:17). In Job 40:9–10 the two terms appear to be used synonymously: "Do you have an arm like God's, and can your voice thunder like his? Then adorn yourself with glory and splendor, and clothe yourself in honor and majesty." To glorify God we must honor Him. One of the ways we do this is through the use of our bodies. In 1 Corinthians 6:19–20 the apostle Paul admonishes: "Do you not know that your body is a temple of the Holy Spirit, who is in you, whom you have received from God? You are not your own; you were bought at a price. Therefore honor God with your body." The fact that the body is a sanctuary that has been indwelt by the Holy Spirit means that everywhere we go is "holy ground." Every aspect of human life is sacred and must be consecrated to God. Yet because we have been bought with a price we are also God's slaves. The slave or servant is one who is under authority and whose life is at the disposal of another (cf. Matthew 8:9; Luke 7:8). Freedom of choice does not give us the liberty to use our bodies in any way that we please. They are to be employed as "instruments of righteousness" (Romans 6:13). Dallas Willard noted that the use of the body for the glory of God is the central expression of the believer's spiritual life and a necessary consequence of being created in the divine image:

> In creating human beings in his likeness so that we could govern in his manner, God gave us a measure of *independent* power. Without such power, we absolutely could not resemble God in the close manner he intended, nor could we be God's co-workers. *The locus or depository of this necessary power is the human body.* This explains, in theological terms, why we have a body at all. *That body is our primary area of power, freedom, and—therefore—responsibility.*[8]

The Christian cannot effectively discharge this responsibility without an understanding of his position in Christ. Through Christ we have died to sin (Romans 6:1–7). As a result of His work we are to consider ourselves dead to the sinful nature, and we must not allow it to direct our actions (Romans 6:12–13). However, if we have died to sin, why does it often seem so alive? The answer is that although we have died to sin, sin itself is not entirely dead in us. The sin principle still continues to exert an influence. This is what Paul usually refers to in the Bible as the "flesh" (translated "sinful nature" in the NIV).[9] If one chooses to yield to its influence, the sinful nature can still control the believer's life. Indeed, if it were not for the counter-influence of the Holy Spirit, such a choice would be inevitable: "So I say, live by the Spirit, and you will not gratify the desires of the sinful nature. For the sinful nature desires what is contrary to the Spirit, and the Spirit what is contrary to the sinful nature. They are in conflict with each other, so that you do not do what you want" (Galatians 5:16–17). The kind of obedience that Paul calls for in these passages is not automatic. Nor does it come without a struggle. The destructive power of the flesh or the sinful nature, although it has been crucified in Christ, always remains a potentially deadly influence (Galatians 5:24; cf. Romans 8:5–8; Galatians 5:13).

Paul's intent in reminding us of the reality of the flesh is not to cause us to despair but to prompt us to rely upon the Holy Spirit. The hope of the gospel is not only the promise of forgiveness, but the hope of genuine transformation. Through Christ we can be changed. As we yield to the Holy Spirit, we can act in a way that reflects the authority of the Father over us. Such a change, however, does not come without a measure of effort. The fact that Paul uses the language of struggle to describe the relationship between the Holy Spirit and the sinful nature indicates that when the believer does experience the Spirit's power, it is not a type of good "possession." Unlike the demonic spirits, whose victims seem unable to resist their prompting, the Holy Spirit works in cooperation with the believer's will and actions. Believers must "put on" the new self and "put off" the old self (Ephesians 4:22–24).[10]

We should not mistake this struggle between the flesh and the Spirit as meaning that these two are equally powerful. The Holy Spirit is far more powerful than the flesh. Indeed, because He is omnipotent, the Holy Spirit could overwhelm us and compel us to obey. Instead He allows us the dignity of choosing to yield ourselves to His empowerment. Why? It would seem far more efficient to exercise a benevolent dictatorship over us by taking immediate and absolute control over our faculties. I believe that His unwillingness to do so is out of respect to the divine image in us. It is our calling to glorify the Father by offering our bodies to Him as a living sacrifice. It is our glory (and His!) for us to do so willingly rather than under compulsion.

Honor God with What You Have

In the parable of the talents in Matthew 25:15–30 Jesus tells the story of a master who entrusted varying amounts of money to each of his servants. When he returned and asked for an accounting he discovered that all but one had doubled the amount. The master condemned the one who failed to earn a return as a wicked and lazy servant (v. 26). The general theme of this parable focuses on stewardship. In the ancient world a steward was a trusted servant who was placed in charge of his master's household. Each servant in the story was to act as a steward over the talents entrusted to him and employ the best interests of his master. They were not all given the same amount, nor were they expected to produce the same results. This is also true of us. God expects us to make the most of all that He has entrusted to us, whether it is our wealth, our spiritual gifts, or our position. The return He expects is proportional to what He has placed at our disposal. When it comes to giving, for example, God expects a level of generosity from us that is consistent with what we have, not according to what we do not have (2 Corinthians 8:12).

Those who exercise spiritual gifts are to do so "with sober judgment, in accordance with the measure of faith God has given you" (Romans 12:3).[11] This sensible standard is not intended to limit us. The poor widow in the temple was commended by Jesus in Mark 12:42–44 for giving more generously than the wealthy, not because she gave a greater amount than all the others, but because she gave all that she had. According to 2 Corinthians 8:3 the poverty-stricken believers in Macedonia not only gave as much as they were able, but gave beyond their ability. Jesus promised His disciples: "I tell you the truth, anyone who has faith in me will do what I have been doing. He will do even greater things than these, because I am going to the Father" (John 14:12). The lesson we learn from these passages is that God has already given us all we need to bring glory to Him.

In his book *The Life You've Always Wanted: Spiritual Disciplines for Ordinary People*, pastor and author John Ortberg tells of the tremendous impact an elderly woman named Mabel had on a friend of his named Tom. Mabel was blind and nearly deaf, and her face was so disfigured by cancer that the supervisors of the nursing home where she was a resident often sent new nurses to feed her to see if they had enough stamina for the job. She had spent nearly twenty-five years in this condition and had few visitors. Tom visited with Mabel several times a week for three years and was deeply touched by her faith, serenity, and joy in Christ. Ortberg comments: "Here was an ordinary human being who received supernatural power to do extraordinary things. Her entire life consisted of following Jesus as best she could in her situation: patient endurance of suffering, solitude, prayer, meditation on Scripture, worship, fellowship when it was possible, giving when she had a flower or a piece of candy to offer."[12] Like the widow in the temple, Mabel cast the few pennies that made up her life into the treasury of God and used them to bring glory to the Father.

The truth is that many of us have it as our ambition to bring glory to God but feel that now is not the proper time. We believe that we could glorify Him more effectively if we had a better job, more money, a different spouse, or any number of changes in our present circumstances. We are like the disciples who, when they were asked by Jesus to feed the multitude, took stock of their meager resources and concluded that there was little that they could do (Luke 9:13). Yet it is by consecrating the little we now have to Him that God is glorified. Those who consecrate what they have to God are given greater opportunity to glorify the Father.

I teach college students who are preparing to serve God in full-time ministry, usually as pastors. They often tell me that they feel overwhelmed by the task. I tell them that it is when they feel inadequate that they are most likely to be used by God. In 2 Corinthians 4:7 the apostle Paul says that "we have this treasure in jars of clay to show that this all-surpassing power is from God and not from us." If our resources for glorifying God often seem limited, it is because they are. Just as Jesus already knew what He planned to do when He asked the disciples to feed the multitude with only five loaves and two fish, our Father knows how to make "his light shine in our hearts to give us the light of the knowledge of the glory of God in the face of Christ" (2 Corinthians 4:6). It is when God Himself is the only explanation for the power in our lives that He receives the most glory.

Avoid the Temptation to Overcompensate

King Saul was one of the most tragic figures in Old Testament history. At the start of his reign he seemed like a promising candidate for royalty. Literally head and shoulders above his peers, he was "an impressive young man without equal among the Israelites" (1 Samuel 9:2). He also seemed to possess a high degree of humility. On the day he was scheduled to be crowned as king, Saul hid among the baggage and had to be compelled to accept the post (1 Samuel 10:22; cf. 9:21). When he was under the power of God's Spirit, he was a formidable opponent capable of great feats of bravery (1 Samuel 11:8–11). He also had the potential to be a compassionate ruler. One of his first acts as king was to forgive those who had challenged his right to rule (vv. 12–13). Yet Saul ended his reign in disgrace, tortured with jealousy and abandoned by God.

Where did Saul go wrong? Two events epitomize Saul's primary failure. The first occurred while Saul was waiting to engage the Philistines in battle at Gilgal. Terrified by the enemy's superior numbers, the armies of Israel had begun to desert and flee into the mountains. The prophet Samuel had told Saul to wait for his arrival, but the prophet had been unexplainably delayed. When Saul saw his terrified troops beginning to scatter, he decided to take matters into his own hands. He called for the burnt offering and the fellowship offering and sacrificed them himself, although that task was reserved for the priest alone. Just as he was finishing Samuel arrived.

When the prophet demanded an explanation, Saul replied: "When I saw that the men were scattering, and that you did not come at the set time, and that the Philistines were assembling at Micmash, I thought, 'Now the Philistines will come down against me at Gilgal, and I have not sought the Lord's favor.' So I felt compelled to offer the burnt offering" (1 Samuel 13:11–12). Who could blame him? Yet instead of praising Saul for his devotion, Samuel condemned him: "You acted foolishly," Samuel said. "You have not kept the command the Lord your God gave you; if you had, he would have established your kingdom over Israel for all time. But now your kingdom will not endure; the Lord has sought out a man after his own heart and appointed him leader of his people, because you have not kept the Lord's command" (vv. 13–14). Saul's behavior betrayed a fundamental lack of faith. Saul did not trust God enough to wait for His deliverance. Even worse, he took matters into his own hands, taking an action that God had forbidden in a misguided attempt to please God.

The second instance is similar. Ordered by God to punish the Amalekites for their treatment of Israel after their escape from Egypt in the time of the Exodus, Saul was told to completely destroy all that belonged to them (1 Samuel 15:3). This was not the first time Israel had been given such a command. When Joshua defeated the city of Jericho they were under similar orders not to take any plunder (Joshua 6:17–18, 21). According to Ralph W. Klein, the Hebrew term used in the command in 1 Samuel 15:3 to "totally destroy" the Amalekites referred to a practice known as "the ban." Klein explained: "The ban was the practice of dedicating the enemy or his goods to the deity by killing the people and burning the animals and property."[13] This was both an extreme form of consecration and an act of divine retribution. Those placed under the ban were also under God's judgment (cf. Deuteronomy 7:2; 20:17).

However, instead of doing as he had been commanded, Saul destroyed only the "despised and weak" (1 Samuel 15:9). The Hebrew term that is translated "weak" in this verse referred to something that was regarded as worthless or contemptible. The other term, translated "despised," is rarer but seems to mean something like "garbage." In effect, Saul disobeyed a direct command and devoted only the garbage to God.

Amazingly, Saul does not seem to have seen anything wrong with this. When Samuel arrived on the scene, Saul rushed out to greet him saying, "The Lord bless you! I have carried out the Lord's instructions" (1 Samuel 15:13). However, the sound of newly captured animals told a different story. Samuel replied, "What then is this bleating of sheep in my ears? What is this lowing of cattle that I hear?" (v. 14). Once again, Saul spiritualized his disobedience: "Saul answered, 'The soldiers brought them from the Amalekites; they spared the best of the sheep and cattle to sacrifice to the Lord your God, but we totally destroyed the rest'" (1 Samuel 15:15). Even if Saul was telling the truth, his desire to "worship" in this way was controlled more by self-interest than by a desire to sacrifice since many Old Testament offerings included a sacrificial meal.[14] These sacrifices were eaten by the worshipers themselves in a feast before the Lord (Leviticus 7:12–15). Like Saul and his men, when we attempt to overcompensate for disobedience in one area of life by doubling our effort in another, we usually concentrate our effort in those areas that suit our own tastes or interests. What appears to others to be a radical commitment and extreme sacrifice may actually be a form of self-indulgence.

Another form of spiritual overcompensation is reflected in what is sometimes referred to as "foxhole religion." I discovered this phenomenon while serving as a pastor. I noticed that some of those who visited our church only seemed to attend when they were facing a personal crisis. They would show up unexpectedly on a Sunday and tell me of some difficulty they were facing—perhaps a sudden illness, loss of a job, or problem with one of their teenaged children—and then ask me to pray for them. They attended for the next few Sundays and then disappeared once the crisis had been resolved. When they finally reappeared, usually months or even years later, I could be fairly certain that new problems had arisen. When times were good they seemed untroubled by thoughts of God. In the face of crisis, however, they turned to Him with renewed zeal.

Eugene Peterson observed: "The most religious places in the world, as a matter of fact, are not churches but battlefields and mental hospitals. You are much more likely to find passionate prayer in a foxhole than in a church pew; and you will certainly find more otherworldly visions and supernatural voices in a mental hospital than you will in a church."[15] In itself, this is not necessarily a bad thing. It is the sick who need the doctor. God often uses moments of desperation to make us aware of our need for Him. For Israel this pattern of behavior became a recurring cycle of neglect of God, distress over difficult circumstances, and then renewed devotion when He finally delivered them (cf. Judges 3:7–31). Its chief danger is that it turns acts of devotion into a kind of bribe designed to enlist God's help only when we sense our need of it. This misguided approach is based upon two major misconceptions. The first is the assumption that we need God less when we do not face difficulties than when we are in trouble. Equally erroneous is the thought that our acts of devotion can be used to manipulate God's favor. We cannot use obedience as a bargaining chip, offering it when we need God's help and withholding it when we do not sense a need for Him.

When Saul argued that his actions were justified because he planned to use what was captured to sacrifice to the Lord, Samuel replied: "Does the Lord delight in burnt offerings and sacrifices as much as in obeying the voice of the Lord? To obey is better than sacrifice, and to heed is better than the fat of rams. For rebellion is like the sin of divination, and arrogance like the evil of idolatry. Because you have rejected the word of the Lord, he has rejected you as king" (1 Samuel 15:22–23). Saul's surface devotion masked an attitude of arrogant rebellion. He had taken it upon himself to modify the commands given to him by God so that they suited his own tastes. Far from being pleasing, they were as offensive to God as witchcraft and idolatry.

A small boy was attempting to persuade his mother to give him a cookie. When his arguments appeared to have no effect, he took her by the hand and pulled her into the kitchen. Standing in front of the refrigerator, he pointed to the memory verse that was fastened to it. He had brought it home from vacation Bible school that very day. "See," he said with determination, "it says: 'If you love me, you will obey me!'" Like him, many of us understand the sentiment expressed in John 14:15 but have misapplied the order of authority. It is we who answer to God, not the other way around. For those who truly seek to bring glory to the Father, there is no substitute for simple obedience. No amount of sacrifice, no matter how costly or impressive in appearance, can substitute.

Our primary calling is to glorify God, not by expressing our devotion to Him in the occasional word or deed, but within the context of life as a whole. If all of life is "holy ground" for the Christian, then no activity is really common. We have the potential to bring glory to the Father in all that we do. As William Law observed: "This is the business of all persons in this world. Men and women, rich and poor, must, with bishops and priests, walk before God in the same wise and holy spirit, in the same denial of all vain tempers, and in the same discipline and care of their souls—not only because they have all the same rational nature and are servants of the same God, but because they all seek the same holiness to make them fit for the same happiness to which they are called."[16] We are called to obedience because we have been called to seek God's glory—and that is the only route that leads to our own happiness as well.

QUESTIONS FOR DISCUSSION

1. Why might the ideas of glorifying and enjoying God seem incompatible with each other?
2. How would you characterize the relationship between the enjoyment of God and the place of duty, effort, and suffering in the Christian life?
3. What is an example of doing the right thing for the wrong reason? What is an example of doing the wrong thing for the right reason?
4. How would you counsel a believer who complained to you that he had "lost his joy"?
5. What does it mean to "glorify" God?
6. What place does the body have in this task?
7. How do some people "overcompensate" for their disobedience to God?

NOTES

CHAPTER 1
"I Believe in God the Father . . ."

1. Kenneth L. Woodward, "Hallowed Be Thy Name," *Newsweek,* 17 June 1996, 75.

2. Leon Morris, *Ruth: An Introduction and Commentary* (Downers Grove, Ill.: InterVarsity, 1968), 282.

3. J. A. Thompson, *The Book of Jeremiah* (Grand Rapids: Eerdmans, 1980), 192.

4. Joachim Jeremias, *The Prayers of Jesus* (Philadelphia: Fortress, 1967), 24.

5. James Barr, "'Abbā Isn't Daddy," *Journal of Theological Studies,* NS, vol. 39, pt. I, May 1988, 28–47.

6. Cornelius Plantinga Jr., "Social Trinity and Tritheism," in *Trinity, Incarnation and Atonement: Philosophical and Theological Essays,* ed. by Ronald J. Feenstra and Cornelius Plantinga Jr. (Notre Dame: Univ. of Notre Dame, 1989), 23.

7. George Lakoff and Mark Johnson, *Metaphors We Live By* (Chicago: Univ. of Chicago, 1980), 56.

8. Charles Hodge, *Systematic Theology,* vol. I (Grand Rapids: Eerdmans, 1977), 339.

9. C. S. Lewis, *Mere Christianity* (New York: Macmillan, 1952), 17.

10. Geerhardus Vos, *Biblical Theology* (Grand Rapids: Eerdmans, 1948), 64.

11. Ibid.

12. Roger Hedlund observed that the fact that God's work in the Bible is carried out in the midst of the nations is an indication of His interest in them: "The nations are the peoples of the world. In particular the peoples surrounding Israel in her Old Testament history. Salvation history which centers in the people of Israel is of par-

ticular consequence to the other peoples. God, if he is not the exclusive Deity of the Hebrews, has a relationship to the world and its peoples. If he is God of the whole world, then he must be vitally interested in the salvation of the Egyptians, the Philistines, the Babylonians, the Assyrians, and kindred nations. He desires not their destruction but their salvation (Isa. 19:19–25; 45:22; Pss. 68:31–32; 86:9; 87). The table of nations (Gen. 10) suggests God's relationship to every human family, language, and people (Gen. 10:5, 20, 31). The covenant with Noah (Gen. 9:9–10) is a universal covenant." Roger E. Hedlund, *The Mission of the Church in the World: A Biblical Theology* (Grand Rapids: Baker, 1985), 25.

13. In this combination *El* underscores the Father's might, while its companion *Shaddai* points to His ability to provide. Martyn Lloyd-Jones explains: "This name describes God in His power over the elements, in His power over nature and creation. Yes, but not merely His power, it particularly emphasizes God's control of all these things for the purpose of His grace and of His mercy, and of His dealings with men and women. For example, He controls the wind, the rain and the snow in order that we may have food to eat. That is the meaning of Shaddai." Martyn Lloyd-Jones, *God the Father, God the Son* (Wheaton, Ill.: Crossway, 1996), 81.

14. J. Barton Payne, *The Theology of the Older Testament* (Grand Rapids: Zondervan, 1962), 147.

15. R. Alan Cole explains: "Exodus 6:3 shows that Israel was quite aware that the patriarchs used the name El-Shaddai (RSV 'God Almighty') for God (cf. the proper name Ammi-shaddai in Numbers 1:12), along with many other titles. So the question of the Israelites does not spring from ignorance, nor is it a trick question framed to test Moses' knowledge of the traditions of his own people. To ask the question, 'Under what new title has God appeared to you?' is equivalent to asking, 'What new revelation have you received from God?' Normally, in patriarchal days, any new revelation of the ancestral God will be summed up in a new title for Him (Gen. 16:13) which will in future both record and recount a deeper knowledge of God's saving activity." R. Alan Cole, *Exodus* (Downers Grove, Ill.: InterVarsity, 1973), 69.

16. Brevard S. Childs, *The Book of Exodus* (Philadelphia: Westminster, 1974), 76.

17. Barbara Kantrowitz, "Raising Spiritual Children," *Newsweek*, 7 December 1998, 62.

18. Nancy J. Duff, "Atonement and the Christian Life: Reformed Doctrine from a Feminist Perspective," *Interpretation*, January 1999, 25.

19. David Blankenhorn, "Houses of Worship: The Fatherhood of God," *The Wall Street Journal*, 19 June 1998.

20. Ibid.

CHAPTER 2
The Role of the Father

1. Jaroslav Pelikan, *The Emergence of the Catholic Tradition (100–600)* (Chicago: Univ. of Chicago, 1971), 193.

2. Quoted by Elizabeth Achtemeir in "Why God Is Not Mother: A Response to Feminist God-Talk in the Church," *Christianity Today,* 16 August 1993, 16.

3. Donald G. Bloesch, *God the Almighty* (Downers Grove, Ill.: InterVarsity, 1995), 25–26.

4. Wolfhart Pannenberg, "Feminine Language About God?" *The Asbury Theological Journal,* vol. 48, no. 2 (Fall 1993).

5. P. C. Craigie, *The Book of Deuteronomy* (Grand Rapids: Eerdmans, 1976), 168.

6. C. F. Keil and Franz Delitzsch, *Commentary on the Old Testament,* vol. 1: *The Pentateuch,* trans. by James Martin (Grand Rapids: Eerdmans, 1983), 323.

7. Leon Morris, *The Gospel According to John* (Grand Rapids: Eerdmans, 1971), 552.

8. Herman Bavinck, *The Doctrine of God,* trans. by William Hendricksen (Grand Rapids: Baker, 1977), 297.

9. J. N. D. Kelly, *Early Christian Doctrines* (New York: Harper & Row, 1960), 129.

10. Millard Erickson, *God in Three Persons: A Contemporary Interpretation of the Trinity* (Grand Rapids: Baker, 1995), 71.

11. Charles Hodge, *Systematic Theology,* vol. II (Grand Rapids: Eerdmans, 1977), 389.

12. J. I. Packer, *Knowing God* (Downers Grove, Ill.: InterVarsity, 1973), 61–62.

13. Ibid., 62.

14. Origen, *On Prayer,* trans. John Ernest, Leonard Oulton, and Henry Chadwick, in *Alexandrian Christianity,* ed. Henry Chadwick (Philadelphia: Westminster, 1954), 269.

15. Louis Berkhof, *The History of Christian Doctrines* (1937; reprint, Grand Rapids: Baker, 1975), 85–86.

16. H. C. G. Moule, *The Epistle to the Philippians* (1897; reprint, Grand Rapids: Baker, 1981), 38.

17. Gilbert Bilezikian, "Hermeneutical Bungee-Jumping: Subordination in the Godhead," *Journal of the Evangelical Theological Society,* 40:1 (March 1997): 63.

18. Gregory of Nazianzus, *The Theological Orations,* ed. Edward R. Hardy, trans. Charles Gordon Browne and James Edward Swallow, in *Christology of the Later Fathers,* ed. Edward R. Hardy (Philadelphia: Westminster, 1954), 199.

19. Ibid., 198.

20. Clark Pinnock, *Flame of Love: A Theology of the Holy Spirit* (Downers Grove, Ill.: InterVarsity, 1996), 36.

CHAPTER 3
The Nature of the Father

1. Stephen Charnock, *Discourses upon the Existence and Attributes of God* (London: James Blackwood, 1875), 111.

2. R. Alan Cole, *Exodus: An Introduction and Commentary* (Downers Grove, Ill.: InterVarsity, 1973), 186–87.

3. Gordon Wehnam, *Numbers: An Introduction and Commentary* (Downers Grove, Ill.: InterVarsity, 1981), 113.

4. Charles Hodge, *Systematic Theology*, vol. I (Grand Rapids: Eerdmans, 1977), 378–79.

5. John Calvin, *Institutes of the Christian Religion*, I.I.1, trans. by Ford Lewis Battles, ed. John T. McNeill, Library of Christian Classics vol. XX, (Philadelphia: Westminster, 1977), 35.

6. Ibid., 36–37.

7. Gerald Bray, *The Doctrine of God: Contours of Christian Theology* (Downers Grove: InterVarsity, 1993), 107.

8. Geerhardus Vos, *Biblical Theology* (Grand Rapids: Eerdmans, 1948), 19.

9. Ibid.

10. Louis Berkhof, *Systematic Theology* (1939; reprint, Grand Rapids: Eerdmans, 1982), 55.

11. Henry Clarence Thiessen, *Introductory Lectures in Systematic Theology* (Grand Rapids: Eerdmans, 1949), 123–24.

12. Westminster Catechism, Question 7.

13. Thomas F. Torrance, *Theology in Reconstruction* (Grand Rapids: Eerdmans, 1965), 31.

14. Douglas Groothuis, *Jesus in an Age of Controversy* (Eugene: Harvest House, 1996), 65.

15. J. I. Packer observes: "The very fact that a Christian prays is thus proof positive that he believes in the Lordship of his God." *Evangelism and the Sovereignty of God* (Downers Grove, Ill.: InterVarsity, 1961), 12.

16. Ibid., 21.

17. Ibid.

18. Richard Rice, "Biblical Support for a New Perspective" in *The Openness of God* by Clark Pinnock, Richard Rice, John Sanders, William Hasker, and David Basinger (Downers Grove, Ill.: InterVarsity, 1994), 48. Rice's chapter title describes this paradigm as a "new" perspective. However, several of its main features were described and critiqued by Herman Bavinck in 1951 in his discussion of immutability in *The Doctrine of God*.

19. Ibid., 52.

CHAPTER 4
The Father Almighty

1. Louis Berkhof, *Systematic Theology* (1939; reprint, Grand Rapids: Eerdmans, 1982), 59.

2. Thomas Watson, *A Body of Divinity* (1692; reprint, Carlisle, Pa.: Banner of Truth, 1992), 61–62.

3. John Calvin notes: "He does not call himself the God of Beth-el, because he is confined within the limits of a given place, but for the purpose of renewing to his servant the remembrance of his own promise; for holy Jacob had not yet attained to that degree of perfection which rendered the more simple rudiments unnecessary for him." *Commentary on Genesis*, 1554. Trans. and edited by John King, 1578. (reprint, Carlisle, Pa.: Banner of Truth, 1975), 165–66.

4. Eugene Peterson, *Leap over a Wall: Earthy Spirituality for Everyday Christians* (San Francisco: HarperCollins, 1997), 65.

5. Ibid., 64.

6. R. Laird Harris, Gleason L. Archer Jr., and Bruce K. Waltke, *Theological Wordbook of the Old Testament*, vol. I (Chicago: Moody, 1980), 257.

7. Geerhardus Vos, *Biblical Theology: Old and New Testaments* (Grand Rapids: Eerdmans, 1948), 40.

8. Richard Rice asserted that God's foreknowledge and sovereign will are not determinative. According to Rice: "God's will is not the ultimate explanation for everything that happens; human decisions and actions make an important contribution too. Thus history is the combined result of what God and his creatures decide to do." For Rice, divine foreknowledge of every human action would make freedom of the will a mere pretense. He argued instead that God's knowledge of the world is dynamic: "Instead of perceiving the entire course of human existence in one timeless moment, God comes to know events as they take place. He learns something from what transpires. We call this position the 'open view of God' because it regards God as receptive to new experiences and as flexible in the way he works toward his objectives in the world. Since it sees God as dependent on the world in certain respects, the open view of God differs from much conventional theology." See Richard Rice, "Biblical Support for a New Perspective" in *The Openness of God*, by Clark Pinnock, Richard Rice, John Sanders, William Hasker, and David Basinger (Downers Grove, Ill.: InterVarsity, 1994), 16–17.

9. Alan A. MacRae makes the following observation regarding Isaiah 44:24–28: "This long sentence begins with an emphatic statement of God's creative power over the universe, followed by condemnation of false prophets and so-called wise men who wish to explain the universe without taking the Creator into account." *The Gospel of Isaiah* (Chicago: Moody, 1977), 26.

10. Charles Hodge, *Systematic Theology*, vol. I (Grand Rapids: Eerdmans, 1977), 546.

The text cited at the end of this quote is taken from the Westminster Confession, III.I.

11. J. P. Hyatt, *Exodus* (Grand Rapids: Eerdmans, 1971), 317.

12. R. C. Sproul, *Essential Truths of the Christian Faith* (Wheaton, Ill.: Tyndale, 1992), 46.

13. Berkhof, *Systematic Theology,* 75.

14. Leon Morris, *The Atonement: Its Meaning & Significance* (Downers Grove, Ill.: InterVarsity, 1983), 179.

CHAPTER 5
The Work of the Father

1. K. A. Kitchen notes: "There is no indisputable evidence that the Hebrew accounts are directly dependent upon the known Babylonian epics, despite a common belief to the contrary. Patriarchal origins in Mesopotamia point back to a common stream of tradition known to be full developed early in the second millennium BC." Kitchen also points out that only about one sixth of the *Enuma Elish* actually deals with creation: "All the rest is occupied by the main theme of how Marduk of Babylon became supreme, plus the list of his fifty names." K. A. Kitchen, *Ancient Orient and Old Testament* (Downers Grove, Ill.: InterVarsity, 1966), 88–89.

2. Howard J. Van Till, "The Creation: Intelligently Designed or Optimally Equipped?" *Theology Today,* October 1998, 360.

3. Ibid., 361.

4. Ibid., 363.

5. Oswald T. Allis, *God Spake by Moses* (Philadelphia: Presb. & Ref., 1950), 14.

6. John Calvin, although writing well before the controversy over evolution, pointed to the order of the creation as evidence for God's direct involvement in the creative process: "No creature has a force more wondrous or glorious than that of the sun. For besides lighting the whole earth with its brightness, how great a thing is it that by its heat it nourishes and quickens all living things! That with its rays it breathes fruitfulness into the earth! That it warms the seeds in the bosom of the earth, draws them forth with budding greenness, increases and strengthens them, nourishes them anew, until they rise up into stalks! That it feeds the plant with continual warmth, until it grows into flower, and from flower into fruit! That then, also, with baking heat it brings the fruit into maturity! That in like manner trees and vines warmed by the sun first put forth buds and leaves, then put forth a flower, and from the flower produce fruit! Yet the Lord, to claim the whole credit for all these things, willed that, before he created the sun, light should come to be and earth be filled with all manner of herbs and fruits [Gen. 1:3, 11, 14]. Therefore a godly man will not make the sun either the principal or the necessary cause of these things

which existed before the creation of the sun, but merely the instrument that God uses because he so wills; for with no more difficulty he might abandon it, and act through himself." *Institutes of the Christian Religion,* I.XVI.2, trans. by Ford Lewis Battles, ed. John T. McNeill, Library of Christian Classics vol. XX (Philadelphia: Westminster, 1977), 199.

7. For an example of one scientist's response to creationist arguments see Donald U. Wise, "Creationism's Geologic Time Scale," *American Scientist,* vol. 86, 1 March 1998, 160–73.

8. Allis, *God Spake by Moses,* 157.

9. Ibid., 158.

10. For more information about intelligent design theory, see *Darwin's Black Box: The Biochemical Challenge to Evolution* by Michael J. Behe (New York: Simon & Schuster, 1998) and *Darwin on Trial* by Philip E. Johnson (Downers Grove, Ill.: InterVarsity, 1991).

11. Derek Kidner, *Genesis* (Downers Grove, Ill.: InterVarsity, 1967), 60–61.

12. Augustine, *On Free Will,* in *Augustine: Earlier Writings,* trans. by John H. S. Burleigh (Philadelphia: Westminster, 1953), 123.

13. John Calvin, *Sermons on Ephesians* (1562; reprint, Carlisle, Pa.: Banner of Truth, 1975), 435–37.

14. "Accordingly, the integrity with which Adam was endowed is expressed by this word, when he had full possession of right understanding, when he had his affections kept within the bounds of reason, all his senses tempered in right order, and he truly referred his excellence to exceptional gifts bestowed upon him by his Maker. And although the primary seat of the divine image was in the mind and heart, or in the soul and its powers, yet there was no part of man, not even the body itself, in which some sparks did not glow." John Calvin, *Institutes of the Christian Religion,* trans. by Ford Lewis Battles, ed. John T. McNeill, Library of Christian Classics vol. XX, (Philadelphia: Westminster, 1977), 188.

15. Philip Edgcumbe Hughes gave an excellent summary of the various ways theologians have interpreted the phrase "image of God" through the centuries in his book *The True Image: The Origin and Destiny of Man in Christ* (Grand Rapids: Eerdmans, 1989).

16. Francis A. Schaeffer, *Art and the Bible* (Downers Grove, Ill.: InterVarsity, 1976), 34.

17. Donald Senior and Carroll Stuhlmueller commented: "Chronologically, of course, creation came first, but salvation is to be given first place theologically. The Bible does open with a dramatic narrative about 'the generations of the heavens and the earth when they were created' (Gen. 2:4 [KJV]), yet the first eleven chapters of Genesis were gathered together at a late period of Israelite history, solemnly to introduce God's law of salvation in the Torah (the five books from Genesis through Deuteronomy). These chapters of Genesis are best interpreted as a theological com-

mentary upon God's way of saving his people Israel." *The Biblical Foundation for Mission*, Maryknoll, N.Y.: Orbis, 1991), 36.

CHAPTER 6
The Care of the Father

1. Alistair Begg, *Made for His Pleasure: Ten Benchmarks of a Vital Faith* (Chicago: Moody, 1996), 107.

2. Myron Chartier, "A Theology of Parenting: An Incarnational Model," *American Baptist Quarterly*, 3, no. 1 (March 1984): 75.

3. Ibid., 76–83. Chartier lists the following traits as reflective of God's parental role: caring, responsiveness, discipline, giving, respect, intimate knowledge, and forgiveness. He argues that these divine actions should also guide human parents in their task: "Care, respond, discipline, give, respect, know, and forgive—these seven mutually interdependent dimensions of love draw some of the lines upon the parental face of God whom we know as love. These same lines need to be recognized by children in the faces of their parents."

4. Robert Leighton, *Commentary on First Peter* (1853; reprint, Grand Rapids: Kregel, 1972), 485.

5. Chartier, "A Theology of Parenting," 77.

6. John Owen, *Hebrews: The Epistle of Warning* (Grand Rapids: Kregel, 1973), 249.

7. C. E. B. Cranfield, *A Critical and Exegetical Commentary on the Epistle to the Romans*, vol. I (Edinburgh: T. & T. Clark, 1975), 266.

8. J. Barton Payne, *The Theology of the Older Testament* (Grand Rapids: Zondervan, 1962), 331.

9. C. E. B. Cranfield, *The Gospel According to St. Mark* (Cambridge: Cambridge Univ., 1966), 385.

10. According to Kirsopp Lake and Henry J. Cadbury: "In general 'widows' came to have a double meaning: (i.) all women who had lost their husbands; (ii.) a selected number of the first class who were appointed to a definite position in the organization of the Church as part of the 'Clerus.'" *The Acts of the Apostles*, vol. IV, English Translation and Commentary by Kirsopp Lake and Henry J. Cadbury in *The Beginnings of Christianity, Part I: The Acts of the Apostles* edited by F. J. Foakes-Jackson and Kirsopp Lake (Grand Rapids: Baker, 1979), 64.

11. William O'Hare reports: "American kids are increasingly likely to grow up without a father in their home. The share of children living in mother-only families has increased from 6 percent in 1950 to 24 percent in 1994. If current rates of divorce continue, the majority of today's children will spend some of their childhood in a single-parent home." According to O'Hare, in the decade from 1984 to 1994 single parents became more prevalent in every state, increasing in cities, suburbs, rural

areas, and among all racial groups. The majority of fatherless neighborhoods is concentrated in urban core areas. See "Life Without Fathers" by William O'Hare, *American Demographics,* July 1995, 60.

12. Charles Spurgeon, *The Treasury of David,* vol. I, part 2 (reprint, McLean: MacDonald, n.d.), 4.

13. R. K. Harrison, *Leviticus: An Introduction and Commentary* (Downers Grove, Ill.: InterVarsity, 1980), 227–28.

14. It should be noted that the poor to which Jesus refers were His own disciples. Matthew's version of this beatitude casts it in a spiritual context (cf. Matthew 5:3). It does not mean that poverty in itself invests those who suffer from it with a unique spirituality or state of blessedness. Furthermore, Jesus' command to the rich follower in Luke 18:22 does not appear to have been a general directive aimed at all the disciples but was called for because it was an unhealthy attachment to wealth that was a form of idolatry. Donald Guthrie explains: "When Jesus advised the rich young ruler to sell his possessions and give to the poor (Luke 18:22), he was not giving a general directive to all his followers, but specific advice to one whose great weakness was too great a love for riches. The incident confirms Jesus' concern for the poor. Furthermore, the somewhat similar statements of Luke 12:33 and 14:33 are not cast in the form of specific advice, but of general exhortation." *New Testament Theology* (Downers Grove, Ill.: InterVarsity, 1981), 943–44.

CHAPTER 7
The Blessings of the Father

1. Charles Hodge notes that the context of this statement deals with the election of Israel as a nation and not with the election of the individual. However, he believes that the certainty promised in this verse is also appropriately applied to the individual believer: "The general proposition of the apostle, therefore, is that the purposes of God are unchangeable; and, consequently, those whom God has chosen for any special benefit cannot fail to attain it. The persons whom he hath chosen to eternal life shall certainly be saved; and the people whom he chooses to be his peculiar people, as the Jews were chosen in Abraham, must for ever remain his people. The purpose once formed, and the promise once given, never can be changed. As in the whole context Paul is speaking, not of individuals, but of the rejection and restoration of the Jews as a body, it is evident that the calling and election which he here has in view, are such as pertain to the Jews as a nation, and not such as contemplate the salvation of individuals." Charles Hodge, *A Commentary on Romans* (1835; reprint, Carlisle, Pa.: Banner of Truth, 1972), 376.

2. Hans Georg Conzelmann, χαρις in *Theological Dictionary of the New Testament,* vol. IX, eds. Gerhard Kittel and Gerhard Friedrich, translated by Geoffry W. Bromiley (Grand Rapids: Eerdmans, 1974), 374–75.

3. Lewis Sperry Chafer, *Grace* (Philadelphia: The Sunday School Times, 1922), 4.

4. We should not think of this as a "legal" obligation, as if the Father were somehow bound by rule of law. Rather, it is an obligation that grows out of the divine nature. God's own veracity ensures that He will do as He promises. When He commits Himself to show grace to someone, He will not go back on His word. To do so would be contrary to His nature.

5. Cranfield commented that the term "stand" is probably used in the sense "stand firm" or "abide." C. E. B. Cranfield, *A Critical and Exegetical Commentary on the Epistle to the Romans,* vol. I (Edinburgh: T. & T. Clark, 1975), 259. H. C. G. Moule expressed a similar view, comparing its usage in this verse with Revelation 6:17 and 1 Corinthians 15:1, "where the context gives the idea of acceptance and safety, as here." H. C. G. Moule, *Studies in Romans* (1892; reprint, Grand Rapids: Kregel, 1977), 100.

6. Charles Hodge, *Systematic Theology,* vol. II (Grand Rapids: Eerdmans, 1977), 675.

7. Richard Baxter, *A Treatise on Conversion* (1657; reprint, New York: American Tract Society, n.d.), 23–24.

8. Millard J. Erickson explains: "Special or effectual calling, then, involves an extraordinary presentation of the message of salvation. It is sufficiently powerful to counteract the effects of sin and enable the person to believe. It is also so appealing that the person will believe." Millard J. Erickson, *Introducing Christian Doctrine* (Grand Rapids: Baker, 1992), 295.

9. B. B. Warfield, "Prayer as a Means of Grace" in *Faith and Life* (1916; reprint, Carlisle, Pa.: Banner of Truth, 1974), 147–48.

10. Donald Whitney, *Spiritual Disciplines Within the Church: Participating Fully in the Body of Christ* (Chicago: Moody, 1996), 136.

11. Louis Berkhof, *Systematic Theology* (1939; reprint, Grand Rapids: Eerdmans, 1982), 617.

12. One proof that baptism does not itself have the power to save is found in Paul's assertion: "For Christ did not send me to baptize, but to preach the gospel—not with words of human wisdom, lest the cross of Christ be emptied of its power" (1 Corinthians 1:17). Paul could not say this if baptism had the power to convey saving grace. In such a case, baptism would have been necessary to salvation.

13. Whitney, *Spiritual Disciplines,* 141.

14. J. C. Ryle, *Practical Religion* (1878 reprint, Grand Rapids: Baker, 1977), 145.

15. Gordon Fee commented, "The whole point of the section, beginning with v. 17 and continuing through vv. 33–34, is to correct a considerable abuse of the church as it is visibly portrayed at the Lord's Supper." *The First Epistle to the Corinthians* (Grand Rapids: Eerdmans, 1987), 564. The self-centered nature of church life in Corinth was epitomized in their observance of the Lord's Supper. They incorporated the communion service into a general "love feast" in which some overindulged

themselves to the point of drunkenness while others were neglected and went home hungry (1 Corinthians 11:21). Such selfishness was a practical denial of the spiritual reality symbolized by the communion service and treated the Lord's Supper as if it were no different from any other meal.

16. William Willimon argues persuasively that the emphasis on the "objective" nature of truth about God employed by many of today's apologists may give a false impression about the nature of divine truth: "Talk of 'objective truth' suggests that the truth is something that any fool can walk in off the street and get without cost or pain. It is a bad legacy of the Enlightenment, which hoped to devise systems of knowledge and morals that that would be immediately available to anyone who could think rationally about such matters." William H. Willimon, "Jesus' Peculiar Truth," *Christianity Today,* 4 March 1996, 22.

17. Saint Augustine, *The Confessions of Saint Augustine,* trans. by Edward B. Pusey (New York: Collier, 1961), 131.

18. Saint Augustine, *On Christian Doctrine,* trans. by D. W. Robertson Jr. (Indianapolis: Bobbs-Merrill, 1958), 7.

19. Ibid.

20. D. Martyn Lloyd-Jones, *Preaching and Preachers* (Grand Rapids: Zondervan, 1971), 302–3.

21. Horatius Bonar, *God's Way of Holiness* (1864; reprint, Guildford, England: Evangelical, 1979), 109.

22. John Newton, *Letters of John Newton* (reprint, Carlisle, Pa.: Banner of Truth, 1960), 148.

23. Ibid., 150.

24. Ibid., 150–51.

25. Ibid.

26. Ibid., 151.

CHAPTER 8
Praying to the Father

1. David Hill, *The Gospel of Matthew* (Grand Rapids: Eerdmans, 1984), 134.

2. Eugene H. Peterson, *Working the Angles: The Shape of Pastoral Integrity* (Grand Rapids: Eerdmans, 1987), 32.

3. Willem A. VanGemeren, "ABBÂ in the Old Testament," *Journal of the Evangelical Theological Society,* 31:4 (December 1988), 397.

4. I. Howard Marshall, *Commentary on Luke* (Grand Rapids: Eerdmans, 1979), 459.

5. In his commentary on Luke, C. Marvin Pate feels that the most likely view is the

eschatological interpretation: "This perspective translates *epiousion* as bread for 'the coming day' or 'for tomorrow.' With this in mind, Jeremias argues that the idea latent in the phrase is that God is requested to give today the bread which belongs to the kingdom of God in the age to come. On this reading, the bread encompasses both physical and spiritual food and, as such, attests to the sufficiency of the kingdom of God. Thus the prayer asks God to permit His disciples to enjoy now the blessings of the end times." *Moody Gospel Commentary on Luke* (Chicago: Moody, 1995), 245.

6. Marshall, *Commentary on Luke,* 460.

7. Charles Ryrie, *Basic Theology* (1986; reprint, Chicago, Ill.: Moody, 1999), 329.

8. R. C. Trench, *Notes on the Parables of Our Lord* (New York: Dutton, 1925), 126.

9. J. C. Ryle, *Practical Religion* (1878 reprint, Grand Rapids: Baker, 1977), 83.

CHAPTER 9
Worshiping the Father

1. Leon Morris, *Reflections on the Gospel of John, Volume I: The Word Was Made Flesh, John 1–5* (Grand Rapids: Baker, 1985), 139.

2. Donald W. McCullough, *The Trivialization of God: The Dangerous Illusion of a Manageable Deity* (Colorado Springs: NavPress, 1995), 110.

3. Graham N. Stanton, "Aspects of Early Christian and Jewish Worship: Pliny and the Kerygma Petrou" in *Worship, Theology and Ministry in the Early Church: Essays in Honor of Ralph P. Martin,* ed. by Michael Wilkins and Terence Paige (Sheffield: JSOT Press, 1992), 85.

4. Robert G. Rayburn, *O Come, Let Us Worship: Corporate Worship in the Evangelical Church* (Grand Rapids: Baker, 1980), 106.

5. Sally Morgenthaler, for example, characterizes the seeker service of Willow Creek Community Church in South Barington, Illinois, as "preevangelistic entertainment, a highly captivating, sixty-minute 'infomercial' for Christianity." She points out, however, that Willow Creek's leaders do not consider their seeker services to be worship. Morgenthaler disagrees with this approach, which assumes that worship and seekers do not mix. She asserts that worship is an effective way to evangelize: "Today when lost people have turned a deaf ear to 'churchianity' but their hearts are being drawn to spiritual things, heartfelt Christian worship can meet their need for both truth and experience, for hearing the 'claims of Christ' and seeing 'Christ in us.' Seekers can pick up a religious experience at any New Age quick-stop. But they won't get Jesus Christ in their take-out bags. Worship such as that in the Philippian jail—exaltation of the God incarnate and present with God's people— this is what seekers really need to see in our churches." Sally Morgenthaler, *Worship Evangelism* (Grand Rapids: Zondervan, 1995), 44, 91–92.

6. Robert E. Webber, *Worship Is a Verb* (Waco, Tex.: Word, 1985).

7. It is true that the apostle addressed some procedural problems related to Corinthian worship, such as the exercise of the gift of tongues and the number of prophecies that should be given in a service, but he clearly was not condemning the Corinthians for their participation in the service and the exercise of their gifts. F. F. Bruce comments: "The upshot of all this is that, when the church meets, it is perfectly proper for each member to contribute to the worship, provided that all things be done for edification." *The New Century Bible Commentary on I & II Corinthians* (1971; reprint, Grand Rapids: Eerdmans, 1986), 134.

8. Parsons Technology–CD. Collection of quotes taken from *The Bible Illustrator,* Parsons-CD.

9. Donald Guthrie, *The Letter to the Hebrews: An Introduction and Commentary* (Grand Rapids: Eerdmans, 1983), 208.

10. Webber, *Worship Is a Verb,* 29.

11. James F. White, *Introduction to Christian Worship* (Nashville: Abingdon, 1980), 72–73.

12. Dallas Willard, *Spirit of the Disciplines: Understanding How God Changes Lives* (San Francisco: HarperSanFrancisco, 1988), 179.

13. Ibid., 180.

14. In an essay comparing the practice of the early church with that of the synagogue, Morris notes: "They worshiped on a different day and perhaps this helps us see that in their worship they had distinctive ideas of their own. They worshiped on the first day of the week rather than on the Sabbath (Acts 20.7; 1 Cor. 16.2), for this was the day when Jesus rose from the dead. They called it 'the Lord's day' (Rev. 1.10). Sunday worship was a weekly reminder of the centrality of Christ's resurrection." Leon Morris, "The Saints and the Synagogue" in *Worship, Theology and Ministry in the Early Church: Essays in Honor of Ralph P. Martin,* edited by Michael Wilkins and Terence Paige (Sheffield: JSOT Press, 1992), 45–46. On the other hand, Graham Stanton suggests that another factor may have prompted the change. It may have been initiated to differentiate the church from the synagogue: "Which came first? The traditional answer stresses that Christian convictions about the resurrection of Jesus were decisive in the shift from Sabbath to Sunday. The historical evidence, however, is not quite so straightforward. For the followers of Jesus in the immediate post-Easter period, proclamation of the gospel to Gentiles and worship on a new day would have been equally dramatic departures from established practice. Whereas in some New Testament traditions proclamation of the gospel to *all nations* is linked inextricably to the resurrection of Christ (Matt. 28:18; Luke 24:47; cf. Rom. 1:3–4, 16; Gal. 1:12–16), traditions about the resurrection do not contain even a hint that henceforth followers of Jesus were to worship on a new day. In my judgment 1 Cor. 16:2; Acts 20:7; Rev. 1:10; *Didache* 14:1 all refer to Sunday worship, but in none of these passages is choice of a new day for worship

explicitly legitimated by reference to the resurrection." Stanton, "Aspects of Early Christian and Jewish Worship," 89.

15. Stanton, "Aspects of Early Christian and Jewish Worship," 98.

16. Donald W. McCullough, *The Trivialization of God,* 103.

CHAPTER 10
Glorifying the Father

1. Herbert M. Wolf noted that Isaiah's criticism in Isaiah 43:23–24 that God's people had failed to bring sacrifices seems at odds with Isaiah 1:10–13, where the Lord complains that His people had "trampled" His courts with a multitude of offerings. Wolf suggests: "Perhaps the Israelites were insincere in their worship. When they did bring offerings, they simply went through the motions of worship, and so God did not consider their empty sacrifices as true sacrifices at all." *Interpreting Isaiah: The Suffering and Glory of the Messiah* (Grand Rapids: Zondervan, 1985), 196.

2. J. Alec Motyer, *The Prophecy of Isaiah: An Introduction and Commentary* (Downers Grove, Ill.: InterVarsity, 1993), 338.

3. D. Martyn-Lloyd Jones, *Spiritual Depression: Its Causes and Its Cure* (Grand Rapids: Eerdmans, 1965), 194.

4. Ibid.

5. Ibid., 195.

6. J. I. Packer, "Richard Baxter on Heaven, Hope, and Holiness," in *Alive to God: Studies in Spirituality Presented to James Houston,* edited by J. I. Packer and Loren Wilkinson (Downers Grove, Ill.: InterVarsity, 1992), 165.

7. In these cases the term referred to the visible manifestation of God, not His divine essence (cf. Exodus 33:20).

8. Dallas Willard, *Spirit of the Disciplines: Understanding How God Changes Lives* (San Francisco: HarperSanFrancisco, 1988), 53.

9. Herman Ridderbos noted that Paul used the term "flesh" in a dual sense: "On the one hand, 'flesh' has for him the significance of what is human in its weakness, dependence on God, and perishableness itself; on the other hand, 'flesh' is the pregnant and very specific description of man in his sin, and the coinciding of being human and being a sinner is therefore expressed in it." *Paul: An Outline of His Theology,* trans. by John Richard De Witt (Grand Rapids: Eerdmans, 1975), 93.

10. Interestingly, Colossians 3:9–10 says that those who are in Christ have already done this: "Do not lie to each other, since you have taken off your old self with its practices and have put on the new self, which is being renewed in knowledge in the image of its Creator." Earlier in this same chapter Paul spoke of the ongoing need to "put to death, therefore, whatever belongs to your earthly nature: sexual

immorality, impurity, lust, evil desires and greed, which is idolatry" (Colossians 3:5). Although we have died to the old self, we must continually put off the old self. We have put on the new self but must continually put on the new self and be renewed in the attitude of our minds (Ephesians 4:23).

11. H. C. G. Moule comments on this verse: "The special direction to be taken by this 'sober-thinking' was the recognition by each Christian of the limits of his own gifts, the reality of the gifts of others, and the position of the individual as only a part of the great community; as well as the ever important fact that 'gifts,' whether many or few, are the sovereign bounty of God." H. C. G. Moule, *Studies in Romans* (Grand Rapids: Kregel, 1977), 207. In his commentary Robert Haldane notes that the kind of pride condemned in this verse takes two forms: "He warns each of them not to form a higher opinion of himself than his faith in God warranted. To this all are naturally prone; but there is an opposite error, assuming the semblance of obedience to this exhortation, which ought equally to be avoided. This is an affectation of humility by speaking of one's self contemptuously. This species of hypocrisy ought to be avoided. When an author speaks of his poor abilities, and tells us he is the most unfit man for the work he has undertaken, he is generally insincere; but if not insincere, he must be unwise; for God never requires us to exercise a talent which He has not bestowed on us." Robert Haldane, *An Exposition of the Epistle to the Romans* (1839 reprint, McLean: MacDonald, n.d.), 558.

12. John Ortberg, *The Life You've Always Wanted: Spiritual Disciplines for Ordinary People* (Grand Rapids: Zondervan, 1997), 28.

13. Ralph W. Klein, *1 Samuel* (Waco, Tex.: Word, 1983), 148.

14. C. F. Keil and Franz Delitzsch, *Commentary on the Old Testament,* vol. II, *Joshua, Judges, Ruth, I & II Samuel* (Grand Rapids: Eerdmans, 1982), 154.

15. Eugene Peterson, *A Long Obedience in the Same Direction: Discipleship in an Instant Society* (Downers Grove, Ill.: InterVarsity, 1980), 158.

16. William Law, *A Serious Call to a Devout and Holy Life,* edited and abridged for the modern reader by John W. Meister, et al. (Philadelphia: Westminster, 1989), 31–32.

BIBLIOGRAPHY

Achtemeir, Elizabeth. "Why God Is Not Mother: A Response to Feminist God-Talk in the Church," *Christianity Today,* 16 August 1993, 16–23.

_____. "The Impossible Possibility: Evaluating the Feminist Approach to Bible and Theology," *Interpretation* 42 (January 1988), 45–57.

Allis, Oswald T. *God Spake by Moses.* Philadelphia: Presb. & Ref., 1950.

Arndt, William F. and F. Wilbur Gingrich. *A Greek-English Lexicon of the New Testament and Other Early Christian Literature.* Chicago: Univ. of Chicago, 1957.

Augustine. *On Christian Doctrine.* Translated by D. W. Robertson Jr. Indianapolis: Bobbs-Merrill, 1958.

_____. *On Free Will,* in *Augustine: Earlier Writings.* Translated by John H. S. Burleigh. Philadelphia: Westminster, 1953.

_____. *The Confessions of Saint Augustine.* Translated by Edward B. Pusey. New York: Collier, 1961.

Barr, James. "'Abbā Isn't Daddy," *Journal of Theological Studies,* NS, vol. 39, pt. I, May 1988, 28–47.

Bavinck, Herman. *The Doctrine of God*. Translated by William Hendricksen. Grand Rapids: Baker, 1977.

Baxter, Richard. *A Treatise on Conversion,* 1657. Reprint, New York: American Tract Society, n.d.

Begg, Alistair. *Made for His Pleasure: Ten Benchmarks of a Vital Faith*. Chicago: Moody, 1996.

Berkhof, Louis. *Systematic Theology,* 1939. Reprint, Grand Rapids: Eerdmans, 1982.

_____. *The History of Christian Doctrines*. Grand Rapids: Eerdmans, 1937. Reprint, Grand Rapids: Baker, 1975.

Bilezikian, Gilbert. "Hermeneutical Bungee-Jumping: Subordination in the Godhead," *Journal of the Evangelical Theological Society,* 40:1, March 1997, 57–68.

Bloesch, Donald G. *God the Almighty*. Downers Grove, Ill.: InterVarsity, 1995.

Bray, Gerald. *The Doctrine of God: Contours of Christian Theology.* Downers Grove, Ill.: InterVarsity, 1993.

Bruce, F. F. *The New Century Bible Commentary on I & II Corinthians,* 1971. England: Marshall, Morgan & Scott. Reprint, Grand Rapids: Eerdmans, 1986.

Calvin, John. *Sermons on Ephesians*. Reprint, Carlisle, Pa., Banner of Truth, 1975.

_____. *Institutes of the Christian Religion*. Translated by Ford Lewis Battles, Edited by John T. McNeill. Library of Christian Classics vols. XX–XXI. Philadelphia: Westminster, 1977.

Chafer, Lewis Sperry. *Grace*. Philadelphia: The Sunday School Times, 1922.

Charnock, Stephen. *Discourses upon the Existence and Attributes of God.* London: James Blackwood, 1875.

Chartier, Myron. "A Theology of Parenting: An Incarnational Model," *American Baptist Quarterly,* 3, no. 1 (March 1984), 73–84.

Cole, R. Alan. *Exodus: An Introduction and Commentary.* Downers Grove, Ill.: InterVarsity, 1973.

Craigie, P. C. *The Book of Deuteronomy.* Grand Rapids: Eerdmans, 1976.

Cranfield, C. E. B. *A Critical and Exegetical Commentary on the Epistle to the Romans,* 2 vols. Edinburgh: T. & T. Clark, 1975.

_____. *The Gospel According to St. Mark.* Cambridge: Cambridge Univ., 1966.

Erickson, Millard J. *God in Three Persons: A Contemporary Interpretation of the Trinity.* Grand Rapids: Baker, 1995.

_____. *Introducing Christian Doctrine.* Grand Rapids: Baker, 1992.

Fee, Gordon. *The First Epistle to the Corinthians.* Grand Rapids: Eerdmans, 1987.

Feenstra, Ronald J. and Cornelius Plantinga Jr., eds. *Trinity, Incarnation and Atonement: Philosophical and Theological Essays.* Notre Dame: Univ. of Notre Dame, 1989.

Foakes-Jackson, F. J. and Kirsopp Lake, eds. *The Beginnings of Christianity Part I: The Acts of the Apostles.* Grand Rapids: Baker, 1979.

Gregory of Nazianzus. *The Theological Orations.* Edited by Edward R. Hardy. Translated by Charles Gordon Browne and James Edward Swallow, in *Christology of the Later Fathers,* ed. Edward R. Hardy. Philadelphia: Westminster, 1954.

Groothuis, Douglas. *Jesus in an Age of Controversy.* Eugene, Oreg.: Harvest Pubns., 1996.

Guthrie, Donald. *New Testament Theology.* Downers Grove, Ill.: InterVarsity, 1981.

_____. *The Letter to the Hebrews: An Introduction and Commentary.* Grand Rapids: Eerdmans, 1983.

Haldane, Robert. *An Exposition of the Epistle to the Romans.* 1839 Reprint, McLean: MacDonald, n.d.

Harris, R. Laird, Gleason L. Archer Jr., and Bruce K. Waltke. *Theological Wordbook of the Old Testament,* 2 vols. Chicago: Moody, 1980.

Harrison, R. K. *Leviticus: An Introduction and Commentary.* Downers Grove, Ill.: InterVarsity, 1980.

Hedlund, Roger E. *The Mission of the Church in the World: A Biblical Theology.* Grand Rapids: Baker, 1985.

Hill, David. *The Gospel of Matthew.* Grand Rapids: Eerdmans, 1984.

Hodge, Charles. *A Commentary on Romans,* 1835. Reprint, Carlisle, Pa.: Banner of Truth, 1972.

_____. *Systematic Theology,* 3 vols. Grand Rapids: Eerdmans, 1977.

Hughes, Philip Edgcumbe. *The True Image: The Origin and Destiny of Man in Christ.* Grand Rapids: Eerdmans, 1989.

Hyatt, J. P. *Exodus.* Grand Rapids: Eerdmans, 1971.

Jeremias, Joachim. *New Testament Theology.* Translated by John Bowden. New York: Scribner's, 1971.

_____. *The Prayers of Jesus.* Philadelphia: Fortress, 1967.

Keil, C. F. and Franz Delitzsch. *Commentary on the Old Testament,* vol. 1, *The Pentateuch.* Reprint, transalted by James Martin. Grand Rapids: Eerdmans, 1983.

_____. *Commentary on the Old Testament,* vol. II, *Joshua, Judges, Ruth, I & II Samuel.* Reprint, translated by James Martin. Grand Rapids: Eerdmans, 1982.

Kelly, J. N. D. *Early Christian Doctrines.* New York: Harper & Row, 1960.

Kidner, Derek. *Genesis.* Downers Grove, Ill.: InterVarsity, 1967.

Kitchen, K. A. *Ancient Orient and Old Testament.* Downers Grove, Ill.: InterVarsity, 1966.

Law, William. *A Serious Call to a Devout and Holy Life.* Edited and abridged for the modern reader by John W. Meister and others. Philadelphia: Westminster, 1989.

Leighton, Robert. *Commentary on First Peter,* 1853. Reprint, Grand Rapids: Kregel, 1972.

Lewis, C. S. *Mere Christianity.* New York: Macmillan, 1952.

Lloyd-Jones, D. Martyn, *God the Father, God the Son.* Wheaton, Ill.: Crossway, 1996.

_____. *Preaching and Preachers.* Grand Rapids: Zondervan, 1971.

_____. *Spiritual Depression: Its Causes and Its Cure.* Grand Rapids: Eerdmans, 1965.

Lockyer, Herbert. *All the Divine Names and Titles in the Bible.* Grand Rapids: Zondervan, 1975.

Marshall, I. Howard. *Commentary on Luke.* Grand Rapids: Eerdmans, 1979.

McCullough, Donald W. *The Trivialization of God: The Dangerous Illusion of a Manageable Deity.* Colorado Springs: NavPress, 1995.

Morgenthaler, Sally. *Worship Evangelism.* Grand Rapids: Zondervan, 1995.

Morris, Leon. *Reflections on the Gospel of John, Volume I: The Word Was Made Flesh, John 1–5.* Grand Rapids: Baker, 1985.

_____. *Ruth: An Introduction and Commentary.* Downers Grove, Ill.: InterVarsity, 1968.

_____. *The Atonement: Its Meaning & Significance.* Downers Grove, Ill.: InterVarsity, 1983.

_____. *The Gospel According to John.* Grand Rapids: Eerdmans, 1971.

Moule, H. C. G. *Studies in Romans,* 1892. Reprint, Grand Rapids: Kregel, 1977.

_____. *The Epistle to the Philippians,* 1897. Reprint, Grand Rapids: Baker, 1981.

Newton, John. *Letters of John Newton.* Reprint, Carlisle, Pa.: Banner of Truth, 1960.

O'Hare, William. "Life Without Fathers," *American Demographics.* July 1995, 60.

Origen, *On Prayer.* Translated by John Ernest Leonard Oulton and Henry Chadwick, in *Alexandrian Christianity,* ed. Henry Chadwick. Philadelphia: Westminster, 1954.

Ortberg, John. *The Life You've Always Wanted: Spiritual Disciplines for Ordinary People.* Grand Rapids: Zondervan, 1997.

Owen, John. *Hebrews: The Epistle of Warning.* Grand Rapids: Kregel, 1973.

Packer, J. I. *Evangelism and the Sovereignty of God.* Downers Grove, Ill.: InterVarsity, 1961.

_____. *Knowing God.* Downers Grove, Ill.: InterVarsity, 1973.

Packer, J. I. and Loren Wilkinson, eds. *Alive to God: Studies in Spirituality Presented to James Houston.* Downers Grove, Ill.: InterVarsity, 1992.

Pannenberg, Wolfhart. "Feminine Language About God?" *The Asbury Theological Journal,* vol. 48, no. 2 (Fall 1993).

Pate, C. Marvin. *Moody Gospel Commentary on Luke.* Chicago: Moody, 1995.

Payne, J. Barton. *The Theology of the Older Testament.* Grand Rapids: Zondervan, 1962.

Pelikan, Jaroslav. *The Emergence of the Catholic Tradition (100–600).* Chicago: Univ. of Chicago, 1971.

Peterson, Eugene H. *A Long Obedience in the Same Direction: Discipleship in an Instant Society.* Downers Grove, Ill.: InterVarsity, 1980.

_____. *Leap over a Wall: Earthy Spirituality for Everyday Christians.* San Francisco: HarperCollins, 1997.

_____. *Working the Angles: The Shape of Pastoral Integrity.* Grand Rapids: Eerdmans, 1987.

Pinnock, Clark. *Flame of Love: A Theology of the Holy Spirit.* Downers Grove, Ill.: InterVarsity, 1996.

Pinnock, Clark, Richard Rice, John Sanders, William Hasker, and David Basinger. *The Openness of God.* Downers Grove, Ill.: InterVarsity, 1994.

Ridderbos, Herman. *Paul: An Outline of His Theology.* Translated by John Richard De Witt. Grand Rapids: Eerdmans, 1975.

Ryle, J. C. *Practical Religion.* 1878. Reprint, Grand Rapids: Baker, 1977.

Ryrie, Charles. *Basic Theology,* 1986. Reprint, Chicago, Ill.: Moody, 1999.

Schaeffer, Francis A. *Art and the Bible.* Downers Grove, Ill.: InterVarsity Press, 1976.

Sproul, R. C. *Essential Truths of the Christian Faith.* Wheaton, Ill.: Tyndale, 1992.

Spurgeon, Charles. *The Treasury of David,* vol. I, part 2, Reprint, McLean: MacDonald, n.d.

Thiessen, Henry Clarence. *Introductory Lectures in Systematic Theology.* Grand Rapids: Eerdmans, 1949.

Thompson, J. A. *The Book of Jeremiah.* Grand Rapids: Eerdmans, 1980.

Torrance, Thomas F. *Theology in Reconstruction.* Grand Rapids: Eerdmans, 1965.

Trench, R. C. *Notes on the Parables of Our Lord.* New York: Dutton, 1925.

VanGemeren, Willem A. "ABBÂ in the Old Testament," *Journal of the Evangelical Theological Society,* 31:4 (December 1988).

Van Till, Howard J. "The Creation: Intelligently Designed or Optimally Equipped?" *Theology Today,* October 1998, 344–64.

Vos, Geerhardus. *Biblical Theology.* Grand Rapids: Eerdmans, 1948.

Warfield, B. B. "Prayer as a Means of Grace" in *Faith and Life,*
1916. Reprint, Carlisle, Pa.: Banner of Truth, 1974.

Watson, Thomas. *A Body of Divinity,* 1692. Reprint, Carlisle, Pa.:
Banner of Truth, 1992.

Webber, Robert E. *Worship Is a Verb.* Waco, Tex.: Word, 1985.

Wenham, Gordon. *Numbers: An Introduction and Commentary.*
Downers Grove, Ill.: InterVarsity, 1981.

White, James. F. *Introduction to Christian Worship.* Nashville:
Abingdon, 1980.

Whitney, Donald. *Spiritual Disciplines Within the Church:
Participating Fully in the Body of Christ.* Chicago: Moody,
1996.

Wilkins, Michael and Terence Paige, eds. *Worship, Theology and
Ministry in the Early Church: Essays in Honor of Ralph P.
Martin.* Sheffield: JSOT Press, 1992.

Willard, Dallas. *Spirit of the Disciplines: Understanding How God
Changes Lives.* San Francisco: HarperSanFrancisco, 1988.

Willimon, William H. "Jesus' Peculiar Truth," *Christianity Today,* 4
March 1996, 21–22.

Wise, Donald U. "Creationism's Geologic Time Scale," *American
Scientist,* vol. 86, 1 March 1998, 160–73.

Wolf, Herbert M. *Interpreting Isaiah: The Suffering and Glory of the
Messiah.* Grand Rapids: Zondervan, 1985.

Woodward, Kenneth L. "Hallowed Be Thy Name," *Newsweek,* 17
June 1996, 75.

INDEX OF SUBJECTS

INDEX OF SCRIPTURE

Moody Press, a ministry of Moody Bible Institute,
is designed for education, evangelization, and edification.
If we may assist you in knowing more about Christ
and the Christian life, please write us without obligation:
Moody Press, c/o MLM, Chicago, Illinois 60610.